FORWARD

"Life is a succession of lessons which must be lived to be understood."
Ralph Waldo Emerson

"Experience is the teacher of all things."
Julius Caesar

"The only relevant test of the validity of a hypothesis is comparison of prediction with experience."
Milton Friedman

There are two basic approaches to running a business in America: You can run your business on what it earns, or you can run your business on debt.

The former approach is basic and old-fashioned: Create a product or service that has value, and sell it in an intelligent way. Then, reinvest your profits in your company for growth. Doing this doesn't mean that you don't need the best business skills that all the most fashionable companies talk about. It just means that you take a conservative approach to what you borrow and invest in.

The latter approach involves, once you get the business started, leveraging large amounts of financing on your customers, and using that to finance growth. The financial services sector has built a whole industry based on this kind of financing, and it has made a great deal of money for banks, brokerages, and financial advisors. It has led to the creation of the rocket science of financial engineering, which has disconnected investment from its sources in business, and, again, made a great deal of money for the financial services industry.

Let us make no mistake: There is nothing morally wrong with debt, with borrowing, or with banking. This book is not here to recall biblical prohibitions about usury, or to make any kind of categorical judgement. People, or businesses, may choose to incur debt or to speculate. What is wrong is when they lose at speculation, but then are saved, or bailed out, from their losses. Capitalism works when people make mistakes, pay for those mistakes, and then learn from them.

Business is about experience, winning and losing. This book is about the experience of doing business without excessive debt, and of growing a successful and significant business in that way. It's about how the Markowitz family did that and how I, Steven Markowitz, continued in that path and still do.

An unfortunate combination of circumstances took me off that path briefly, and got me involved with the other kind of finance. It's not a pretty story, and the subsequent litigation, as told in the book, shows just how far off the rails our legal system has gotten in terms of supporting fair dealing in business and finance.

But the book will also place my own story in the context of the whole trouble with the financial services industry, its unwillingness to operate according to the most basic principles of ethical business practices, and the industry's penchant for promoting debt. We also take a look at what this and the over use of leverage has done to our country's economy as a whole.

Bad Debt and the American Economy

Our first chapter takes a look at what happened to the American economy in 2008, with an entire country plunged into recession because its banks had taken bad mortgage loans and turned them into complex financial products that they had then sold off. The worldwide market for these products, worth trillions of dollars, crashed, and millions of people lost their savings as the investments they had made became worthless. Unfortunately, the entire ethic seen here has not changed, and we could well see another crisis of this type again, despite the vain work of our politicians.

The series of bailouts that have propped up the banking industry in the U.S. have removed significant parts of the discipline of failure that capitalism requires to succeed. Its origins could be traced to relatively small bailouts, for example the 1979 $1.5 billion bailout of Chrysler. Proponents of bailouts will actually use the Chrysler bailout as an example of success in not only saving a company, but also paying back the government with interest. However, such bailouts promote the view that companies that are too big to fail can count on future bailouts if their bad business decisions fail. This leads to even more imprudent behavior by large companies and banks.

Bailouts since 2008 dwarf the one given Chrysler. We have since seen bailouts with taxpayer funds of tens or even hundreds of billions of dollars, a result of the slippery slope we travel. More perversely, the banks that were too big to fail in 2008 are now even larger.

This book presents a sharply critical view of the use of debt to finance nonproductive endeavors. Such debt, along with the low interest rate policies of the Fed, has been a boondoggle for some, including the financial services industry.

This book is here to propose a change to a different set of business values.

Bad Debt and the Financial Advisor

Financial advisors were just as much involved in the debacle of 2008 as were bankers and brokers. They helped promote the ethic of bad debt and risky investments, and they worked closely with companies promoting speculative financial products. By doing this, they earned lucrative commissions, and although the financial advisor industry claims it is moving away from this practice, it is not moving to an oath-based system like the one doctors and lawyers use. Professionals are supposed to place care of the client at the center of their work, but financial advisors often do not do this. My own example is an instructive tale of what happens when they don't, and of how the law protects them. Our second chapter takes a hard look at the financial advisor industry and how it works.

Role of the Inventor/Entrepreneur

Chapter Three takes a look at what, instead, does work, and should work in our economy. Creative invention and entrepreneurship have played significant roles in the development and success of the United States. Examples include: Benjamin Franklin's inventions like the Franklin stove, the lightning rod and bifocals. A few decades later, Eli Whitney invented the cotton gin increasing agricultural productivity. In 1888, George Eastman gave the world the Kodak camera, and in the twentieth century, Thomas Edison produced hundreds of inventions. Contemporary entrepreneurial inventors include computer technology moguls Bill Gates and Steve Jobs.

While entrepreneurs often earn personal wealth, they add significantly to the wealth of the country as well. The businesses created from these inventions help to enrich a great part of the community, and of course many benefit from their products and services offered as well. This shared creativity is a main benefit of capitalism.

But being an inventor also means being a good businessperson if the developed products are to be brought to the larger community. My father, Jerome Markowitz, brought those qualities of creativity and good business together and he founded the business that my family has grown and remains an important one today – we tell the story in Chapter 3.

Once, when I was a teenager, my father's business was troubled by a shortage of copper wire caused by a labor dispute. Copper wire was the key ingredient of the toroidal coils required to produce the electronic organs he had invented and that his company manufactured. I asked about the consequence of not being able to obtain the wire. The answer was that without coils our organs could not be manufactured. The ramification, even to a young boy, was that the business would close down.

My father then shared his solution to the problem. He had purchased in advance a substantial quantity of copper wire that was stored at his factory. I still recall the relief I felt with this conservative and proactive approach to an economic issue.

Business skills and creativity are the basis that makes success. A controlled amount of debt can be good debt – can help the business to grow. All of this is made clear in our story.

Bad Debt and Destructive Growth – Good Debt and Healthy Growth

Chapter Four makes a comparison between our company and how we grew it conservatively and organically with good debt, with what happened to Nortel, another high-tech firm that, in the hands of the bankers, took on a load of debt it couldn't repay, and expanded much too rapidly as a result.

The chairmen of the Federal Reserve Alan Greenspan and Benjamin Bernanke have taken the part of the bad-debt bankers. Instead of focusing on a stable money supply and low inflation, as their able predecessor Paul Volcker did, they intervened in efforts to stop economic downturns. Their interventions helped propel negative reactions like the Asian monetary crisis of the latter 1990s, as well as the Dotcom and Datacom bubbles and busts a few years later. Nortel was a victim of the Datacom bubble and bust phase.

That's not what Allen Organ Company did. My father invented a new kind of electronic organ, and a business in electronics grew up around it. We took on an acquisition in Datacom using our own funds. When it had problems, we handled them without borrowing. That approach lead to a long-term profitable investment and positive outcome for investors.

Similarly, in Chapter Five, we show how the company was taken private without incurring debt, and with the help of a responsible financial advisor. And Chapter Six shows how we financed expansion responsibly.

A Disastrous Move in the Wrong Direction

Following chapters chronicle how I was obliged, for specific circumstances, to set aside this healthy, conservative, and prescient philosophy in one instance, and how it led to disaster. The story of how our funds were invested with two different financial advisors, how they were placed in a speculative and dangerous investment, and how that investment was not carefully tended, is a cautionary tale. My experience fits perfectly into the context we have given of irresponsible government, banking and law.

Chapter 12 takes a close look at how the case law applies in litigation like mine against financial advisors, and asks some hard questions about whether the case law is appropriate to the system is supposed to regulate.

Chapter 13 shows how the bad debt environment has poisoned the economic system as a whole. The disastrous increases of the money supply over the years, along with excessive federal borrowing, have led to perilous economic volatility, while cheap money has fed the greed and speculation of the financial world.

The Way Forward

We remain a proponent of a less fashionable, an old-fashioned, traditional approach to doing business, to regulating finance, and to running our economy. Capitalism works, but speculation is risky, and speculators should fail if their risks don't pan out. By controlling risk, maintaining reasonable expectations for growth without incurring bad debt, business can thrive.

Governments can do the same. We went off course back in the 1960s when President Lyndon Johnson was determined through his expansive and expensive Great Society programs to eliminate poverty, an effort that did not succeed. He was also determined to win a widening war in Vietnam that was also an expensive endeavor, another failed effort. These two simultaneous expensive efforts, known as "guns and butter," had consequences. It led to pressure on the U.S. dollar a few years later that resulted in President Nixon disconnecting its relationship to the value of gold. This then led to the significant inflation of the 1970s.

Similarly, in recent years, the Fed's activist approach fueled the housing bubble whose popping continues to inflict malaise on the economy. It also incented people into high-risk investments in search of yield, as well as the increased use of debt worldwide, debt which governments around the world have had to acquire. The bailouts, along with low interest rate policies, rewarded banks and the financial services industry even though they played significant roles in creating the 2008 meltdown.

All of this goes against the business values proffered in this book – bad debt, bad policy, and the undermining of the economy. We need to change the way we do business, to get back to good debt, and good policy, and that is what this book militates for.

Steven Markowitz

Note Regarding Glenmede Trust Company

Part of this book deals with our litigation with the Glenmede Trust Company. We contacted Glenmede by letter before publishing the book and offered to let them read and comment on it. We offered to include these comments in the book.

After waiting a month, we received no reply from Glenmede. We note this for the record.

S.M.

Chapter 1

Introduction – Standing Up to the Bankers

This story is about just one of the many Americans burned by banks and wealth managers during the economic meltdown that began in 2008. Our financial system not only permitted, but helped promote excessive risk-taking by the financial services industry, which had a role in the losses suffered.

In addition, governments and central banks tempted investors into excessive risk-taking through their interventionist policies that included increased monetary liquidity and low interest rates. The macro result was a global financial crisis caused by the drying up of the credit markets. As securities markets of every kind plunged, the number of Americans who suffered vast loss of wealth was huge, but never completely tallied.

But many in the financial services industry had a different outcome. Besides the profits they had obtained by selling high risk paper and facilitating ill-advised mergers, they were rewarded with bailouts, huge injections of liquidity that supported balance sheet recovery, and ultimately regulations that did not materially change the conditions that caused the crisis. The low interest rate policies continued today by central banks are an ongoing form of bailouts allowing banks to profit, in some cases by loaning the same funds back to governments, at higher rates.

Many thousands of individuals lost their life-savings in the crisis. Of these, many suffered from poor financial planning and advice, whether from their bankers or financial advisors. No one bailed out most of these victims.

However, unlike most Americans, I did not accept one of the losses as being an accident or bad luck of the markets. This investor took his financial advisor and banker to court and partially won. But, more important than that individual victory, this investor has a lifetime of experience in healthy finance – the development of a different, conservative philosophy of investment that works without depending on speculative bubbles or the financial services industry.

This book exposes the incompetence, dishonesty and lack of accountability of the financial services industry. It is a story of how a conservative investor who shunned that industry for years got unwittingly sucked into the vortex of "lemming style" investing that characterized the years from 2001-2007.

Having profited from a conservative philosophy for investments for decades,

I would have avoided major loss from the 2008 meltdown, had I not been the victim of financial advisors whose supposed expertise in the field led to foolish, high-risk asset placement, incompetent service and ultimately a cover-up.

Although a court found that my advisor acted against my interest and that the advisor "... did a poor job in effectuating its investment decision...", "... did not diligently attempt to obtain the auction rights for 12 months", and "... was disingenuous", I was only able to recuperate pennies on the dollar for losses on the investments managed by that financial advisor. Our legal system is either incapable of holding, or refuses to hold, the financial industry accountable for its misdeeds.

Speculation Causes a Financial Crisis

The financial crisis of 2007[1] began when, in June of that year, Standard & Poor's and Moody's Investor Services, both responsible for rating the quality of financial instruments, downgraded over 100 bonds that had been backed by second-lien subprime mortgages. This was highlighted in March of that year when international bank HSBC announced that one portfolio of its purchased subprime mortgages' pool evidenced much higher delinquency than had been built into the pricing and rating of these products.

Speculation in "Structured Products"

At issue was the quality of the credit behind the mortgages and ultimately their pooled-collateralized investment securities offered. Greedy bankers, desperate for yield, had provided mortgages to consumers who had little means to pay them. Often, borrowers did not have to provide proof of financial capabilities to obtain the loans.

The bankers who sold these mortgages to consumers then quickly sold them off to larger banks that sliced and diced them into repackage bonds called Collateralized Debt Obligations (CDOs). These CDOs were complex financial products that few understood, including Standard & Poor's and Moody's Investor Services who were responsible for rating the quality of these bonds. Nonetheless, the bonds found willing buyers who were looking for regular income and increased yield. Unfortunately, they turned out to be high risk investments, irrespective of their ratings.

The downgrade of these mortgage-backed bonds sent a shudder through the entire financial system. Banks worldwide had been creating mortgages of this type, wrapping them into collateralized bonds and other kinds of financial instruments, and then selling them with high credit ratings to unsuspecting buyers. Given the breadth of the bond sales, the possibility that these instruments weren't creditworthy put the entire world market for structured securities into a tailspin. Credit of all kinds dried up and the large Wall Street Banks very survival became at risk.

End of Cheap Money for Financing

The drying up of credit was a disaster for any number of financial institutions. There had been cheap credit available for years, based on the choice of the Federal Reserve and other central banks to keep interest rates exceptionally low to gin up the economy. The relatively new structured financial products added to this orgy of cheap credit

In addition, while the very low interest rates maintained for an exceptionally long period had given banks access to cheap money for this extended time, it also cut into their returns for relatively safe investments. In search of higher yields banks lent that money at higher risk to many who could not repay the loans. These risky bonds were then made salable due to the inappropriate bond ratings supplied by the rating agencies.

The banks, which became rich when the risky mortgages were given, were now at risk of failing due to their poor decision to increase their leverage. When the collateralized bonds true risk became known, their sale was no longer possible, which not only put an end to the housing bubble, but also put at risk the survival of the large banks. Leverage has put a stake in the heart of many businesses even during minor economic downturns. With the economic tsunami that hit in 2008, leverage placed at risk the very survival of most major American banks and with them the overall world economy.

Bankers' greed for rewards

With leverage, banks around the world had plunged far more risk capital into these mortgage-backed loans and structured products than they could possibly maintain. With no regulations to stop them, bankers made as many loans and investments as they possibly could during the housing bubble. Each time they were rewarded by fat incentives and profits tied to the completion of these financial products, not the long-term viability of the loans. In addition, bank compensation policies rewarded executives and traders based on short-term gains, irrespective of long-term consequences to their business or greater public.

As a result of these perverted policies, bankers lent far more than they had a right to risk. Some of the overleveraged institutions simply failed, like Bear Sterns and Lehman Brothers. Others, like Citigroup, were rescued by government bailouts or in the case of insurance giant AIG, were nationalized (or nearly nationalized). Other banks who survived the carnage received backdoor bailouts in the form of cheap taxpayer-sponsored loans. The fear of "systemic risk," in which a large bank failure would send the entire global monetary system into chaos, was the justification of the bailouts as those banks were deemed 'too big to fail.'

Politicians Take Over

There were no criminal charges brought against the financial services actors who were behind the speculation. Instead, the government took extensive regulatory actions, theoretically to prevent such a crisis from happening again. This culminated in the Dodd-Frank Act of 2010, which was a vast compendium of regulatory changes intended to gain more control over the banking system. In reality, this act favors larger banks who can better afford its cumbersome regulations.

At this writing, Dodd-Frank is three years old and only about 30 percent of all the regulations it calls for have been implemented by U.S. government agencies. It will likely take a decade before any real effect from Dodd-Frank is felt. Meanwhile, banks have begun trading and speculating again with the lion's share of profit at major banks in 2012 coming from speculative trading activities.[2] Central banks continue with historically low interest rates that pressure banks and individuals to once again take on more risk in search of yield.

Politicians have created lots of new regulatory posts and increased the power of agencies like the Securities and Exchange Commission to send in inspectors, but our financial system remains essentially unchanged. Banks that were too big to fail in 2008 are even bigger today. This makes the likelihood of another crisis requiring additional governmental bailouts significant.

The Victims and their Advisors

Of the thousands of Americans who lost their lifesavings in the crash, many had been given a false sense of security because they worked with a financial advisor. We will discuss later in the book the details of what that really means.

But there is every reason to assume that financial advisors and wealth management firms were just as caught up in the frenzied search for yield as were the bankers. At the same time, since much of this industry's fees are based on a percentage of the assets managed, they directly benefited from the asset bubbles created.

As a Deloitte industry analyst puts it:

"For wealth managers, the period 2004 to 2007 was characterized by ever-higher asset prices and aggressive growth strategies. Throughout these boom times, wealth managers experienced significant growth in the size of assets under management and increasing revenue margins…The global financial crisis, however, triggered a staggering 24 percent drop in profitability.[3]"

Part of the reason for the drop in profitability was the fact that clients had ceased to trust their financial advisors, having suffered losses during the crisis. Advisors had what the industry referred to as an "eat what you kill," attitude to relationships with clients. Nearly 100 percent of major firm's business was commission-based, so advisors could just sell a lot of products and make healthy incomes. Consumers who suffered in the crisis ceased to trust advisors who "ate what they killed," and have since been more likely to seek advisors who earn fees based on specific services.[4]

While the industry has been moving more to fee-based work, financial advisors don't have to use this model. Under current rules, advisors can adhere to either type of business, depending on how clients pay for their services. The commission-based system encourages advisers to steer clients into costlier products that earn them fatter commissions. They may call themselves 'advisors', but they are effectively sales reps.

There is considerable debate, which we will discuss in Chapter 2, about who is an advisor and how advisors should function. But, in my own case and that of many before and during the financial crisis, the financial advisor was more concerned about commissions than about my financial future. Like the bankers who sought rewards for making deals, the advisor placed my funds in an obscure instrument that, once the crisis hit, became illiquid and plunged in value. However, the firm that purchased these investments assured me that there was "no downside risk" to the bonds.

This book will recount my own suffering and eventually how I was able to recuperate at least some of what I lost through litigation. But the book will also place my own story in the context of the whole trouble with the financial services industry, its unwillingness to operate according to the most basic principles of ethical business practices, and the industry's penchant for promoting debt.

The book will also tell the story of how my family and I built a company based on viable business principles and low debt. Fending off the assaults of bankers who, especially during boom years, sought to drag us into the unsustainable debt vortex, we financed growth organically and, in doing so, built new businesses with the funds that we earned.

We will, oppose to the malign and tottering edifices of the financial services industry, proffer the principles of a conservative financial philosophy that actually creates real and long-term value.

---

[1] For a summary of the academic view of the crisis, please see "A Bird's-Eye View, The Financial Crisis of 2007–2009:Causes and Remedies," Viral V. Acharya, Thomas Philippon, Matthew Richardson, and Nouriel Roubini, February 2009

[2] "Trading boosts Morgan Stanley earnings," Financial Times, July 18, 2013; "Goldman Sachs and JP Morgan see profits surge in 2012," The Daily Beast, January 16, 2013

[3] "Winning in wealth management," Deloitte 2009

[4] "Younger generation is scarce among financial advisors," Crain's Cleveland Business, April 29, 2013

Chapter 2

Are You a Financial Advisor?

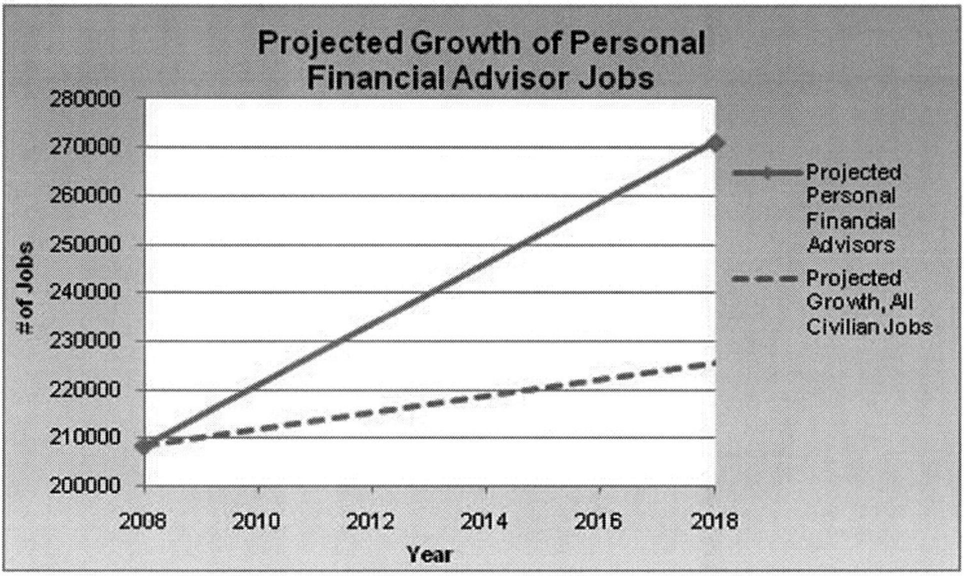

Source: Labor Department statistics

As the chart above shows, there are currently about 240,000 financial advisors in the U.S., and that number is growing rapidly.

Demand is high for financial advice. "In this economy, people have a greater sense of wanting and needing more control over their nest eggs," said Charles T. Moses Jr., interim dean of Clark Atlanta University's School of Business. "They are turning to financial experts to help them manage their investments and plan for retirement.[1]"

But even these Labor Department statistics are based on a relatively narrow definition of the financial advisor – those who have specific qualifications to do the job. In fact, anyone can claim to be a financial advisor of one sort or another.

The problem is that there are many sorts of financial advisors, and only some of the different types are actually regulated by an organization, legislation, or authority. Even those that are regulated have only limited responsibility to

---

[1] "Job outlook bright for personal financial planners," Atlanta Journal –Constitution, September 9, 2013

the client. The fiduciary standard, which is intended to protect the client, is in practice full of holes.

A medical doctor has a very strict duty of care with regard to his or her patients. A lawyer also must abide by fairly strict standards in terms of client responsibility. We may joke as much as we like about lawyers, but the fact remains that they have fairly limited liberty of action.

But a financial advisor has, in effect, little if any duty of care at all. Now we need to pay strict attention to the words "in effect," for some types of financial advisors are regulated and also, in theory, have limited liberty of action. The problem is that, unlike for doctors or lawyers, the rules allow far too much leeway when it comes to financial advisors.

This is not to say, either, that many financial planners, financial advisors, retirement planners, etc. are not perfectly ethical, trustworthy business people. Indeed, a John Hancock 2012 study found that affluent U.S. investors tend to trust their advisors more than their doctors or accountants.[2] But this is because these advisors have earned the trust of their clients, building relationships based on clear and honest explanations of investment recommendations, being responsive and being transparent about their practice and how they are compensated.

The problem is that financial advisers often don't have to do any of these things. And more than a few times they leave clients very unhappy.

- According to SEC statistics, the agency filed 147 enforcement actions against advisors and investment companies in 2012; one more than the record set in 2011.

- According to FINRA (Financial Industry Regulatory Authority) statistics, in the five years from 2008 through 2012, investors filed 19,444 complaints against brokers/financial advisors.

- The North American Securities Administrators Association reported that enforcement actions at the state level against brokers and advisors nearly doubled in 2012, compared with the previous year.

Of course, these are just the unhappy investors who actually took legal action or officially complained to some agency. Undocumented are the thousands more who work with advisors of every type, get unsatisfactory results, and just don't do anything about it.

---

2 "John Hancock Survey, " company press release, June 6, 2012

The Hierarchy of Financial Advice

What happens, for example, when your broker recommends a stock or other investment and it goes the wrong way? There is nothing at all to be done because a broker recommendation doesn't legally bind them in any way.

This is something that investors in the stock market pretty much understand. Stocks are volatile; your broker has lots of ideas, and you know that some of them just aren't going to work out because investing is risky. If you pay a broker, you might do it because a fair number of that broker's ideas do pan out and lead to a profit, enough to make it worthwhile for you to give the broker a higher commission than you would pay to an Internet-based trading site where you make your own decisions.

There is currently debate, stimulated by the recent financial reform legislation, about holding brokers to a higher standard, but as of this writing it has not been implemented.

Most brokers try to manage investor money to increase aggregate value since more commissions are potentially available for them. The acceptance of these commissions in exchange for advice puts a broker on a higher level of responsibility, and he or she must register with the SEC (or a state authority) as an investment adviser.[3] One must bear in mind that there are differences between an investment adviser, a financial advisor, a financial planner, etc. But this is the 'first degree,' one might say, of the hierarchy.

Citing from the SEC document:

"Unlike the laws of many other countries, the U.S. federal securities laws do not prescribe minimum experience or qualification requirements for persons providing investment advice. They do not establish maximum fees that advisers may charge. *Nor do they preclude advisers from having substantial conflicts of interest that might adversely affect the objectivity of the advice they provide.* (Italics ours) Rather, investors have the responsibility, based on disclosure they receive, for selecting their own advisers, negotiating their own fee arrangements, and evaluating their advisers' conflicts of interest.[4]"

So, there it is. A registered investment adviser, one with the certification of the nation's highest authority, no doubt framed on his or her wall, has no effective responsibility to the investor. Is it surprising, therefore, that a great

---

3 "Regulation of Investment Advisers by the U.S. Securities and Exchange Commission," SEC, March 2013

4 "Regulation of Investment Advisers by the U.S. Securities and Exchange Commission," SEC, March 2013

number among them makes deals with banks and brokerages to sell certain investments, and then sells investors whatever earns them the most money?

To do advisors justice, however, the SEC document continues, with the changes made by the Dodd-Frank Wall Street Reform and Consumer Protection Act of 2010:

"Fundamental to the Act is the notion that an adviser is a fiduciary. As a fiduciary, an adviser must avoid conflicts of interest with clients and is prohibited from overreaching or taking unfair advantage of a client's trust. A fiduciary owes its clients more than mere honesty and good faith alone. A fiduciary must be sensitive to the conscious and unconscious possibility of providing less than disinterested advice, and it may be faulted even when it does not intend to injure a client and even if the client does not suffer a monetary loss."

A great deal of jurisprudence has been devoted to defining the nature of the fiduciary relationship. This legal formula is intended to guarantee the investor who trusts an advisor a much higher level of responsibility than the investor would have demanded from a broker. However, as we will see later in this book, the actual responsibility of the fiduciary remains open to legal debate. It is difficult and expensive for smaller investors to attempt to seek legal redress for a breach of this responsibility.

One example of the fiduciary duty is that the advisor cannot buy securities for his or her account prior to buying them for a client. The advisor must also do his or her best to make sure investment advice is made using accurate and complete information, or basically, that the analysis is thorough and as accurate as possible. Additionally, the advisor needs to place trades under a "best execution" standard, meaning he or she must strive to trade securities with the best combination of low cost and efficient execution.

Each of these fiduciary stipulations is subject to broad interpretation. Is the information complete? Who can say? Who can judge whether the analysis has been as "thorough and as accurate as possible?" How does an investor determine if the advisor has been diligent in making a trade? Investing is an art, not a science – otherwise all the "scientists" would be rich… No one can judge investment strategy by objective criteria.

But the title "investment adviser" is not the same as the title, "financial advisor", which is a degree higher in the hierarchy. As we've seen, the latter title is used somewhat indiscriminately – it is not restricted in any way – but there is:

- **The National Association of Personal Financial Advisors**: NAPFA's membership requirements include proof that a financial advisor can produce a comprehensive financial plan for a client. Proof is demonstrated through peer review of a financial plan submitted by the prospective NAPFA member. A NAPFA member is subject to the fiduciary standard and may not receive compensation for investments made. All his or her work is fee based.

- **The National Association of Insurance and Financial Advisors** – This is largely for insurers, who, however, are free to act as financial advisors. Many of these hold the Chartered Financial Consultant designation, which is awarded by the American College. It does address a range of financial planning topics and requires the passage of multiple exams. Candidates must possess three years of business experience (two if they hold an undergraduate degree) and abide by a code of ethics.

- **Certified Fund Specialist or Chartered Mutual Fund Counselor** - Professionals who earn the CFS title have completed a portion of the Certified Financial Planner program and focus on assisting clients with setting up investment portfolios for retirement and estate planning. However, a bachelor's degree is not required.

- **Certified Trust and Financial Advisor** - The American Bankers Association confers CTFA certifications to trust and wealth management professionals who offer fee-based services. To qualify for CTFA certification, individuals must meet specific levels of experience (depending on their level of education), pass a comprehensive exam, and agree to abide by a code of ethics.

- **Certified Financial Planner** - This designation is conferred by the Certified Financial Planner Board of Standards. Certification is rigorous. It involves a lengthy education requirement and follows the successful passage of multiple exams completed over a two-day period dealing with personal finance subjects, including investments, insurance, and estate planning. Candidates are required to possess a bachelor's degree and three years of relevant experience, and must adhere to a code of ethics.

- **Financial Planning Association** - The Financial Planning Association is a leadership and advocacy organization connecting those who provide, support and benefit from professional financial planning. The FPA has nearly 100 chapters throughout the United States representing tens of thousands of members involved in all facets of providing financial planning services. There is no certification process related to becoming an FPA member, although the organization requires members to adhere to its Code of Ethics.

This is not a comprehensive list and there are hybrid designations like "retirement planner," that also use the title financial adviser. Of those listed, the ones that investors are most likely to take seriously as a partner are financial planners and NAPFA-certified advisors. In 2012 the two designations essentially merged. "The National Association of Personal Financial Advisors announced Tuesday that as of January 1, NAPFA would only accept the certified financial planner (CFP) designation for people who applied to be NAPFA-registered financial advisors. 'NAPFA's decision to support the broader recognition of a single, defining designation for the financial planning community makes sense. Less confusion means more consumer confidence, and the CFP designation hits the mark as a strong, baseline standard,' NAPFA Chair Lauren Locker, who is herself a CFP, said in a statement. About 85 percent of NAPFA membership already held the CFP designation when this announcement was made.[5]

The Trouble with the Fiduciary Standard

NAPFA-certified advisors take a fiduciary oath:

"The fiduciary oath taken by NAPFA-registered personal financial advisors means the advisor shall exercise his/her best efforts to act in good faith and in the best interests of the client. The advisor shall provide written disclosure to the client prior to the engagement of the advisor, and thereafter throughout the term of the engagement, of any conflicts of interest, which will or reasonably may compromise the impartiality or independence of the advisor. The NAPFA fee-only financial planner, or any part in which the advisor has a financial interest, shall not receive any compensation or other remuneration that is contingent on any client's purchase or sale of a financial product. The NAPFA fee-only planner does not receive a fee or other compensation from another party based on the referral of a client or the client's business."

This should be reassuring. But we continue to see news items like the following:

[5] NAPFA statement dated December 4, 2011

"The CFP Board has been embroiled in controversy since last November, when then-chairman Alan Goldfarb resigned after allegations he may have violated provisions of the board's standards of professional conduct. He was sanctioned in June by the Board's ad hoc Disciplinary and Ethics Commission for misrepresenting his compensation model.

In the time since his resignation, Goldfarb has been outspoken in denying that he mischaracterized his compensation. In a listing on the FPA website, he described his compensation initially as fee-only and later, in a revision, as 'salary'; he was also part-owner of a broker-dealer firm that could also receive commissions. 'Nothing I did in the last five years had anything to do with selling on a commission basis,' he said.[6]"

Without making any allegation about the conduct of Mr. Goldfarb, it would seem intuitively as a conflict of interest to own a broker-dealership and to be a purely fee-based financialadvisor. It is important to understand that Mr. Goldfarb is at the top of the financial advice hierarchy. This kind of conduct goes to the inherent problem in the use of the fiduciary standard for regulating the work of financial advisors. It is simply too subjective. While Mr. Goldfarb believes that he did nothing wrong, the Board of his own Professional Organization doesn't agree. How is the application of the fiduciary standard to much more complex issues, like the investment in a certain type of instrument, going to be determined? How can an individual investor be confident that an advisor is acting in an inappropriate fiduciary manner?

To cite the words of Supreme Court Justice Felix Frankfurter:

"*To say that a man is a fiduciary only begins analysis; it gives direction to further inquiry. To whom is he a fiduciary? What obligations does he owe as a fiduciary? In what respects has he failed to discharge these obligations? And what are the consequences of his deviation from duty?*[7]"

Perhaps the most obvious issue that arises with the fiduciary standard applied to a financial advisor is that the advisor is often the director of a wealth management firm (or advisory service, etc.), or at the very least an employee of that firm reporting to high level executives. Therefore, the advisor also has a fiduciary duty to the best interests of the company, its shareholders, and/or its stakeholders. There is almost inevitably a conflict between the financial advisor's fiduciary obligations to the client and those owed to the company for which he or she work. This is rarely pointed out in this context, but it has often been cited as an issue in corporate law:

---

6 Untitled Article from Financial Planner, September 3, 2013

7 SEC v. Chenery Corp., 318 U.S. 80, 85-86 (1943).

"Fiduciary relationships present a problem of legal classification. They lie in a gray area between the more clearly defined worlds of government regulation and private ordering through contract. They plausibly can be characterized as a species of either. Because the fiduciary acts on another's behalf, the relationship implies a beneficiary needing protective regulation. But fiduciary relationships also are volitional and inevitably entail a measure of private ordering, in many cases a large measure. As a result, the same fiduciary relationship may be the subject of two sharply contrasting descriptions with contrasting normative implications.

Depending on the factors emphasized, either legally mandated self-sacrifice or unconstrained pursuit of self-interest in an environment of free contract may be implied.[8]"

This closer look at the fiduciary standard and the financial advisor designations with the highest standards of education and conduct suggests that self-regulation, which is the effect of the imposition of the fiduciary standard, does not work for the financial advisory industry. Too much of the law still places the onus of decisions on the client without legally obliging any duty of care from the advisor in the way one would expect it from a doctor or a lawyer.

As part of the Dodd-Frank legislation, it is now possible to obtain extensive background information on an advisor from the SEC and from FINRA. Known as Part 2b or the "Brochure Supplement" among regulators and financial compliance personnel, this resume seeks to provide all of the information that a consumer should know about the person who is helping them make important decisions that will affect their future financial security.

More importantly, the Brochure Supplement provides a standardized way for investors to receive information on any financial advisor with whom they are considering working. In particular, every advisory firm must provide, among other things, the educational background, business experience, and disciplinary history (if any) of each employee who provides advisory services to a client. In addition, all advisory firms are required to organize and present this information in the same order and with the same headings as specifically identified by the SEC. FINRA now has both individual disclosures and background from advisors and a new disciplinary actions database that will make disciplinary information more accessible to the general public. This is a step forward, but does not resolve the issue of just who is, and who isn't, going to be a trusted financial advisor. It also does not guarantee diligent behavior.

---

[8] William W. Bratton, Self-Regulation, Normative Choice, and the Structure of Corporate Fiduciary Law, George Washington Law Review, 1084, 1100 (1993).

Chapter 3

A History of Value Creation – The Markowitz Family

Young Jerome Markowitz at work.

Finance and business have, historically, been two separate activities. Until the late 20th century, finance had been largely at the service of business. Investment banks existed essentially to provide creative solutions for businesses that required capital to expand or for some other productive purpose.

Since the beginning of the 20th century the finance industry has taken off on a trip its own, finding ways to profit in more "creative" endeavors. The creation of financial instruments that have no direct relationship to a business or its operations has become a huge field, dominating the profits of Wall Street and other financial centers. It is now possible to make investments in financial derivatives, for example, that are entirely divorced from any relationship to a business or its fundamentals, one that depends entirely on the fluctuations of certain indexes or currencies.

Excesses and the frenzied search for yield (as reviewed in Chapter 1) have turned this more contemporary kind of finance activity into short-term search for gains without concern for the medium or longer term consequences. This hunt for yield has found willing facilitators in central banks worldwide, who in recent years have manipulated interest rates to historically low levels in efforts to fix all kinds of economic and/or social maladies. While these policies can increase overall liquidity in the economy, they also bail out corporations and individuals who made imprudent financial decisions and also helped create the economic calamity in the first place, this at the expense of those who were more prudent. The bailouts of the banks in the fall of 2008, under the direction of Hank Paulson, turned into a windfall for the financial services industry including the major investment banks.

There are other consequences to the easy money policies pursued by central banks including the US Federal Reserve. The low interest rates have significantly lowered the returns on relatively safe investments, such as money market funds, while at the same time cajoling investors into seeking higher returns through more risky investment strategies. This promotes bubbles, including equity valuations, while at the same time increasing the opportunities for the financial services industry to create more profit for itself. These policies are not only looked on favorably by the large banks, but also by business schools whose students are trained to seek the rewards possible in the financial services industry. The best and brightest today rarely look to the manufacturing sector for careers given the opportunities in the financial services industry.

But there is another kind of business with another kind of finance mentality associated with it. It is an older style of business that has lost favor in both Wall Street and with the major business schools. It involves rolling up ones sleeves to create wealth by productive endeavors, avoiding financial manipulation and its associated tools.

For example there is the fundamental investing championed by Warren Buffett and his school, which looks for companies that are creating value and supports their growth with finance. My family history is another example of a similar philosophy put into practice, both in the creation of Allen Organ Company, the investments and risks it has taken along the way, and the investments my family has made in other growing companies that focuses on creating real value.

Jerome Markowitz; Creative Invention as Value

My late father, Jerome Markowitz, was a successful inventor who built a business around his innovative ideas. He was a child of Romanian immigrants that started a clothing apparel business that continues to this day to be run by another part of the family tree. (Paris Accessories, New York, NY)

Jerome did not join the family soft-goods business. He had a different itch that needed to be addressed. History has proven his passion to have benefited many over the decades.

Jerome Markowitz was a self-taught engineer. Early in life he had the need to build the latest technological gadgets that included radios and a television. He became a ham radio operator, a hobby many technologists of that day took on.

During the 1920s and 1930s, hardware-based electronic technology was in its formative stage, in some respects similar to that of PC technology in the mid-1970s. The mid-1970s spawned the personal computer industry and software companies. The 1920s and 1930s spawned technologists and companies that would create products utilizing vacuum tube technology. One of those technologies created by my father was the electronic organ.

My grandparents sent my father to Allentown Prep School and later to Muhlenberg College in Allentown, Pennsylvania. Their goal was to have Jerome join the family business. This would not happen and his educational experiences would not play a significant role in the success Jerome ultimately obtained.

In 1937, while a senior at Muhlenberg College, Jerome suffered from an attack of appendix-related peritonitis, at the time an often fatal occurrence. After missing more than a month of college due to the illness he decided to leave school to pursue his passion, to create a pipeless organ using advanced technology of the time. That decision led Jerome to ultimately create Allen Organ Company, a technology and manufacturing company that remains under family ownership today.

The First Electronic Pipeless Organ

My father's first invention was the Stable Audio Oscillator, patented in the late 1930s that would enable Jerome to produce a pipeless organ using electronic tone generation. To perfect this technology he initially spent many days working with pipe organs learning the physics behind their sound production. He combined this knowledge with his technological expertise to create a musical oscillator, a kind of frequency generator with similar technology to that he used to build his radio equipment.

Jerome's early work was accomplished in one of his father's nearby factories. There he enlisted the aid of Norman Koons, a factory maintenance man with expertise in mechanics. Together in 1939 they built Allen Organ opus 1 and eventually sold it to a local church.

The Second World War put the business on hold until 1945. During the War Jerome worked for the US government in Hawaii on the then secret radar systems.

After the War Jerome raised money through friends and family to start the business and Allen Organ Company was born. He began hiring workers to build and sell organs. As sales grew he moved to a larger rented facility in downtown Allentown, Pennsylvania. He also continued with his first love, inventing. For example, in 1949, he introduced the Gyrophonic Projector. The 'Gyro' was a rotating speaker system designed to add liveliness to the electronically generated sounds of Allen instruments. This and other inventions helped the business prosper.

By 1953 Allen Organ Company was making a profit and expanded to the point where it needed additional manufacturing space. That year the Company purchased and moved into a closed textile plant in Macungie, Pennsylvania that offered room to grow. This is the same location where the much larger factory still resides.

Allen Organ Company was differentiated from competitors by tailoring organs to meet the specific needs of individual customers and creating unrivaled sound quality. Most competitors then opted to produce organs that were more 'off-the-shelf', focusing on cost over quality. In addition, Allen focused on building electronic organs that mimicked the sound of windblown pipe organs, rather than sounds that were more appropriate for popular music. Allen organs were therefore best suited for serious musicians; concert halls and churches. The instruments became renowned for their ability to produce pipe organ sounds, bringing these tonal qualities to lower price points than could be achieved with pipe organs.

The Company's success continued to the point that it was able to launch a successful IPO (Initial Public Offering) in 1961 that attracted an additional 500 investors. This improved the Company's balance sheet, giving it capital to expand in the coming years. In the early 1960s these funds were used to expand the Macungie factory as organ sales grew.

In 1966, the Company created a subsidiary operation, Rocky Mount Instruments, in Rocky Mount, North Carolina. This division produced portable keyboards, portable amplifiers and other novelty instruments. Its keyboards became popular with rock musicians during the late 1960s and 1970s. RMI keyboards were used by many world-famous bands and musicians including The Loving Spoonful, The Doors, Stevie Wonder, Rick Wakefield, just to name a few. As a teenager working at the Company I had the pleasure to meet some of these rock legends.

By the late 1960's Allen Organ Company had sold more than 30,000 organs with its products available on six continents. The Company continued to fund expansion during the 1960s, initially with funds from the public stock offering and later from internal cash flow.

Irrespective of the added liquidity Allen achieved and its stronger financial position, the Company did not change its culture or conservative financial philosophy. It did not outrageously increase executive salaries, spend money on unproductive physical plant or pay high dividends even though the family was the Company's largest shareholder. Instead, excess funds were retained in the Company for future investment opportunities. That decision would lead to profound benefits for the Company and shareholders within a few short years.

The First Digital Organ

Irrespective of the success Allen achieved during its first 20-plus years, as a technologist Jerome understood that he had taken audio oscillator technology that he invented to the pinnacle of its capabilities, first with vacuum tubes and later transistors. He yearned for the next jump in sound-producing technology.

In 1966, North American Rockwell (later Rockwell International), was a prime contractor in America's Apollo space program. While America was still a few years from landing a man on the moon, Rockwell understood that this program's funding would begin to drop off significantly by the early 1970s. They needed to find other businesses in order to grow and searched for commercial uses for the technology that it developed for the Apollo program.

One of the ideas Rockwell generated was to create sound with digital technology, a process that was to become known as sampling. With sampling, any sound such as an organ pipe is recorded, then converted into digital numbers, stored in computer memory and played back as very close replicas. Jerome quickly realized that this technology could more precisely reproduce complex pipe organ sound than the approximate and more difficult to control analog oscillator technology he invented decades before.

Even after the digital organ idea was developed, implementing a commercially viable product was a substantial challenge in the late 1960s. A digital organ would require multiple custom large-scale microcircuits, devices that were not available for use in commercial products at that time.

Rockwell had expertise in designing and producing the required Metal-Oxide Semiconductor/Large-Scale Integrated, or MOS/LSI microcircuits. However, they had no expertise in designing, producing, or selling organs. They therefore set out to form a joint venture with an organ manufacturer to co-develop and sell digital organs.

Rockwell demanded that its joint venture partner pay for the expensive development of the technology, including the custom MOS/LSI circuits. They approached all of the large organ builders at that time including Hammond, Baldwin, Wurlitzer and Conn. While these companies were very interested in the radically new technology, they were unwilling to fund its development due to the huge risk that would be involved. These rejections nearly killed the digital organ project before it got started.

Almost as an afterthought, Rockwell then approached the relatively small Allen Organ Company with the joint venture offer. Because of Jerome Markowitz's understanding of sound technology, the Company's financial capability, and the Markowitz family's large ownership position in Allen stock, the Company entered into the joint venture agreement with Rockwell in 1967 to develop the digital organ.

The Rockwell joint venture involved considerable risk to Allen Organ Company, requiring a capital commitment of over $2 million – a huge investment for a company with total sales at the time of less than $10 million annually. But my father decided that the digital innovation was so significant to be worthy of the risk. He bet Allen's future on funding this advanced product's development, funding it from cash flow and retained earnings without taking on massive debt.

In 1971 Allen launched the world's first digital organ. The product was an instant success, but also included technological hick-ups, not unexpected with a radically new technology.

In 1972 Allen was awarded the prestigious *IR-100 Award* making the Allen

Digital Computer Organ one of the most significant technological innovations of the year. Also confirming the significance of this product and technology, years later the first Allen Digital Computer Organ would find a home in the Smithsonian Institution in Washington DC. The fact that the Allen Digital Computer Organ preceded competitors' digital organs by 15 years helps demonstrate the significant technological lead Allen obtained from this investment.

Jerome Markowitz receiving IR 100 award in Chicago, IL, 1972.

In addition to the sales success of the digital organ, Allen gained ownership to the pioneering digital sound production patents. Allen later licensed these patents to some of the largest musical instrument manufacturers in the world. This further strengthened Allen's balance sheet, a fact that would ultimately allow it to make yet another risky and even larger investment in the 1990s that would also significantly benefit Allen's stockholders.

A Different Approach to Finance

Allen's organ sales grew throughout the 1970s, 1980s and 1990s. These strong sales, along with the royalties it received from the digital organ patents, made Allen even stronger financially. Once again, in keeping with the conservative financial philosophy, my father kept the earnings within the Company. It did not pay huge dividends or outrageously high executive compensation. This decision would again offer the Company significant benefits when it sought to finance a major corporate expansion in the mid-1990s.

I joined Allen Organ Company in 1975 after graduating from Penn State University. I had the benefit of working in various departments at the Company as a teenager, which allowed me to come into the Company with "nuts and bolts" knowledge of the product and business.

My initial responsibilities included negotiating patent license agreements for the digital organ patents. In addition, I was made responsible for running the Company's international division for organ sales. I became the Company's president in 1990. By then my father had already turned over significant operational responsibility to me. He passed away in 1991 after a year and a half battle with cancer.

After becoming Allen's president I continued the conservative financial philosophy inherited from my father. At the same time, like my father, I continued to look for investment opportunities that could reward shareholders. My DNA required that such investments be internally financed.

The Company has always taken pride in being vertically integrated and we continue to manufacture all of our products in the United States, long after it became the business school mantra to subcontract such work overseas. We maintained our place in the local community and kept Americans employed. In fact, ten employees worked for Allen for over fifty years. In addition, many employees have passed jobs on to sons, daughters, brothers and sisters, and even to grandsons and granddaughters.

We took a paternalistic view of our responsibilities to the community and employees long before the term "Corporate Social Responsibility," became a buzzword. And our approach to finance is part of this philosophy and a requirement for carrying it out.

Allen has been able to maintain its US manufacturing because of our willingness to invest on an ongoing basis in plant and equipment. These investments were made possible by Allen's conservative financial philosophy that shunned debt.

Employees at work at the Allen factory.

Throughout the 1980s and continuing today, we moved to automate production, upgrading to new technologies that were more efficient. This enabled us to remain competitive even while maintaining a paternalistic management style. However, such investments are expensive. If financed externally, they become problematic during inevitable economic downturns. By internally financing them we felt comfortable that we could weather the inevitable economic storms that a dynamic economy brings to any business.

Before becoming president of Allen, during the mid-1980s, I recall taking potential financial investors for a factory tour. During one tour the group that included bankers stopped me and commented that while the factory looked beautiful, we were foolish for not increasing our return on investment by outsourcing manufacturing. While their suggestion may have benefited my family and Company shareholders in the short-term, the long-term effects on the business, community and employees would have been devastating. Ringing assets out of a company for short-term gain is a major reason for the gutting of so much of American manufacturing in recent decades.

Investment in Product Diversification

While, like my father, I take a paternalistic view of the Company's responsibility to employees and the community, I do not ignore my responsibilities to shareholders, the Company's owners. I am a capitalist and have always looked for opportunities to increase returns in a way that does not conflict with what I see as our responsibility to employees and the community.

By the early 1990's Allen Organ Company was the leader in the church organ market with the largest market share. The mass-market home organ business that Allen historically avoided had significantly shrunk with large companies including Wurlitzer, Baldwin, and Conn no longer in business. This limited growth opportunities within the music business.

With strong organ sales and a strong balance sheet, I made the decision to use the Company's strengths as a platform for corporate diversification. Allen had already started a program to organically diversify into the subcontract assembly business. We were assembling our own printed circuit boards and other complex electromechanical assemblies for organs. We therefore started a contract manufacturing division at the Macungie, Pennsylvania plant, Allen Integrated Assemblies (AIA), offering manufacturing services including electronic circuit board and electro-mechanical assemblies to other companies. This was a logical extension for Allen given our expensive production equipment and complex skills required to manufacture our organs' subassemblies. AIA, which continues to operate today as an Allen division, used these assets as a base to grow the new business. By the late 1990s AIA was producing thousands of circuit board assemblies annually, half of which were sold to outside companies. AIA's primary focus is on small to medium production size runs for customers that require quality, quick turnaround, and flexibility, the same requirements Allen has for assemblies used in organs.

By the late 1990s, Allen Organ Company was organized among four industry segments: musical instruments; electronic assemblies; data communications; and audio equipment (our efforts to diversify into the audio field were ultimately unsuccessful). The story of our Eastern Research data communications subsidiary, which was a significant part of Allen's history from 1995 to 2006, is told in the next chapter of this book.

Components being inserted in circuit boards by AIA.

Allen Organ Company today continues to be a highly regarded supplier of both organs and electronic assemblies. All employees are US based. What's more, continuing a tradition used to fund the development of the digital organ and later Eastern Research, I used some of the equity the family acquired from the sale of Allen's Datacom subsidiary to invest in a number of high-tech companies through a specialized private equity fund, Goldin Ventures. Goldin Ventures nurtures technology companies during the difficult period between start-up and market validation.

The success that we have gained to date, as well as my continued investments in growing companies, has been made possible mainly because my father and I didn't listen to the bankers and their siren song of easy money. While it is possible that the bankers' advice would have been even more profitable for the Markowitz family, the success that we have obtained is a proof statement that capitalism can succeed with conservative business philosophies and corporate responsibility.

Chapter 4

Beating Back the Bankers: A Conflict of Values

In 1994, I was president of a relatively small, but successful publicly-traded company that was listed on NASDAQ. Allen Organ Company, then with annual sales of about $29 million, operated in two markets: Musical Instruments and the then recently started contract electronic assemblies business. Our story is told earlier in this book in Chapter 3.

I made the decision in 1995 to expand into the data communications field by purchasing a small company called *Eastern Research* (ERI), which then had sales of less than $2 million, along with two of its small sister companies.

This was a logical business extension for Allen since producing sophisticated electronics assemblies were already a significant part of the digital organs we manufactured. In addition, with the digital technology included in our digital organs, I already had considerable experience in advanced technologies. Just as important, the data communications area was at that time becoming the next big transition for technology, as well as an important field for the overall economy. ERI, which specialized in products that delivered voice and data services to corporate customers, seemed a good investment opportunity at a time when the growth of the Internet was raising expectations for Datacom needs on a global basis.

The Datacom acquisition would prove to be exciting, but also a greater challenge than I originally anticipated. ERI went through periods of significant growth, but also suffered a large financial loss in one period due to an unforeseen meltdown that occurred in its market. However, because of our conservative investment philosophy, highly competent ERI management and a hands-on view of the industry, we saw ERI through this period and it went on to reach sales of $65 million annually when we sold it in 2006.

The time we acquired ERI coincided with the early stages of the Datacom bubble in the United States. The developing mania led to over-investment and speculation in companies that supplied equipment and services to providers in this market. This bubble would ultimately result in a catastrophic downturn in the industry just a few years later when it popped.

A Cautionary Tale – What the Bankers do

The mania that surrounded the Datacom field in the mid-to late 1990s led to an over-availability of investors and investments for companies serving the market. The financial services industry was quite willing to help and profit from Datacom companies loading up on debt, selling equity shares at inflated prices, and promoting mergers to take advantage of what was a bubble. When the market crashed in 2001, hundreds of these companies went broke or struggled on with shrinking sales and high debt payments for years.

Nortel Networks - Stock Price 2000-2013

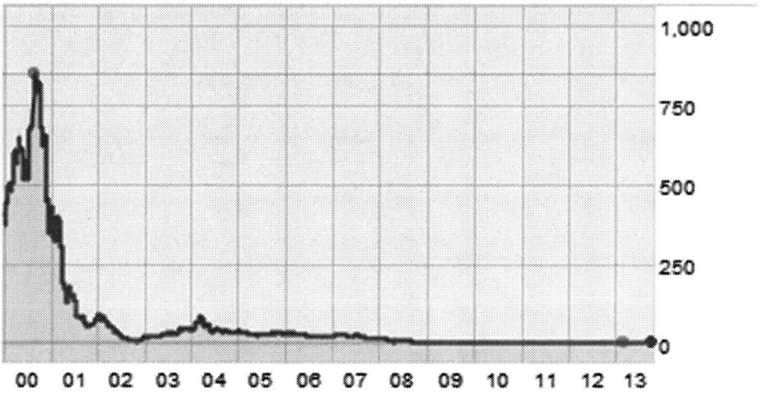

Source: Google Finance

Canada's Nortel Networks, as the graph above shows, provides a good example of what went wrong during and after the Datacom, as well as Dot-Com, booms.

The giant Canadian company, Nortel, was a poster child for the Datacom industry's bubble growth and subsequent meltdown. Nortel's origins stretch back to the Bell Telephone Company of Canada that, together with its US counterpart, received the patent rights for telephone technology from Alexander Graham Bell in the late 19th century.

In 1999, Nortel was a global leader in telephony, data, eBusiness and wireless solutions for the Internet. Nortel offered network solutions for two business groups: Service Provider and Carrier, and Enterprise. Nortel's Service Provider and Carrier Group was the global leader in Internet Protocol, high-speed access, long distance, optical and wireless networking. The enterprise solutions group provided Internet Protocol-based communications solutions that enabled interpersonal electronic communications for all kinds of businesses.[1]

Nortel Networks, like other Datacom companies, went on an acquisitions spree in the late 1990s. They often used its equity shares or debt to finance these acquisitions with the company's acquisitions including (cited from the annual report, 2000):

- In October 1999, Nortel announced the acquisition of Clarify, a provider of front office eBusiness solutions. Clarify stock holders would receive 1.3 common shares of Nortel stock for each share of Clarify common stock. Nortel stated that Clarify's leadership in eBusiness combined with Nortel's high performance Internet technologies would create powerful applications that could serve both the Carrier and Enterprise customers.
- In February 1999, Nortel announced the acquisition of Qtera, a producer of ultra-long-reach optical networking systems.
- Also in February 1999, the company announced the acquisition of Dimension Enterprises, an engineering and business strategy consulting firm, for $65 million in cash. Dimensions was supposed to help Nortel design and engineer Internet data centers that house eBusiness transactions.
- In March 1999, Nortel announced its agreement to acquire CoreTek, a pioneer in strategic optical components, for $1.43 billion in Nortel common shares. Nortel indicated that CoreTek's tunable lasers would strengthen Nortel's ability to deliver a flexible high-performance optical Internet.
- In April 1999, Nortel and Architel Systems announced an agreement whereby Nortel would acquire all common shares of Architel for about $395 million in Nortel common shares. Architel was a global leader in software systems that allowed service providers to offer Internet and other next generation Internet Protocol services.
- In January 2000, Nortel announced plans to acquire Promatory Communications, a developer of Digital Subscriber Line (DSL) platforms for high-speed Internet access. The aggregate purchase price for the common shares of Promatory was roughly $778 million on a fully diluted basis.

Nortel shares reached a peak of $1,230 per share in March 2000, taking account of a 10-for-one share consolidation.

With the benefit of history, Nortel's acquisition binge, as well as acquisitions made by other companies in the Datacom industry during that period, was not only ill-advised, but disastrous. Overactive merger and acquisition activities often occur during bubble periods when access to debt is not only cheap and easy, but promoted by the financial services industry that profits from each of the transactions.

In Nortel's case, the acquisition activity occurred despite the fact that it was, even in 1999, incurring significant losses. While 1999 revenues were up 26 percent from 1998 to $22.2 billion, net income only increased from a loss of $569 million in 1998 to a loss of $197 million in 1999. Long-term debt remained relatively unchanged at $1.6 billion, and the long-term debt to equity ratio dropped only 1 percent from 1998 to 13 percent. Due to increases in long-term receivables and the acquisitions, cash flow from operations dropped significantly from a decrease of $112 million in 1998 to a decrease of $1.4 billion in 1999. This last item particularly should have been a cautionary indicator to management and shareholders, and yes, the bankers.

Nortel became leveraged (increased debt) well beyond any predictable revenue and income growth in future years that would allow repayment of the debt. When the Datacom boom went bust in 2001, its share price plunged and Nortel has spent years "recovering" from the high level of debt. It went into the Canadian equivalent of Chapter 11 in 2009.

While Nortel shareholders lost billions, the bankers made millions on its acquisitions and financing activities. Bankers are typically compensated by receiving a percentage of financed activities that they help facilitate. Unfortunately this compensation practice gives bankers incentive to focus on the short-term, an attitude that is often in conflict with the long-term interests of a company and its shareholders. In Nortel's case, the combination of poor internal management and bad advice from the financial services industry resulted in significant wealth destruction and the loss of many jobs.

By the late 1990s the overall Datacom industry was in the midst of significant growth, fueled by a bubble that was in part caused by the *Telecommunications Act of 1996*.

- This Act significantly amended the *Communications Act of 1934*. Major reasons behind the 1996 Act were to address the growing Internet business in broadcasting, as well as spectrum allotment for broadband communications.
- The Act promoted cross-ownership of various telecom assets with the goal of increasing competition and facilitating startups who desired to enter the market.
- It also included deregulation of the broadcasting and telecommunication markets.

An unfortunate result of many government intrusions into the economy are unintended consequences. One unintended consequence of the *Telecommunications Act of 1996* was that it helped create the illusion, promoted by many entrepreneurs and bankers, that the need for data transmission bandwidth was nearly limitless. Infamous hockey stick graphs with upward projections for future bandwidth requirements were included in many PowerPoint presentations to potential investors that fueled a mania for investing in Datacom companies. These presentations were high on hype and often devoid of substance. The hype helped fuel the Datacom boom, an orgy of over-investment and speculation in companies that supplied, or would supply, services and equipment to providers.

A large proportion of the startups, and even some established companies, became insolvent when the market melted down in 2001, an inevitable result of popping bubbles. Nortel was but an example of the companies destroyed in the wake of this popped bubble.

Those of us involved in the Datacom industry during the bubble years heard all sorts of anecdotal comments concerning the mania that existed. There was a 'lemming' mentality from potential investors who were afraid of missing out on the gold rush. For example, it was said that $100 million could be raised from investors merely with a hyped-up PowerPoint presentation. Another example was that supposedly Datacom companies could be valued based on a multiple of the number of engineers they employed. These examples were preposterous, but were promoted in part due to the willing partnership the industry found in the financial services industry. As history has shown, this mentality guaranteed a tragic ending for many.

ERI – A Different Story

Our experience with Eastern Research (ERI) was quite different than most Datacom companies during the bubble years. While ERI would require significant investment and a different strategy than what was required for our Musical Instrument business, we brought to ERI our heritage of basic, conservative and fundamentals-based approach to running a company. We did not allow bankers and financiers, who had no experience on the operational side of business, to persuade us to forego good business judgment that we believed was required for companies to be successful in the long term.

During the time that Allen Organ Company owned the Morristown, NJ-based ERI, it produced multi-service cross-connect and access gateways that provided intelligent networking solutions for wireless and wireline network operators. In 1995, when Allen acquired ERI, the world was at the early stages of the expansion of the Internet. It was logical to assume that demand for networking gear and technology would increase significantly in the coming years. It was not logical to assume that this demand would be infinite. By avoiding the bubble mentality that infected the Datacom industry, Allen's conservative management philosophies helped ERI survive the meltdown when so many other companies failed.

Prior to any business acquisition, buyers perform due diligence on target companies during which the potential acquirer learns about the intricacies of the target business, including its technology, human resources, its market, and actual financial situation. During due diligence should an acquirer learn of significant issues or problems with the target, the buyer may back out of the deal, typically without penalty.

As unfortunately often occurs and irrespective of our due diligence, we learned after the acquisition that ERI had more significant requirements than we initially contemplated that needed to be addressed for the company to achieve our desired growth strategy. While ERI had advanced technology and great people, it was weak in an overall business strategy and missing important product portfolio pieces. Addressing these issues would require further investment in ERI.

From the beginning, it was not my intention to actively manage ERI since I did not have the time, or quite frankly the skills, to manage the Datacom subsidiary. My plan was to be involved in topline strategic decisions only. However, within months after the acquisition I understood that ERI was in need of a strong executive to create a sound strategic plan in order for it to grow, but did not have such a person internally.

Since I was an outsider to the Datacom industry, I did not have the contacts in the industry to locate a qualified executive for ERI. I therefore engaged the services of an executive search firm to assist me with this task.

The executive search firm located several potential candidates for ERI that I interviewed. One, who I ultimately hired to be president of ERI, Mike Doyle, was already a seasoned Datacom executive. He became ERI's president in April, 1997. The decision to bring in Mike was perhaps the most important one that I made for ERI. Mike, who remained president of ERI until we sold the company, was a key reason for its success. He not only had the ability to run all aspects of ERI's operation, but as important, Mike brought with him a conservative view of managing a business that was simpatico with mine.

The relationship Mike Doyle and I began in 1995 continues to this day. Using the same conservative philosophy, we started a venture group after the ERI divestiture, Goldin Ventures, to help young technology companies grow, as will be discussed later in the book.

As a seasoned executive, Mike had the crucial ability to create a strategic plan for

ERI. This plan was not only important for ERI's success, but was also required as a roadmap for me and Allen's Board of Directors to use in running and funding ERI.

Creating the strategic plan for ERI began shortly after Mike became its president. The first version of the plan took literally hundreds of hours for Mike and the ERI team to prepare. It covered every aspect of ERI, including R&D, marketing, HR needs, etc. and was included in a binder that was in excess of 100 pages. After being approved by me, it was presented to Allen's Board of Directors and approved. That plan was reviewed annually to track metrics and to be updated as required.

Along with Allen's Board, I made the decision to invest in ERI's growth based on its strategic plan and given its overall potential in the growing Datacom market. That plan would not overspend nor mortgage the Company future by taking on debt. It included reinvesting ERI's profits back into this division to fund its growth. As a result, ERI grew organically and based on products that filled real market needs.

The details included in its strategic plan allowed all ERI managers to have a clear understanding of the goals and financing philosophy for the company. As a result, when the Datacom bubble popped, while ERI was significantly impacted, it was not only able to survive, but actually returned to profitability only three quarters later. That success was a direct result of competent management, prudent spending, and being able to pivot quickly as market conditions changed.

Helping manage ERI was very rewarding, but at times a challenging task. It required risk and patience. In 1994, ERI had sales of less than $2 million annually and those sales were highly concentrated in just a few customers. After Allen's acquisition, ERI added marquee customers that included Lucent, Telstra, Sprint/Nextel, and Korea Telecom. This success in the early years justified Allen's acquisition decision, as well as making further investments in ERI.

ERI rewarded Allen's investment with significant growth. By 2000 its sales had increased to about $30 million. Making this growth more remarkable was the fact that it was not achieved through special customer financing or other financial gimmicks that were common in the Datacom field. Such financial incentives were used by managers to help them reach quarterly sales targets used to determine their bonuses. However, this focus on short-term numbers damaged the long-term viability of many companies. For example, customer-financing often led providers to purchase more Datacom equipment then they actually required. When the market softened or worse, melted down, the equipment manufacturers were either forced to take back their products or to try to collect from companies that had become insolvent.

As ERI grew, along with the overall Datacom market, I came under increasing pressure from some investors, industry experts, and bankers, to add gas to the fire by significantly increasing Allen's investment in ERI to further ramp up its growth. I did not succumb to this pressure because of my conservative business philosophy that included a jaundiced view of debt. That decision would be proved correct in 2001.

Up until the latter part of 2000, ERI was growing at a steady pace with sales then at $30 million for the year. However, signs of impending problems were beginning to show in the industry. In 2001 the Datacom market melted down even quicker than it had grown. Sales for many companies basically dried up instantly as the bubble popped due to an oversupply of equipment, shrinking product demand and the inability to further finance debt, a requirement to keep the bubble going.

ERI was not spared from the carnage. Its sales dropped from $30 million in 2000 by 16% to about $25 million in 2001. This resulted in ERI having a loss for the year of $8.3 million costing Allen Organ Company an overall loss of $7 million for the year. This was a painful time for ERI and its employees, as well as Allen Organ Company and me personally. ERI had to cut its costs to reflect the new realities of the business. This meant a reduction in headcount and combining two Datacom facilities by closing our Southampton, Pennsylvania, building, a move that required a $530,000 restructuring charge in the second quarter of 2001.

During this time period, ERI re-evaluated its strategy for the future. Our initial target market, like many other Datacom companies during the second half of the 1990s, had been the Competitive Local Exchange Carriers (CLECs). CLECs had significantly grown in number since 1996 when the Telecommunications Act of that year created a uniform national law to allow local exchange competition. This had the unintended consequence of stimulating the formation of many more CLECs than the market could ultimately bear. The formation of these CLECs, with easy financing from venture capitalists, equipment vendors and IPOs, was a significant contributor to the Datacom bubble of the late 1990s, which then turned into the "bust" of 2001–2002.

Mike and I had concerns about the long-term viability of CLECs even before their implosion occurred. As a result, ERI already had a plan in place to pivot from the CLEC market when the downturn started. This included targeting two alternative markets for ERI: cellular networks and international carriers. One of our first major cellular deals was with Nextel (then Sprint Nextel) for cell tower switching equipment. We were also successful in finding markets for our equipment with international carriers. In fact one of our vice-presidents moved to Asia for an extended period to direct operations there. This led to successes with significant carriers including Korea Telecom and Telstra of Australia.

Thanks to our change in strategy, the meltdown in 2001 was for ERI and Allen Organ Company, a period of significant challenge that was relatively short-lived. While many Datacom companies were forced to shut down as a result of the popped bubble, ERI not only survived, but began to thrive, becoming profitable after only two quarters of losses. In fact, ERI made a profit of over $2 million during 2002. This remarkable turnaround was a testament to the ERI products, its employees and management. It was also made possible because Allen did not saddle ERI with excessive debt. Finally, because of the respect that Mike Doyle gained within Allen's Board and me personally, we were confident in the ERI team's ability to navigate this very difficult period.

Debt is not always a destructive financing method. It can be used by companies to appropriately fuel growth if used productively. During bubbles, including the one that fueled the Datacom market in the second half of the 1990s, too much debt was used to fund exorbitant salaries, bankers' fees, inappropriate mergers and other unproductive expenditures. Even a small downturn in a market can be disastrous for companies with excessive debt. However, when a bubble pops, it can kill an entire industry, as it basically did with Datacom.

ERI was also able to become profitable by 2002 irrespective of the carnage in industry through being nimble, quickly taking the following actions:

- Pivoting away from CLEC's and to the international markets. Changing target markets allowed us to pursue sales to companies that were still liquid and growing. International service providers were selling to markets not distorted by the US Telecommunications Act of 1996.
- Focusing on the cellular market. The cellular market still had significant growth ahead of it. These providers continued to require equipment to grow their networks even after the US Datacom meltdown occurred.
- Rationalizing cost structure. Irrespective of how quickly we were able to pivot ERI's market focus, the pace at which the sales downturn occurred in 2001 required that we make difficult decisions. This included a staff reduction and merging locations. As difficult as this was, because we had strategic and spending plans in place that all employees understood and bought into, the ERI team was fully cooperative with these difficult efforts.
- Operating under new market conditions with fewer competitors. Because of the steps ERI took during the meltdown and because the company was not saddled with excessive debt, it was able to survive this traumatic period. Given that many companies serving ERI's markets did not survive, the competitive landscape improved significantly in ERI's favor.

ERI's growth continued after 2002. Sales rose 53 percent in 2004 year from the previous year, to nearly $55 million, accounting for more than 50 percent of Allen's consolidated total revenue.

By 2005 ERI had grown to an annual sales rate of $62 million and Allen was approached by several large companies interested in purchasing ERI. One Datacom company, *Sycamore Networks,* purchased ERI in 2006 for $92.5 million.

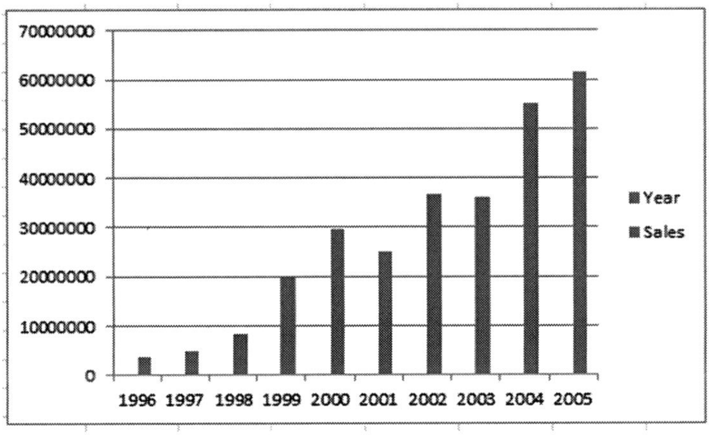

ERI's success rewarded Allen's shareholders with a good return on investment. In addition, ERI provided, despite the difficulties in 2001, a relatively stable work environment for employees during the 10-plus years it was owned by Allen. Certainly we offered far more stability than companies like Nortel, which let go tens of thousands of workers. In fact, most of the employees who were with ERI when Allen made the acquisition in 1995 were still there when the company was sold in 2006. At the time of the divestiture, ERI had approximately 275 employees compared to only about two dozen ten years earlier.

Fending off the bankers

Prior to the Datacom industry's 2001 meltdown, from 1999 through 2001, I met with investment bankers to consider options for the growing ERI that included spinning it off through an initial public offering (IPO). The bankers included US Bancorp Piper Jaffrey, SoundView Financial Group, BankBoston Robertson Stephens, Lehman Brothers, and Chase. In fact I was meeting with Lehman Brothers in New York the day Lucent Technologies' stock began its meltdown, heralding the huge correction that ended the Datacom boom.

I often found suggestions received from bankers disturbing and unrealistic. Some gave Allen astronomical valuations for ERI. During a time when ERI had sales of about $20 million, some bankers offered valuations for the company of hundreds of millions of dollars. These valuations were, no doubt, based on a value that could be obtained in the bubble stock market. They bore no relationship to the company's actual earnings and prospects.

One interesting comment I recall receiving from some bankers was that ERI was a good company, but it was not losing enough money that they felt was necessary to fund the type of growth investors were then demanding. These bankers wanted ERI to expand through the use of increased spending and debt in a similar manner Nortel did. This did not match up with my conservative business philosophy, or for that matter that of ERI's President, Mike Doyle. And, of course, after the Datacom bubble popped, the unrealistic valuations in the industry came tumbling back to reality, as the Nortel share price chart shows.

As a side note, most of the technology investment bankers I met with prior to the Datacom meltdown closed their offices after the markets' collapse. But it's hard to feel sorry for these folks, many of whom made huge fees on the financing activities that help fuel the bubble, then the bust.

Clearly one of the reasons ERI survived when so many other companies in the field failed was because Allen did not follow the bankers' advice. Our conservative financial philosophy and competent ERI management allowed ERI to quickly return to organic growth. When, in 2006, Sycamore acquired ERI for cash, they were confident in its value. At the time, Sycamore Networks President and CEO Daniel E. Smith said that the acquisition would combine Eastern's proven network access technology with Sycamore's extensive expertise in core optical switching, resulting in an integrated portfolio of solutions that would enable wireless and fixed-line operators to significantly increase the efficiency, agility, and scalability of their next-generation networks.

While this book reviews conflicts between the financial services industry and those they are supposed to serve, it is not an indictment of all within the industry. While the financial services industry is compensated in a manner that often puts it in conflict with those they serve, strong character of individual bankers can overcome this potential problem. My experience with the firm Raymond James shows this positive potential, as outlined in Chapter 5. Raymond James was ultimately chosen by Allen to negotiate and complete the sale of ERI to Sycamore Networks.

The ERI story is one of real value, not speculative value. Producing such real value is what business and finance should partner to make happen. Instead, as the next chapter discusses, the financial services industry often has its mind on more parochial needs.

---

[1] Nortel Networks, Annual Report, 1999

Chapter 5

When Bankers Do Their Job

This book is intended to decry excesses and abuses in the financial services industry – the general failure of that industry to serve clients best interests while allowing speculation to replace real value creation. It also reviews personal experiences that showed a lack of competence in the industry.

The book is not meant, however, to be an indictment of all participants in that industry. Our experiences with Stefan Jansen, of Raymond James, were of a different order. Unlike most of the bankers I met with over the years, Jansen demonstrated patience and a willingness to work for long-term benefit of his clients.

Going Private

Allen Organ Company had been a public company for approximately 40 years, trading on NASDAQ.

The 1960s were a time of growth for Allen. Access to capital through the public markets helped facilitate that growth. The fact that we were a public company in the late 1960s also allowed Allen make the multimillion dollar investment that involved great risk, but resulted in development and introduction of the world's first digital musical instrument, a decision that would propel the Company into successful growth for decades and enhance digital sound technology in general.

Allen success in the 1970s and 1980s from the digital organ ultimately help fund its diversification, including the highly successful investment in the Datacom industry.

But, at the turn of the century a significant change occurred to the required governance of public companies that made us seek change to our corporate structure strategy. One of the meltdowns that occurred at the turn of the new century was that of the troubled energy giant Enron of Texas. The Enron failure took down not only many investors and Enron employees, but also the huge accounting firm Arthur Andersen.

The government responded to the Enron debacle in its typical way: more regulation. The result was the Sarbanes-Oxley act of 2002. Those of us that managed smaller public companies at the time saw this Act and the many burdens it placed on companies as a boondoggle. It would not stop future fraud, but instead would be a gravy train for the accounting industry.

For Allen, attempting to comply with Sarbanes-Oxley would have cost hundreds of thousands of dollars and made producing a quality product in the United States more difficult. Given our relatively small number of shareholders, we were able to avoid the costs of the Act by taking the Company "dark", trading shares on pink sheets.

Sarbanes-Oxley gave us a powerful incentive for the next step, to ultimately take the Company private. It was not the first time we gave that direction consideration.

Fending Off the Bankers

During the years that Allen was a public company, various bankers contacted us from time to time suggesting that the Markowitz family take the Company private. The bankers obviously also sought to earn the large fees associated with that kind of transaction.

The bankers all pitched a leveraged buyout, a form of buyback of outstanding corporate shares that was trendy at the time (see the book *Barbarians at the Gates*[1] for the best-known examples).

The plan typical was:

- The Markowitz Family through a newly formed company would buy out other Allen shareholders using various forms of debt to fund the purchases.
- The new private company would then have substantial debt on its balance sheet, unlike the public entity that was nearly debt-free.
- The family would totally own the private company and would also receive cash, of course funded by debt.
- The newly structured private entity would use its future cash flow to pay off the debt required to take the entity private.

The bankers presented sophisticated spreadsheets and models purporting to forecast how the debt would be paid down in future years and how the family would profit from the transaction. None, however, took into account potential unforeseen business changes, such as downturns in either the market or overall economy, or skyrocketing expenses such as employee healthcare benefits. Such unforeseen circumstances are a normal part of any business and should clearly have been part of the scenarios. But the bankers, in their eagerness to earn fees, tried to paint as rosy a picture as possible to motivate the family into doing the buyout.

But we weren't taken in. The family's conservative financial philosophy resulted in avoiding the type of debt structure suggested by bankers that would have been required to take the Company private. This policy ultimately served the Company, its outside shareholders, its employees and the founding family well in the long term.

Many companies that took on the heavy LBO debt burdens failed after the buyouts, as unforeseen circumstances occurred making debt repayment impossible. While bankers prospered and insiders were able to take funds out of these companies, the related communities and employees suffered. Many American industries were gutted by LBO-derived excess debt, taken on, in fact, not to improve the companies' long-term capabilities, but to provide short-term gain for a few.[2]

Stefan Jansen (seated) attending ERI function with ERI VP John Sculley.

A Rational Approach

Shortly after the Datacom meltdown occurred, Allen was contacted by *Raymond*

James and its banker Stefan Jansen. Jansen not only had financial expertise, but also expertise in the Datacom field.

It was telling that Jansen initially contacted Allen during a time when the Datacom market was in a severe downturn and as a result there was no near-term possibility of business for Raymond James. Jansen, however, stayed in touch with Allen for some years, assisting ERI at various times without earning any fees.

We liked Jansen's different, rational approach, and so Raymond James was ultimately chosen by Allen to negotiate and complete the sale of ERI to Sycamore Networks. Contact with Stefan Jansen and his associates at Raymond James always included good communications in all respects and the bankers handled themselves with diligence and integrity.

Allen ultimately took the musical instrument and contract manufacturing businesses private in 2006, but without placing debt on the business. This was accomplished by the founding family using its proceeds from the sale of ERI to purchase the organ and contract assemblies businesses, the total operations of the Macungie, PA factory. These businesses continue to operate today under family ownership.

---

[1] Harper Collins, New York, 2009

[2] The literature on leveraged buyouts is extensive. See, for a useful summary, "The Causes and Consequences of Leveraged Buyouts," Michael R. Garfinkel, Federal Reserve Bank of St. Louis, 1989

Chapter 6

Goldin Ventures – Expansion Financed Organically

The first major business risk taken by the family was when Jerome Markowitz dropped out of college to pursue his invention of an electronic organ and started a business. From the late 1930s, with a hiatus taken for World War II, through the mid-1960s, this phase of the Company was defined by improving the oscillator organs' technology and growing the business.

The next major risk opportunity taken by the Company that defined its next major expansion was in 1967 when my father decided to fund and co-develop the world's first digital organ (actually the world's first digital musical instrument). This huge and ultimately successful bet helped define the Company's success and growth for the next 25 years. It would ultimately help fund the next major risk opportunity that the Company would take.

The third major risk opportunity was taken with the 1995 acquisition and venture into the Datacom industry. This decade-long journey was a major force behind the Company's growth through 2006, when the division was sold.

When Allen's ERI division was sold to Sycamore Networks, Allen signed an agreement with the buyer that we would not hire ERI employees for a specified period of time. This is typical when a company is sold since its employees are key corporate assets. Certainly, ERI's president, Mike Doyle, was one of the key employees.

Towards the end of Sycamore's due diligence of ERI, I asked if they planned to keep Mike on after the acquisition. They informed me this was not in their plans and I therefore asked permission to hire Mike for other plans that I had. They granted the request.

Given the relationship Mike and I developed over the years, the success we had at ERI, and our common business philosophies, I felt comfortable that we could duplicate the success achieved at ERI in other ventures. And that led to the next phase in the family's risk-opportunities search.

Mike and I started Goldin Ventures shortly after ERI was sold and the family had taken the musical instruments and assemblies business private. Goldin Ventures was the next manifestation of the family's philosophy to take prudent risk when presented with opportunity, while at the same time continuing avoiding debt.

Initially the game plan for Goldin Ventures was to leverage our abilities in the

Datacom field by purchasing spinoffs from larger Datacom companies, such as Lucent and Nortel, or to take majority positions in small technology companies. This plan did not pan out for two reasons. First, the large Datacom companies had little interest in spinning off cash-flow positive divisions of the size we desired. Also, attempting to purchase majority interests in smaller privately owned companies proved problematic due to the difficulty aligning sellers' and Goldin Ventures' view of valuations.

We then modified Goldin's approach to instead focus on minority investments in relatively young technology companies that already had revenue, as well as a logical plan to achieve growth and profitability. Taking minority interests in companies made the valuation negotiations (price) less contentious.

Goldin Ventures had morphed into a later stage angel-type investor with specialized capabilities. Because of our operational backgrounds, we not only offered capital, but also assistance to young companies that typically include technical people with minimal operational experience. For some of our investments we are involved with helping create their strategic plans.

Goldin Ventures sifts through as many as 100 companies in order to find one target that we feel is appropriate for investment. We look for companies with sound product ideas, committed and hard-working management, and sales traction. Another important issue is the compatibility between the target's business philosophies and our own. We favor companies that have conservative views of how businesses should be operated and managed.

At this writing, Goldin Ventures has invested in six companies. As is typical with early-stage investments, patience is required as these companies are nurtured and grow.

VanGogh Imaging

One example of a Goldin Ventures investment is VanGogh Imaging. They are a high-tech company providing affordable and easy-to-use embedded vision solutions for high-volume applications that can use mobile devices to capture, display and measure objects in 3D.

The 3D computer vision market took off when Microsoft introduced the Kinect technology to the market in 2010. This was the first affordable real-time 3D sensor and triggered interest in a large number of new applications. VanGogh Imaging adapted this camera technology for its first application in the agricultural industry and is working on additional applications including 3D printing.

The potential for VanGogh's technology is large and includes applications in the medical, manufacturing, security, consumer electronics and entertainment industries. VanGogh's embedded vision technology captures, measures, recognizes, and displays objects and scenes accurately in real time. Previously, mobile applications did not consider using 3D computer vision technology due to cost and complexity. Advances in cameras, projectors, and algorithms have dramatically reduced the cost and complexity of 3D computer vision with improved accuracy.

VanGogh is a technology "play" (investment). Like any advanced technology it is difficult for investors to fully understand the products' internal workings, which typically occur within integrated circuits or complex algorithms.

After due diligence, we invested in this company because of its management's broad vision to make its technology a standard within the 3-D recognition field. In addition its management has previously been successful in creating and running technology-based companies. Some investors from those earlier ventures are also investing in VanGogh. Finally, I felt comfortable that the principle's vision of corporate morality fit with my own.

Wizehive

Wizehive is another Goldin investment. Its products empower people to get customized business applications up and running quickly, often in less than an hour. These business applications gather various types of data to help get work done efficiently. This includes creating forms, customizing workflows and automating tasks in a shared and secure online database.

Users of Wizehive's products include educational institutions and nonprofits for scholarship applications and online contests. Its customers include Consumer Electronics Association, Society of Petroleum Engineers, Global Health Corps, and others.

After due diligence of the company, we felt confident about Wizehive's product and management, as well as the market it serves. It also became apparent that Wizehive's management philosophies were simpatico with ours.

Since making the investments, Wizehive, as has VanGogh, have communicated with us quarterly about their activities and results in a forthright and timely manner. How a company communicates with investors after investments are made is an important indicator of how management views its relationship with outside investors. Timely and accurate communications help demonstrate a partnership type approach, a positive sign.

An advantage for the early stage type investments Goldin makes is that none have included third-party intermediaries, i.e. brokers or bankers. While this eliminates fees and potential hidden motivations of such agents, these direct transactions require significantly more diligence on the part of investors. Such investments certainly involve risk. However, assuming that the investor's due diligence on the target companies and their management is thorough, the risk then focuses on the chosen markets, products and execution skills of management, and not on financial manipulation by others.

Early-stage investing, the business of Goldin Ventures, requires patience and involves risk. At the writing of this book is too early to judge the likelihood of success for any of the investments. However, we are generally pleased with the directions of all of the companies.

Chapter 7

The Trouble with Financial Advisors

If we've seen in the previous chapter how serious bankers can do their jobs well as advisors, we now have the telling example of the contrary. This is what can happen when they don't and it's a forceful example of what's wrong with the financial services industry.

Engaging Professional Investment Advisor

Before the sale of ERI, the publicly traded stock of the Allen Organ Company constituted the lion's share of my family's assets. This stock was owned by a Trust set up by my father before he passed away for the benefit of my mother. My mother (who has since also passed away) and I were co-trustees of the Trust.

Because the family's assets were mainly Allen stock, there were relatively few liquid assets. That lessened the need for outside financial investing advice and so we didn't call on it for the family's investing. This was apart from my dim view of its potential value.

I continued adhering to the basic philosophy that wealth is best accumulated by creating and managing successful companies. With this philosophy the family's liquid assets would be placed in low risk investments with the main goal being preservation of capital for future productive growth opportunities. I did not seek to use financial tools to maximize the value of these accumulated liquid assets.

- This is the same philosophy that enabled Allen to invest in the risky, but highly successful, Digital Organ project.
- It is the same philosophy that enabled Allen to invest in the data communication subsidiary. While highly risky, it also proved very beneficial to shareholders, employees, and the family.

But, after the ERI sale the Trust would have significantly more liquid assets, in addition to owning the private musical instrument and contract-assemblies businesses. I therefore decided to engage the services of a professional investment firm for two reasons:

- Our family's increased liquidity.
- With my fiduciary responsibility to the Trust I felt it prudent to seek the services of professionals.

That decision turned out to be disastrous.

I understood that the ERI sale would occur in September 2006. So, in the summer of 2006 I initiated a search for a financial advisory firm. Also, that summer I engaged Wachovia Bank (now Wells Fargo Bank) as a temporary advisor for the Trust while searching for a longer-term advisor. Wachovia's Glenn Thomas, Relationship Manager, was the Trust's contact at the bank. Wachovia was informed that their engagement was temporary, but that they would have the opportunity to compete for the longer-term engagement.

During the period that Wachovia was the temporary financial advisor they were informed that the Trust wanted the most conservative investment for its assets. Wachovia proposed a STIM (Short-Term Investment Management) for the investments that would include "*7 day Muni Floaters.*" Upon receipt of Wachovia's proposal, I questioned Thomas as to whether there was any risk for the investments via email dated August 16 (emphasis added).

> "Thanks for the info. As I read the info on STIM, **I believe there is downside risk. Am I correct?** If so, I'd like to be in a money market type investment, given the fluid nature of my planning. What can Wachovia offer in this area and what would the fees be?"

Wachovia responded that same day via email stating that there was no risk (emphasis added).

> **"There is no downside risk in the STIM that we would contruct for you**. **We would use 7-day Muni Floaters** which would give you a tax-free high current rate. Principal is guaranteed and matures weekly. **The only risk that you have is reinvestment risk, i.e. as the weekly rates go down your rate would go down as well**. But the reverse is also true. Also, this means then you would only be able to make distributions from this type of account with notice of about a week. My advice would be to use this type of account.
>
> Beyond the STIM, today we could provide a rate of 4.60% taxable on your existing Trust money market account. Assuming a 35% tax bracket that would be about 3.00% net after tax. This is a more traditional bank money market account. FYI, this is a promo rate that I could offer until 8/31 and the rate would then be good for 60 days. I do not know what the rate would be at the time of you closing. The guarantee that I will give you is my best efforts to get you the best available deal. However, I could put the 4.60% rate on the account any day before 8/31 to protect you if the Trust could deposit $250,000.00 of new funds into the account. The new funds are a requirment to get the rate.
>
> A long winded answer to is there risk. "

As we will see, Wachovia's claim that there was no downside risk to the assets in the STIM proved incorrect and the initial source of a great deal of trouble to come.

After appointing *Wachovia* as temporary advisor I interviewed four firms for the longer-term advisor role. One was Wachovia, a large bank with offices located near where I lived. While they managed the account on a temporary basis, I eliminated them as a longer-term choice because they had a significant personnel change during the search process. In addition, I felt Wachovia was too large of an organization for the Trust's needs.

Raymond James was, of course, another logical choice. However, I eliminated them because the people involved with wealth management were different from the bankers I used in the ERI transaction and the group that would have worked with the Trust was located in Georgia. In hindsight, eliminating Raymond James may have been an error given the successful relationship Allen already had with them.

I also considered a smaller local financial services company located near Allentown, Pennsylvania. This firm was not chosen because I felt their organization was too small for the Trust's varied needs.

Finally, my choice fell on Glenmede, a regional and mid-sized financial services company located in Philadelphia, PA.

Glenmede put on a full court press to obtain the Trust's account. On November 28, 2006 at Glenmede's office in Philadelphia I met with employees including Vice Presidents Dave Schwartz, Bob Kiep, Chuck Aulino, ant Hobie Porter, as well as Laura Larosa, a key person in their fixed income department, Chief Investment Officer Gordon Fowler and CEO Al Piscopo.

I chose Glenmede as the Trust advisor given the strength of their presentation that promised personal service. In addition I believed they were the right size for the Trust's needs.

Glenmede and Asset Transfer

After choosing Glenmede, the Trust's assets had to be transferred to them from Wachovia. On December 11, 2006 Wachovia was informed of the Trust's decision and that Glenmede would contact Wachovia to arrange the assets transfer. This process and the failure to properly complete it proved to be a source of significant problems later.

From December 11 on Glenmede took over the management of all aspects relating to transferring Trust assets from Wachovia. Glenmede sent updates to me concerning the transfer progress during the first few weeks of 2007.

According to Glenmede the transfer was competed as of February 1, 2007. This was confirmed by an email on February 1, 2007 from Glenmede's Trust Administrator and First Vice President David Schwartz, who informed me that it had received all assets (emphasis added).

> From: DAVE.SCHWARTZ
> Sent: Thursday, February 01, 2007 10:58 AM
> To: Markowitz, Steve
> Cc: ROBERT.KIEP; Eckhart, Nathan
> **Subject: Funding of Trust Complete**
>
> Dear Steve,
>
> We received a check for $180.95 from Schwab (Cornerstone), **so we now have everything here**.
>
> Regards,
> David
>
> David R. Schwartz
> First Vice President
> The Glenmede Trust Company, N.A.
> 1650 Market Street, Suite 1200
> Philadelphia, PA 19103-7391

While this Glenmede confirmation should have been the end of any issue relating to the Trust's transfer of assets from Wachovia, Schwartz's claim proved to be false. This would become a key issue in a litigation later initiated by the Trust against Wachovia and then Glenmede. The Trust would not be informed that Schwartz's statement was false until April of 2008, 14 months later. It is difficult to comprehend that such a statement from an advisor could be made, and later proven false, without appropriate corrective action taken – yet this is what happened.

<u>More Communications Issues</u>

From January 2007 through March of 2008 Glenmede seemed to be acting with diligence for the Trust. Trouble was brewing, but we knew nothing about it.

Between January 2007 and March 2008 Glenmede mailed the Trust monthly reports. None indicated a problem concerning any Trust assets. Quarterly meetings were also held between the Trustee (me) and Robert Kiep, Portfolio Manager, and again no threat to Trust assets was mentioned in any of these meetings.

In 2008, as the macro financial crisis began, I had concerns that I brought to the attention of Glenmede included in my email of March 15 and Glenmede's response below.

SM question (emphasis added)

> From: smarkowitz
> Sent: Saturday, March 15, 2008 10:04 AM
> To: ROBERT.KIEP
> Cc: Eckhart, Nathan
> **Subject: Trust Investments**
>
> Hi Bob.
>
> I've been in Europe for a week (returning Monday) and have had the opportunity to view the current financial markets' "challenges" with a more international perspective. Unfortunately that perspective does not make me feel any more comfortable.
>
> As the financial issues became more significant, about a month ago I internally set up two metrics to follow when attempting to determine if a spiraling effect might occur:
>
> 1) a run on the dollar, and 2) a major bank failing. Since both situations have started, I'm not going to move the goal posts.
>
> What percentage of the portfolio is currently in equities? I would like to hold on increasing this amount until the financial markets become more stable.
>
> **Also, is there any significant risk to any other Trust investment outside of the equities position?**
>
> Steve

Glenmede response (emphasis added):

From: ROBERT.KIEP
Sent: Monday, March 17, 2008 9:06 AM
To: Steve Markowitz
Subject: Re: Trust Investments

Attachments: Asset Allocation for Jerome Markowitz Trust.pdf

Steve;

I can really appreciate your views on the dollar and financial markets. What's nice is that our exposure to equities is 22% (see attached) and we have allot of cash available for investment. **Phone me when you get back into the country**.

Best Regards,
Bob

(See attached file: Asset Allocation for Jerome Markowitz Trust.pdf)

Robert P. Kiep, III
Glenmede
Philadelphia, PA

Kiep's response still had no mention of problems for any Trust asset. There was, however, a huge surprise that was to come from Glenmede less than three weeks later.

Kiep requested and set up the Trust's quarterly review at Glenmede's Philadelphia office for April 3, 2008. Prior to that meeting there was no mention of problems with any Trust asset. In fact, the invitation to the April 3 meeting included a Glenmede offer of tickets to the Philadelphia Phillies game after the meeting, which I declined. Given the bombshell that Glenmede was to drop on me at the meeting, it was fortuitous that I did not accept that invitation.

April 2008 - Bond Bombshell

I arrived on April 3 at Glenmede's offices with no suspicion of what was to follow. It proved to be a fateful meeting.

Upon arrival I was given a meeting agenda that included meetings with Bob Kiep, Gordon Fowler (Chief Investment Officer) and Laura LaRosa (Director of Fixed Income). Kiep started the meeting by reviewing relatively mundane issues relating to the Trust account. Then, almost as an afterthought, Kiep indicated that there were problems with Trust investments that would be reviewed later by Glenmede's Laura LaRosa.

After I'd listened to a general review of the economy from Gordon Fowler, LaRosa joined the meeting and explained that she was in charge of bond trading at Glenmede. She then dropped the bombshell concerning a large percentage of the Trust's assets held at Glenmede (approximately 25 percent). According to LaRosa, certain Trust assets were held as Auction Rate Securities (ARS).

This was the first time I had ever heard the term Auction Rate Securities or this type of investment. I learned that the Trust's ARS's were municipal bonds that included long-term nominal maturities, but whose interest was reset on a monthly basis through auctions. These bonds were treated by the financial markets as cash equivalents, since they could be redeemed at full par value every 35 days at the auctions.

LaRosa indicated that the ARS market froze up in recent weeks and these Trust assets were now illiquid. In fact she stated that some of these Auction Rate Securities could remain illiquid for up to 30 years.

I asked LaRosa how and why this problem to Trust assets had occurred. She explained that these bonds had come to Glenmede from Wachovia approximately 14 months earlier. Glenmede had been trying to sell them since, but could not because Wachovia did not transfer to Glenmede the required auction rights. Further, while Glenmede made many attempts during that period in an effort to obtain the auction rights, Wachovia had been totally uncooperative and unresponsive.

At the conclusion of meeting I asked Glenmede to provide me with more details showing Wachovia had been uncooperative. My goal was problem resolution. I needed to obtain additional facts from Glenmede to better understand the problem and causes behind it.

Glenmede knew before the meeting that the Trust bonds issue was significant. Even before I returned home from the April 3 meeting, LaRosa sent an email to Robert Kiep, the Trust Relationship Manager at Glenmede that was forwarded to the me stating (emphasis added):

> "***Note the date on our first email to Wachovia 2/8/07!!!!!!! Over a year ago. Constant phone calls after that yielded nothing****.* *The only real reason that they finally helped us is when I mentioned that Jefferson Hills* [one of the ARS's] *and I told them that I would report to the Markowitz' that they knew the bond was going into default and did nothing to help. The PERFORM report with the sample portfolio is coming over shortly.*"

LaRosa that same day sent an email to me stating (emphasis added):

> *"**This was the first email that we sent out. When we got no response we started calling and we called regularly throughout the whole year with no response to any of our inquiries.** I will forward other emails that I have a soon as I come up for air."*

These communications supported the contention LaRosa made during April 3 meeting concerning Wachovia's lack of cooperation. LaRosa's assistant, Richard Gale, provided further confirmation of this. Yet, months later, and only after Glenmede had been sued by the Trust, would it admit that their story concerning Wachovia was false. But, for the time being the evidence pointed at Wachovia's lack of cooperation. So my immediate reaction was anger at Wachovia.

I contacted Wachovia on April 4, 2008, one day after the Glenmede Philadelphia meeting. I emailed Glenn Thomas, the Trust's Account Representative at Wachovia, informing him of the illiquid Trust bonds. The email requested that Wachovia purchase the bonds from the Trust given their failure to cooperate with Glenmede (emphasis added).

> "*As you are aware, the Trust's assets were transferred from Wachovia to Glenmede Trust Company in January 2007.* ***I have been informed by Glenmede that they made multiple attempts since that time to get the required sign offs from Wachovia to transfer the auction rights related to these bonds in order to trade the bonds in question. For reasons that are not clear, Wachovia did not cooperate with the need in providing these approvals until recently and the bonds have become illiquid.***"

Thomas responded quickly, informing me that he turned over my communication to Wachovia's legal department – it was evident to me what that suggested! Wachovia's Assistant General Counsel, Pamela Pearson, responded putting the blame on Glenmede stating (emphasis added):

> "*While we understand your frustration with the current liquidity issues concerning your investments,* ***these assets were transferred out of Wachovia's management more than one year ago, and as a result we were divested of the ability to advise you or to affect a liquidation of the securities on your behalf.*** *As a result, we are unable to grant your proposal that Wachovia repurchased the securit*ies."

Who was telling the truth? While Wachovia's comments seemed logical, their response failed to address Glenmede's contention that Wachovia had the auction rights needed to sell the bonds, but did not make them available to Glenmede.

I forwarded Wachovia's letter to Kiep for Glenmede's comments. Kiep responded indicating that Glenmede's Corporate Counsel (James Belanger) had reviewed the Wachovia letter. He insisted that the fault was Wachovia's, reiterating what the Trust much later learned was a false claim: "*We did go to Wachovia requesting the auction rights in early 2007. There were emails and numerous phone calls*."

I expressed concern to Kiep about the way problem resolution was preceding. In response, Kiep informed me that the matter was turned over to Glenmede's Corporate Counsel and Vice President, James Belanger, who would get back to me directly.

On May 7, 2008, I was contacted by Belanger who stated:

- He would prepare a "ghost letter" for my signature to be sent to Wachovia to help pressure them into buying back the problematic bonds.
- He also recommended that if that letter did not work, the Trust should sue Wachovia.

The fact that high level Glenmede executive was getting involved, who also happened to be its Corporate Counsel, offered me some confidence that Glenmede was working diligently towards problem resolution. However, this conclusion, too, would later prove to be incorrect.

Battle Lines Form

On May 9, 2008, Belanger sent me an email with items to be included in the threatening letter to Wachovia (emphasis added):

> From: JIM.BELANGER
> Sent: Friday, May 09, 2008 3:21 PM
> To: smarkowitz
> Cc: ROBERT.KIEP; LAURA.LAROSA
> Subject: Wachovia letter
>
> Mr. Markowitz
>
> Here is a draft letter to Wachovia that asserts your displeasure with the negligent behavior of Wachovia.
>
> The points to put forward are 1. Once notice is received, trading is supposed to stop. Any subsequent trades were unauthorized.
> 2. **Wachovia has been unresponsive. This may be their normal standard, but it has been so egregious as to be a liability to them.**
> 3. Finally, the premise upon which they created this portfolio was grossly misleading. Given the outcome, they bear some continuing responsibility.

There are two areas where information should be filled in. The trades after receipt of the letter at the end of 2006 and before January 22, 2007. I did not have that information. The second is the specific securities that you want them to take. If you need help with either I am sure that Bob and Laura can assist.

Its unfortunate that Wachovia has chosen to stonewall on this issue.

Given the amount at risk, this should be resolvable by them.

(See attached file: markowitz.doc)
James R. Belanger
Corporate Counsel
The Glenmede Trust Company

It is instructive that Belanger's email was copied to both LaRosa and Gale. Neither corrected any fact included in the email, even though we would later learn that they knew the highlighted portions were false.

As our advisor with fiduciary responsibilities to the Trust, I believed Glenmede's claim that Wachovia was uncooperative given it was repeated in writing, as well as by a Glenmede officer and its Corporate Counsel, Belanger. So, on May 12, 2008, I sent a letter to Pearson at Wachovia that reiterated Glenmede's claim (emphasis added):

> "***It is a fact that Wachovia ignored the repeated request from Glenmede to provide the auction rights to the securities. I have been advised that this amounts to gross negligence by Wachovia. In support of these fact are numerous email and written requests to Wachovia for the necessary rights to sell the securities, all without response.***"
>
> In addition, the letter stated: "***In summary, I believe that I have just cause to take Wachovia court and that others may share my predicament.***"

All information included in the above letter to Wachovia concerning the illiquid bonds was supplied by Glenmede. Wachovia's response (or lack of it) to my letter indicated that it was unwilling to participate in problem resolution and that led to my decision to initiate a lawsuit against Wachovia on behalf of the Trust based on what I later learned was false information supplied by Glenmede. In hindsight, it is incredible that Glenmede stood by while I initiated a lawsuit against Wachovia based on their false accusation.

The First Time in Court

In August, 2008 the Trust initiated a lawsuit against Wachovia. The main claims against Wachovia were based on information supplied by Glenmede that included (emphasis added):

> 16. Petitioner's new investment advisor attempted to sell the said Jefferson County Municipal Investment, as well as other investments made by the Respondent, **but was unable to do so without the authorization of the Respondent**.
>
> 17. Respondent did not give the required authorization to sell until March 2008, **despite repeated requests by Petitioner's investment advisor to do so**.

After initiating the lawsuit, the Trust began taking discovery on Wachovia that included collecting documents and calling depositions of various Wachovia employees including Glenn Thomas, who was the Trust's Account Manager at Wachovia and Roshel Isakharov and Michael Kennedy.

Wachovia also took discovery that included depositions of Glenmede's Richard Gale and me, the Trust's Co-Trustee.

Information obtained in depositions indicated that Auction Rate Security bond trading was esoteric with few outside controls. It also became apparent that Wachovia employees who actually dealt with the Trust, including Glenn Thomas, did not understand the investments made for the Trust.

This lack of knowledge at the customer service level was similar to what occurred in the macro market meltdown that involved Collateralized Debt Obligations (CDO's). Many investors found themselves with losses to their investments that even their own bankers did not understand. Michael Lewis wrote a detailed account of the macro meltdown and issues in *The Big Short,*

Discovery also indicated a lack of diligence by Wachovia that included:

- Wachovia's Glenn Thomas email and committed to the Trust that Wachovia would invest Trust assets in "*7 day Muni Floaters*" that could be traded every seven days. The Trust learned that the ARS's Wachovia instead invested in could only be traded every 35 days.
- Wachovia's Glenn Thomas represented to the Trust in an email dated August 16, 2007, that these investments had no risk. *"There is no downside risk in the STIM that we would contruct for you."* Given what happened to the Trust's ARS's, this representation was obviously not true.

- Wachovia also purchased one ARS for the Trust in December 2007, even after receiving notice of cancellation for being the Trust's advisor. Wachovia blamed this on an employee vacation issue.

It was only after the litigation was well underway that we learned that Glenmede had played a major role in causing Trust assets to become illiquid.

Chapter 8

The Advisor Didn't Do The Job

Wachovia had made mistakes – there was no question about that. But, as we learned too late, the principal fault in our bonds becoming illiquid lay with the longer term advisor I engaged in late 2006, Glenmede. That advisor, who was supposed to protect the client's interests, did something entirely different.

When the Trust initiated the lawsuit against Wachovia, we believed that our advisor, Glenmede, had been diligent in trying to sell the Auction Rate Securities during the 14-month period between January 2007 and March 2008. This is was what they told us repeatedly.

We also believed that its Corporate Council, James Belanger, on behalf of Glenmede, was acting as a fiduciary for the Trust. Both beliefs proved incorrect. It became apparent through discovery that Glenmede's repeated claim that Wachovia's lack of cooperation caused the bonds to become illiquid was false. More specifically, we learned that had Glenmede been diligent in efforts to obtain the auction rights, the bonds could have been sold at full face value from February 2007 through February 2008, as there were many successful auctions before the market froze up.

The Advisor Acts Against Our Interests

During the first quarter of 2009 we learned that Glenmede was attempting to protect its own interests instead of the Trust's by misrepresenting the actions of its bond traders and those of Wachovia. This is, of course, entirely opposed to the way a financial advisor is supposed to act.

With the discovery that Glenmede had been disingenuous with the Trust concerning Wachovia's lack of cooperation and its own failure to sell the bonds, we asked Glenmede to be involved with a settlement that would make the Trust whole for the illiquid bonds. Glenmede, through James Belanger, refused our settlement overtures.

Belanger instead informed the Trust that Glenmede's position was that the Trust should continue its litigation against Wachovia and that after it was completed, Glenmede would somehow help right the wrong. This suggestion was outrageous to me for several reasons. Glenmede's lack of diligence, incompetence and misrepresentations were not only involved with the bonds becoming illiquid, but also led to the Trust suing Wachovia based on false information Glenmede had supplied us.

For obvious reasons we didn't have much trust in Glenmede after their bad faith. In addition, the Trust had been paying for the litigation against Wachovia, not Glenmede. Therefore, in April 2009, Glenmede was made a codefendant in the Trust's suit against Wachovia. Glenmede was also fired as the Trust's advisor with Trust assets being transferred to another firm.

Based on what the Trust had learned through discovery in the Wachovia litigation, the Trust's complaint against Glenmede included (emphasis added):

> 23. Glenmede represented that it would and did undertake to sell said assets at auctions that were held periodically in regard to the Jefferson County and Mobile County investments.
>
> 24. Despite this representation, **Glenmede did not take appropriate steps to sell said assets with the result that the markets have ceased to exist and the trust is left with poor quality investments in Jefferson County and Mobile County as noted above.**
>
> 25. **Glenmede misrepresented that it was in fact taking appropriate steps to sell said assets when in fact, little or nothing was done to sell said assets.**
>
> 26. **Numerous successful auctions were held for both the Jefferson County and Mobile County securities over the space of the next year or so yet Glenmede failed to participate in any of them with the result that the Trust still has the assets which are now not of investment grade and are poorly rated by the major bond rating agencies.**
>
> 27. Respondent failed to take the steps necessary to secure the auction rights to said securities and dispose of said securities and failed to properly represent and handle the assets of the Trust.
>
> 28. Respondent represented that it had expertise and knowledge in the field of auction rate securities and investments when in fact, the personnel assigned by Respondent had little knowledge of these markets and were unable to properly participate in the auctions and dispose of the assets.

<u>Discovery Tells the Tale</u>

The litigation now included expanded discovery on Glenmede and this enabled the Trust to obtain documents and collect interrogatories and sworn depositions of the following Glenmede employees. All except one were later called as witnesses at trial.

- Al Piscopo – Glenmede's then CEO
- James Belanger - Senior Vice President and Corporate Counsel
- Robert Kiep - First Vice President and Relationship Manager
- David Schwartz – First Vice President and Trust Administrator
- Laura LaRosa - Director of Fixed Income
- Rich Gale - Assistant to Laura LaRosa

This discovery ultimately supported and strengthened what had already been learned during the Wachovia discovery: The main reason the Trust ARS's were not sold before the market froze up was due to Glenmede's lack of diligence and incompetence. Further, Glenmede engaged in a cover-up to the Trust in an effort to protect its own interest and not that of the Trust.

Given what was learned about Glenmede's actions and in an effort to simplify the litigation, the Trust settled with Wachovia in October 2010 for a relatively small sum. The litigation then proceeded solely against Glenmede.

Glenmede's own testimony will be used in this chapter to paint a dark picture that started with incompetence and lack of diligence, then evolved into deceit and cover-up. It also shows Glenmede's poor internal controls and that it was not following related federal regulations or its own internal procedures relating to client services.

Glenmede's Competency Issues

Discovery indicated that certain Glenmede employees lacked basic skills required to properly manage the Trust's funds. When the Trust's bonds became illiquid, Glenmede then began a cover-up scheme in an effort to have its lack of diligence blamed on Wachovia.

During its first sales meeting with the Trust in Philadelphia in November 2006, Glenmede clearly wished to demonstrate to the Trust its know-how for handling the Trust's investments. Glenmede brought in several high-level employees to meet the Trust including Al Piscopo, its CEO. This had been very impressive. But discovery and trial testimony would raise questions about the firm's competence.

David Schwartz was a Trust Administrator and 15 year employee at Glenmede, as well as a Vice President when he worked with the Trust. He also had a degree in law. I was impressed that a person with these credentials would be working with the Trust. So I ask in hindsight: How could a person with this kind of experience and know-how be responsible for allowing these troubled assets to be administered so poorly?

During discovery, it became clear that Schwartz lacked even basic understanding of the Trust's Auction Rate Securities that he was charged with bringing into Glenmede, as well as other relatively simple organizational issues.

For example, at trial, Schwartz testified that he did not know if Glenmede's Operations Department was responsible for bringing client assets into Glenmede. Making this lack of basic Glenmede operations knowledge more curious, Schwartz was in the courtroom while Glenmede's CEO, Gordon Fowler, already answered that simple question. This response indicates a callous attitude and lack of basic knowledge by Schwartz concerning operations at a company for which he was an executive.

[Fowler (emphasis added)]

Q - Sir, when you were the chief investment officer of Glenmede, did you, **was it under your purview to determine that the assets coming into Glenmede could be handled by Glenmede?**
A - **Actually, that would have been a decision that is largely an operational decision.** And that would have been determined by someone in our operations area. I might have evaluated it from a sort of, is this an appropriate investment type of, of thing. But operational-type of issues, I would not have evaluated.

[Schwartz (emphasis added)]

Q. - Okay. ***Isn't it correct that the operations department determines if Glenmede could handle the investments?***
A. ***- I don't know.***
Q. - ***Well, where you here the last time when Mr. Fowler testified and said exactly that, the CEO of Glenmede?***
A. - ***If he said that, it's true.***

While Schwartz was the Glenmede employee responsible for bringing Trust assets in from Wachovia and he kept the Trust informed of progress, he did not inform the Trust of any problem with the transfer, even though he admitted that should have been his responsibility.

[Schwartz Deposition (emphasis added)]
A. - "As administrator, ***I opened the account and facilitated the transfer of the assets from the prior advisors to Glenmede****."*

[Schwartz Deposition (emphasis added)]
Q - Schwartz 5, that purports to be an e-mail from you to Mr. Markowitz, copying Mr. Kiep and Mr. Porter, dated January 8 of '07. Correct?
A. - Yes.
Q. - And what were you conveying in this e-mail?

*A. - **I was keeping the new client apprised of the transfer process, to let him know it was in process, and that we had, our operations person had checked with the prior custodians.***
*Q. - Let me ask a different way. **Did you ever learn of any difficulties with any of the Wachovia assets transferred to Glenmede?** [Prior to this lawsuit]*
*A. - **No.***

[Schwartz Trial Testimony (emphasis added)]

*Q. - Mr. Schwartz, **if there was any problem in getting the assets over from Wachovia, would you have notified the trust?***
*A. - **Yes.** The securities transfer people tell me if there's undo delay and I tried to keep the client appraise the back."*

Schwartz also testified at trial that he did not even know what an Auction Rate Security was! Yet he was the employee responsible for bringing Trust assets into Glenmede and a substantial portion of these Trust assets were in Auction Rate Securities.

[Schwartz Trial Testimony (emphasis added)]

*Q. - Okay. **Sir, in January of'07, and you know what auction rate securities were?***
A. - no.

[Schwartz Deposition (emphasis added)]

Q. - Okay. Do you know what an auction rate security is?
A. - No. [September 22, 2009, 1 ½ years after the Trust's Auction Rate Securities were transferred into Glenmede.]

As a National Bank, Glenmede is subject to the *Code of Federal Regulations*. Under section 9.6 point (a) of this Code it states: "***Before accepting a fiduciary account, a national bank shall review the prospective account to determine whether it can properly administer the account.***" Given Schwartz's lack of knowledge of ARS, it is hard to imagine how this requirement was followed concerning these Trust assets.

Lack of knowledge seems to have been endemic at Glenmede. Richard Gale was a key player in trading Trust bonds and became involved with the cover-up concerning Glenmede's supposed interactions with Wachovia. He reported to Laura LaRosa who was the head of Glenmede's fixed income and bond trading.

LaRosa made Gale responsible for selling the Trust bonds. During trial, LaRosa testified that selling Auction Rate Securities was a relatively simple matter typically given to lower-level employees.

[LaRosa Trial Testimony (emphasis added)]

Q - Given that he worked for you, why did he respond to Mr. Eckhart and not you?
A - ***Rich would typically handle auction rate securities*** *and those -- and floating rate notes because it wasn't-- you don't need a lot of sophistication to handle this.* ***This is something that typically we give to the more junior people on the desk to handle. That's not, it's not a big deal. -There's no real skill in handling that****.*

[LaRosa Trial Testimony (emphasis added)]

Q - You indicated that you assigned Mr. Gale-and please correct me if I'm wrong ***-- you assigned Mr. Gale the duty to take care of the auction rate securities because you do not need sophistication and no real skill is needed****?*
A - ***Anybody can tender an auction rate bond, but we didn't have him as the auction rate guy****. Anybody who had them in an account could do it. At Glenmede that was a fixed income person.*
Q - ***Were you here earlier in this case when Mr. Gale testified that it was the most, one of the most difficult things he ever did****?*
A - ***This was a particularly difficult thing for him****.*

Given LaRosa's testimony it must be assumed that Gale lacked some basic skills. Why then was he given the task to manage the sale of the Trust's ARS?

In fact, Gale testified during deposition that he could not recall ever requiring more than a month to obtain auction rights. Given it took approximately 14 months to obtain the auction rights for the Trust bonds indicates either a lack of diligence or competence.

[Gale Deposition (emphasis added)]

Q. - ***Were there any situations where it took a year to acquire the bidding rights prior to the Markowitz trust account****?*
A. - ***I do not recall any situations where it took in excess of a year.***
Q. - ***How about in excess of a month?***
A. - ***I don't specifically recall an instance it took longer than a month.*** *I do not recall a situation where it took longer than a month.*

Laura LaRosa was Glenmede's Director of Fixed Income during the time it managed the Trust assets. She had been employee at Glenmede for over 15 years. Rich Gale reported to her. Given the significance of the problems Glenmede had in obtaining the auction rights and selling the Trust's Auction Rate Securities, it was remarkable that she did not even recall discussing the matter with any Glenmede employee.

[LaRosa Deposition (emphasis added)]

Q. - During the 2007/2008 period, ***did you ever indicate to Ms. Wirts or anyone else at Glenmede prior to April of '08 of any particular problems you were having trading any bonds within the Markowitz portfolio****?*
A. - ***I don't recall****.*

[LaRosa Deposition (emphasis added)]

Q. - Okay. Rich Gale reported to you?
A. - Correct.
Q. - ***Did, at what point did Rich Gale indicate to you he was having problems liquidating those bonds****?*
A. - ***That, I can't be sure of****.*

With the amount of funds involved with the problematic Trust bonds this is surely an issue that she might have kept track of.

And Glenmede CEO, Al Piscopo, also claimed to have little knowledge of various matters (Sometime before the trial Piscopo was replaced as Glenmede's CEO by Gordon Fowler). During his deposition Piscopo showed a significant lack of knowledge on many issues asked. It is left to the reader to interpret this.

Piscopo (emphasis added)

Q. - Was the subject of ***auction rate securities*** *ever discussed that you can recall at the management committee meeting?*
A. - ***I don't remember****.*

Piscopo (emphasis added)

Q. - Okay. Were the ***issues concerning the Markowitz Trust ever*** *discussed at a management committee meeting?*
A.- ***Not that I remember****.*

Piscopo (emphasis added)

Q. - Here is what's been marked as Piscopo 2. ***Do you recall receiving Piscopo 2****?*
A. - ***No, I don't****.* [Piscopo 2 is a letter dated March 25, 2009, to Piscopo from Steve Markowitz concerning the Trust ARS.]

Piscopo (emphasis added)

Q. - And this indicates an upcoming meeting I believe with Mr. Markowitz and Mr. Eckhart of the Markowitz Trust, and indicates that you are going to speak at, you were going to be at the meeting about 2:00 o'clock. ***Do you recall being at that meeting?***

A. - ***No.***

Piscopo (emphasis added)

Q. - In regard to his dealings with the Markowitz Trust prior to this, the suit being filed, ***did Mr. Belanger report anything to you about what was going on in regard to the Markowitz Trust****?*

A. - ***I don't remember****.*

Piscopo (emphasis added)

Do you know, does Glenmede have a document called a policies and procedures manual?
A. - Yes.
Q. - Are you familiar with it?
A. - Yes.
Q. - ***Okay. Does this manual list Glenmede's responsibilities to its clients?***
A. - ***I don't know****.*

Piscopo (emphasis added)

Q. - That's all I ask. Do you know, does Glenmede have a document called a policies and procedures manual?
A. - Yes.
Q. -Are you familiar with it?
A. - Yes.
Q. - Okay. ***If it is determined that Glenmede does have a conflict of interest with a client, how does Glenmede resolve the issue? What does the manual indicate, do you know?***
A. - ***No, I don't.***
Q. - Okay. ***What would you expect Glenmede to do to resolve a conflict of interest?***
A. - ***It depends****. You're saying a conflict between we, as a corporate organization, and our client?*
Q. - Yes.
A. - Where we have a conflict?
Q. - Yes.
A. - How would I expect to resolve that? ***I guess I would want us to acknowledge it to the extent we were aware that we, as an organization, had a conflict****. I'm not sure I know what the ultimate resolution might need to be.*
Q. - ***Okay. Do you know if Glenmede and the Markowitz Trust developed a conflict of interest over these bonds?***
A. - ***No.***

During the period that the Trust engaged Glenmede through trial, James Belanger was its Senior Vice President and Corporate Counsel. He reported directly to Glenmede's CEO and sat on Glenmede's Management Committee and Risk Management Committee. Belanger was also the Compliance Officer with responsibility of ensuring that Glenmede adhered to federal codes required of National Banks.

Belanger became involved with the Trust in May 2008 when I expressed concern to Glenmede about the lack of progress in pressuring Wachovia to buy back the problematic bonds. Belanger informed me that he was brought in to assist the Trust with problem resolution.

Evidence presented in discovery and at trial showed that instead of serving the interests of the Trust, Belanger went into "circle the wagons" mode helping perpetuate the covering up concerning Glenmede's lack of diligence with respect to the illiquid bonds.

Given that Belanger was Glenmede's Compliance Officer, his response to related deposition questions was telling.

[Belanger's (emphasis added)]

*Q. - **Now, you sit on the management committee of Glenmede, do you not?***
*A. - **I do.***
Q. - Do you sit on any other committees within Glenmede?
A. - Yes.
Q. - Which ones?
A. - I sit on the risk management committee, I sit on the vendor management committee, I sit on the security committee; those are the only ones that I can recall.
*Q. - **Okay. What's the function of the management committee?***
*A.- **I'm not sure I can precisely tell you.***

[Belanger's (emphasis added)]

*Q. - Yeah. **Is there someone at Glenmede whose responsibility it is to ensure that the firm follows prudent business practices as investment, as an investment steward for its clients**, or is it just basically the whole management committee that oversees that?*
*A. - **I don't know**.*

Belanger's "lack of knowledge" was broad. If a client cannot have the expectation that Glenmede will carry out its instructions, it is difficult to imagine Glenmede accepting a fiduciary responsibility for it.

[Belanger's Deposition (emphasis added)]

Q. - ***Did Mr. Markowitz have a right as the customer of Glenmede to assume that Glenmede was going to carry out his instructions?*** *That's the first question.*
A. - ***I don't know.***

In yet another telling exchange during his first deposition, Belanger indicated he did not know if Glenmede had a policy relating to conflicts of interest that may arise with clients. This is remarkable coming from Glenmede's Corporate Counsel and Compliance Officer.

[Belanger's (emphasis added)]

Q. - I asked about conflicts of interest, and whether how, if you could define the types of conflicts of interest that may arise, and then I'm going to ask you what Glenmede does about such problems.
A. - Conflict of interest could arise if the company had a monetary interest in an investment. A conflict of interest could arise... I'm hard pressed to come up with another example beyond that.
Q. - ***All right. Does Glenmede have a policy as to what to do in the event conflicts of interest do arise?***
A. - ***I'm not sure.***

Who did know? Who takes responsibility? No one at Glenmede seems to have known!

At Belanger's second deposition on July 15, 2010 he testified that he did not know why Robert Kiep, who was charged with managing the Trust's account, was not made aware of the problem with bonds during the 14 month period they were supposedly trying to obtain the auction rights. Given that this response occurred over two years after the bond market froze up indicates at best an unwillingness to search for truth.

[Deposition (emphasis added)]

Q. - ***Why wasn't Kiep made aware of the problem with the auction rights for 14 months?***
A. - ***I don't know.***

<u>Lack of Diligence</u>

A key issue in the litigation was: Why did the Trust's Auction Rate Securities become illiquid and who was responsible for the bonds not being sold before the markets froze up. During trial the Judge, J. Brian Johnson, made the following comments (emphasis added):

Okay. So now we have 14 months, something took 14 months that should've taken about a month. I want you to think about whether you're willing to agree that, because I'm not - I sit here waiting for things that matter and everything else is a waste of time, as far as I'm concerned.

I want to focus on what the question for me is. The big question.

Isn't the question then, who was responsible for that delay and within that, you know, whether there was a reasonable explanation for the delay? So we know there's a delay. The question is, was there reasonable explanation that was no one's fault or was it someone's fault? And, if so, whose responsibility was it? Was Wachovia? Was a Glenmede? Was it trustees? Was it all of them? Isn't that really what I'm looking At --

The Judge's opinion issued 11 months later seemed to lose sight of these important questions.

Glenmede testified that it discovered the Trust assets transferred from Wachovia included Auction Rate Securities in January 2007, almost immediately upon receiving them. They also determined within weeks of receiving these bonds that they did not want to keep them as an investment for the Trust and decided to sell them. Gale's trial testimony confirmed this.

[Gale (emphasis added)]

Q - ***And was that in January of '07 when you made that discovery?***
A - ***I think it was in late January, really, really early February that we found those auction rights.***
Q - ***When you noticed that the auction rate securities were there, you went to Ms. LaRosa?***
A - ***Correct.***
Q - Okay. And you discussed that-- again, I don't want to put words in your mouth. What did you discuss with her?
A - I brought it to her attention that there were auction rights that we found in this portfolio. And I, basically, the initial conversation was me just telling her that there were auction rights in this portfolio.
Q - And did you also have a discussion with her that these were not the kind of assets that you normally held in portfolios like this?
A - There's other assets that we would prefer to hold.
Q - Okay. And was it determined - excuse me. I think you answered this, but I want to make sure. ***There was a determination made at that time to dispose of those assets****?*
A - ***We, we decided that we were going to try to liquidate the securities*** *to try to get the auction rights, participate in the auctions and move them out of the portfolio.*

[Gale (emphasis added)]

Q - ***And you started that process right away?***
A - ***Correct.***
Q - ***In January, February of '07****?*
A - ***That's correct.***

After Gale's testimony, his supervisor LaRosa testified at trial on the same issue concerning when Glenmede decided to sell the problematic bonds. LaRosa tried to equivocate in a rather transparent attempt to avoid the obvious question: If Glenmede made the decision in January 2007 to sell these bonds, why did it not succeed? The answer is relatively clear: It is because Glenmede did not actually try to sell the bonds until the market froze up and then created the false Glenmede story that Wachovia was uncooperative.

[LaRosa (emphasis added)]

Q - ***Was Mr. Gayle incorrect when he said he came to you and said that he wanted to get rid of these?***
A - My guess is that we would prefer to not hold auction rates rather than to hold seven~day floaters.
Q - ***Right. And that's in that January, February, 2007 time frame you're answering, correct?***
A - ***I would guess, if that's what he said, then that is what he said, that's what he did.***

[LaRosa (emphasis added)]

Q - ***And the discretion in this case was, it was a determination made to get rid of these bonds, right****? The Jefferson-- specifically, the Jefferson and Mobile bonds?*
A - That ***eventually*** *we wanted to get out of all the auction rates in the account; that's correct.*

With LaRosa's equivocating, the Trust's attorney repeated the question. Finally, the Judge interjected indicating that he understood the issue. Unfortunately, the Court's decision issued many months later did not confirm this understanding.

[LaRosa (emphasis added)]

Q - Okay. And because of that possibility is part of the reason why in January and February of '07, Mr. Gale came to you in and a determination was made--
THE COURT*: -* ***I think I have it.***

LaRosa also testified at trial that after the markets froze up she threatened Wachovia with contacting the Trust about the missing auction rights and this got Wachovia's attention. There are two problems with that testimony. First, evidence presented at trial indicated that she was able to obtain the auction rights within one week of actually attempting to do so in March 2008. This also raises the question as to why she did not use this threat as a lever before the bond market froze up.

[LaRosa (emphasis added)]

Q - Then you said further in that e-mail, I believe -- and I don't have it in front of me. Maybe the second page-- quote, ***The only real reason that they--- meaning Wachovia --finally helped us is when I mentioned the Jefferson Hills and I told them that I would report to the Markowitzes that they knew the bond was going into default and did nothing to help****, end quote. Did you write those words?*
A - That's, that is correct. Those are on that email. But this is what I meant by that~~ or, maybe to interpret that: When a client leaves a firm, there is very little desire on the part of the old firm to help the new firm because now they are no longer a client. So at some point, we were down to just our last couple and we really wanted to get out of them because bad news was coming out about, about the auction rate market, ***so I decided to, at that point, see if maybe we could get some help from Mr. Markowitz****.*
Q - But you never did ask him for it until April, did you?
A - That's when the problem started happening, sir.

[LaRosa (emphasis added)]

Q - Excuse me?
A - The reason that they transferred the rights over finally was because I invoked the fact that I really wanted to get them done, get the rights in, get it over with or I would call the client and have the client call and complain*.*
I don't-- I think that was okay to do. I think that was the right thing to do, at that point.
Q - So when you sent this to Wachovia, you had not yet told Mr. Markowitz about it -- right? – you were threatening to do so?
A - Probably.

At this point LaRosa was asked a key question concerning the 14 month delay in Glenmede's obtaining the auction rights. Her response -- that this inaction was because the markets were functioning normally -- was closer to reality than the false story given to the Trust that it was due to Wachovia's lack of cooperation.

Q - Okay. Any reason why you didn't make that threat in the 14 months previously?
A - The auction rate markets were functioning normally up until the beginning of 2008 sometime*. Either the late winter of 2008 or the spring of*

2008. I don't remember exactly when it was. But the point is that this was going on for a while and we wanted to get them, we wanted to get it over with At this point.

Gale's trial testimony confirmed that when he and LaRosa finally contacted Wachovia about the auction rights in March 2008, they were able to obtain the rights within a week. The ease in which Glenmede was able to obtain these rights is further evidence that their lack of diligence caused the bonds to become illiquid.

[Gale Trial]

A - We called Sharon Malia, yeah.
Q - And within a week or so of that time, she put you in touch with the appropriate people at Wachovia, did she not?
A - She put us in touch with different people than the first time that we spoke to her.
*Q - **But you were satisfied within a week or two of that that you had those auction rights, didn't you?***
*A - **We got the auction rights probably about a week after we reached out to her**.*

The testimony by LaRosa and Gale confirms their lack of diligence and honesty with the Trust concerning why the Auction Rate Securities became illiquid. Glenmede's then CEO Al Piscopo expressed concern during his deposition about the Trust not being informed of Glenmede's problems selling the Trust ARC's.

Piscopo (emphasis added)

*Q. - And I'm asking **if you have a difficulty in trading or otherwise dealing with those aspects, do you feel that Glenmede has a responsibility to advise the client**?*
*A. - **I would imagine, responsibility, I think that relationships involve a fair amount of communication**. The breadth of this communication is going to depend on the specifics of any individual situation and the complexity around whatever kind of assets we may be talking about. Often these are really quite complex.*

Piscopo (emphasis added)

*Q. - Well, there is, **assuming that there had been an order to Glenmede to liquidate securities in January of '07, and as of April of '08 it still had not occurred, do you think there was an obligation in that 14 month period to at least tell the client it wasn't occurring and why?***
*A. - **I would presume someone might have spoken with the trustees**.*

While Glenmede's Corporate Counsel Belanger also attempted at trial to equivocate, he testified that Glenmede should have communicated with the Trust earlier about the problems Glenmede had selling the bonds.

Belanger (emphasis added)

Q - Mr. Belanger, let's look at page 86 of this deposition. I'm sorry. That's the wrong page, too. I'm sorry. It's the wrong deposition. Let me get you the second one. Actually, it's the top of page 87 of your second deposition. That's the first one, I believe, sir. Is that the one in my office? That's the first one. This is the second one. ***I asked you, do you believe that Glenmede's delay in informing the Trust was inappropriate in any way? Could you tell the Court what you answered?***
A - ***In any way, given the nature of the question, sure, it would have been good client service to have communicated with the client.***

Given Glenmede's actions, good client service does not seem to be a real requirement for the firm.

At trial Belanger was also questioned about the 14 month period during which Glenmede did not sell the problematic bonds. The Judge interjected, asking Belanger about the reasonableness of Glenmede not selling the Trust bonds within that period. Belanger indicated that not selling these bonds within a six-month period might be a concern. This is a rather remarkable admission given that, if Glenmede had contacted the Trust after only six months of receiving the bonds concerning their problems liquidating them, these bonds still could have been liquidated since the market was then functioning normally.

Belanger (emphasis added)

THE COURT - Let's do this. I would just like -- ***I think we've been all around this question. What's your final answer to the fact that there were 14 months from January '07 to April of '08 and what is your answer to why -- well, his question is whether or not you had an obligation. That's the first question.***
THE WITNESS - Well, I believe that this is a situation where they lacked the option rights and were working on the issue. These weren't, these were all investment grade securities that were paying interest and were not in default, so there was nothing inappropriate about keeping them and they were working on the issue to try to get rid of the securities. So it's one of those "Where do you draw the line?" kind of situations ***where after a month, no, there's no big concern, after six months, you might be more concerned and after 14 months, yeah, in hindsight, that looks like you should have raised your hand sooner and let Mr. Markowitz know that we were having this issue. I'm not sure we had the obligation to inform him of that operational issue, but it would have been good client service.***

Part of the discovery served on Glenmede included "Requests for Admissions". With Admissions a litigant asks questions of the other party who is then required to admit or deny them. Admissions are designed to simplify presenting uncontroverted facts at trial. The following Admissions by Glenmede were read into the trial record.

42. Successful auctions for the Mobile County ARS were held on May 9, June 13, July 18, August 4, and September 26, 2007. Glenmede did not liquidate the ARS at those auctions (emphasis added).

    Response: Admitted that there were five successful auctions for the Mobile County ARS from May to September 2007 and that Glenmede did not liquidate the ARS at those auctions because it could not. For clarification, Glenmede believes the August auction was held on August 22, not August 4.

43. Successful auctions for the Jefferson County ARS were held on May 17, June 21, July 26, and August 30, 2007. Glenmede did not liquidate the ARS at those auctions.

    Response: It is admitted that Glenmede did not liquidate the ARS at those auctions, because it could not.

55. From February of 2007 through January of 2008, there were 11 successful auctions involving the Mobile County ARS and 11 successful auctions involving the Jefferson County ARS.

    Response: It is admitted that during this time period, there were 11 successful auctions involving the Jefferson County ARS. It is denied that there were 11 successful auctions involving the Mobile County ARS; to the contrary, there were 10.

These Admissions of uncontroverted facts indicate that if it wasn't for the incompetence of Glenmede in obtaining the auction rights, a process that began in January 2007 and was not completed until March 2008, the two problematic bonds could have been liquidated at full value. Yet the Judge's findings would ignore these Admissions.

Chapter 9

Advisor Bad Faith

It seems relatively elementary that in order to properly manage a client's account that a financial advisor needs to know its risk tolerance. Glenmede not only admitted to the importance of this, but also that key Glenmede personnel responsible for trading Trust assets did not know its risk tolerance.

Gordon Fowler, Glenmede's CEO, testified at trial as to the importance of its bond traders knowing a client's risk tolerance.

Fowler (emphasis added)

Q - Would you expect the bond traders, people in the fixed income department*, to understand and know what the terms of the investment policy statement are?*
A - I would expect the bond traders bond portfolio managers to know what policy guidelines they are working under.
Q - Would you also expect them to know the risk tolerance of the account?
A - I would expect them to know the risk tolerance.
Q - So you would agree with me, if in fact Ms. LaRosa had no idea what the risk tolerance of this account is, somebody fell down somewhere here?
A - If Ms. LaRosa had no idea of the risk tolerance, if that wasn't communicated either in form of policy or whatever, there would potentially be an issue there*. But I would want to know more facts on that.*

However, Laura LaRosa who was ultimately responsible for trading the Trust's bonds testified that she did not know the Trust's risk tolerance.

[LaRosa Deposition (emphasis added]

Q. - Okay. ***Were you aware of what the risk tolerance of the Markowitz Trust was?***
A. - ***I was never told what the risk tolerance was****.*

[LaRosa Deposition (emphasis added)]

Q. - Okay. ***How did you get the input as to what the risk tolerance and investment goals of the trust were****? Who gave it to you?*
A. - ***That's something that we discussed with the client when we meet with the client.***
Q. - ***Well, do you remember discussing that with Mr. Markowitz?***
A. - ***No. I do not remember discussing that with Mr. Markowitz.***

*Q. - **Do you know what the risk tolerance of the Markowitz Trust was?***
*A. - **I don't know. I don't have firsthand knowledge of it.***

Kiep testified in deposition that he understood the conservative financial posture and low risk tolerance of the Trust, as well as its desire for liquidity. However, LaRosa's testimony along with her department's lack of diligence that allowed the Trust's Auction Rate Securities to become illiquid indicates at best poor communications within Glenmede.

[Kiep (emphasis added)]

*Q. - **What was your understanding of the risk tolerance of the Markowitz Trust?***

*A. - **That Steve didn't want to take a lot of risk**, that this was an income generating, to be more of an income generating company because his mother was the income beneficiary, and that growth was a secondary...*

*Q. - **Would you agree, then, that the market tolerance for risk was lower than many clients of Glenmede**?*

*A. - **Yes**.*

[Kiep (emphasis added)]

*Q. - All right. And specifically on page 3, which I think is the page you had, that is the page, do you agree with me **one of the most important objectives for the account included liquidity?***

*A. - **It's written on here.***

*Q. - Okay. **And why was that important?***

Q. - Why did you understand that was important to the trust in generating this?

*A. - **Because Mrs. Markowitz is older, and at some point in time she would pass away and there may be needs for estate taxes and the like**.*

Were these bonds equivalent to Money Market Accounts?

When Wachovia was made the temporary financial advisor for the Trust it understood the Trust's low risk tolerance. Wachovia therefore invested a substantial portion of the Trust assets in Auction Rate Securities since these bonds acted like money market accounts up until March 2008.

Various Glenmede employees confirmed the high level of liquidity of Auction

Rate Securities during discovery and at trial. In addition, they confirmed that the Trust's Auction Rate Securities were in the cash portion of the Trust investments at Glenmede.

[Gale Trial (emphasis added)]

Q - What happened after you brought the auction rate securities to Ms. LaRosa's attention?
A. - We talked about it and decided that we were going to start the process to get the auction rights and tendered securities at the following auctions.
Q. - As of January 2007, when you had this discussion with Ms. LaRosa, were auction rate securities considered inappropriate?
A. - I don't think so. We had received them into other clients' accounts and we didn't think that they were inappropriate because ***they were investment grade short-term investments that were functioning like a money market vehicle.***

[Gale Trial (emphasis added)]

Q. - ***Mr. Gale, you said that the auction rate securities were functioning like a money market vehicle in'07*** *- January of '07, right?*
A. - Yes.
Q. - Okay. And a money market vehicle, functioning like a money market vehicle means what?
A. - This is, I think this goes back to the issue of being a shorter term or reset, so that most of the money market funds will hold vehicles that reset their interest rates.
Q. - ***Money market funds you can liquidate at any time, correct****?*
A. – ***Correct.***

[Gale Trial (emphasis added)]

Q - Do you -- strike that. Now, ***during this time frame, from January, February of '07 until March of '08, there were numerous successful auctions for Jefferson, Jefferson, Mobile securities, were there not? The market wasn't frozen.***
A - ***That's correct.***
Q - ***Okay. But you were unable to participate in any of them; is that right?***
A - ***That's correct.***

[LaRosa Trial (emphasis added)]

Q - And do you remember Mr. Gale coming to you and saying, There's these auction rate securities and I think we need to get rid of them?
A - Well, I don't know in particular that I remember it was right at that moment.

Q - It was at some point, though?
A - It wasn't about we have to get rid of them. ***These were cash substitutes or money market substitutes that were usually held in cash management accounts, which is how they came to us in the first place because they were in a cash management account in Wachovia which is what the aim of having the portfolio was so they were moved over to Glenmede****. They were still considered cash management substitutes or money market substitutes.*
Q - ***Was Mr. Gayle incorrect when he said he came to you and said that he wanted to get rid of these?***
A - ***My guess is that we would prefer to not hold auction rates rather than to hold seven day floaters.***
Q - ***Right. And that's in that January, February, 2007 time frame you're answering, correct?***
A. - ***I would guess, if that's what he said, then that is what he said, that's what he did.***

[LaRosa Trial (emphasis added)]

Q - During the time period from January, February of '07 until March of '08, when this difficulty with the auction rights was occurring, did you think it was important to tell the relationship manager?
A - Not really. There wasn't any -~the market was functioning perfectly normal, so there was really no need to discuss anything with the relationship manager. ***Again, this wasn't something that was a risky security.*** *This was a money market-type substitute.*

LaRosa was partially correct. The Auction Rate Securities should have been a cash substitute and would have been if it were not for Glenmede's lack of diligence in obtaining the auction rights required to sell them. Both Belanger and LaRosa testified at trial that the liquidity issues and impairment of the value of the problematic bonds did not occur until the markets froze up, over a year after Glenmede received and decided to sell the bonds.

Belanger (emphasis added)

Q - But isn't that what Glenmede's defense is throughout this case, that it was market forces, it wasn't us?
A - I believe Mr. Markowitz's claim is that he's stuck with an illiquid asset and the reason that it's an illiquid asset isn't because we purchased an illiquid asset for him, it's because the market no longer exists.
Q - ***And because you didn't sell it within the 14 months, correct?***
A - ***That's correct.***

At the end of this portion of LaRosa's testimony, the Judge interjected indicating that he understood that had Glenmede acted the bonds could have been turned into cash. Unfortunately, by the time the Judge issued his decision months later, he either had forgotten or ignored this important point. He later corrected his error.

[LaRosa (emphasis added)]

Q - So every 35 days, if there's a 35-day thing, they could turn, literally turn into cash; is that right?
A - For the most part.
Q - And you believe that was the case from January of '07, when they came to Glenmede, until March or so of '08?
A - That's correct.
Q - Correct? Now that was true if, in fact, you could participate in those auctions, correct?
A - That's correct.
Q - ***But isn't it true that Glenmede could not participate in the auctions because, in your words, and this-- in Glenmede ...***
A - ***The option rights were not transferred to us.***
Q - So because of that, they were not cash equivalents -- isn't that right? -- because you couldn't participate in the auctions?
A - Well, I mean that's --no, they-- no. The security didn't change its stripe just because of that. There was -- in the Trust, just so you know, they held only this type of security that would be set to short term interest rates and that was the main key of the Trust, was to make sure that the interest rates were always being set on a short term basis, so everything they held was being set at a short term basis.
Q - ***At any time during those 14 months, 12 months, whatever it was, if you had the option rights, could you have turned those into cash?***
THE COURT: ***Yes. I know the answer.***
MR. BERGSTEIN: Thank you.
THE COURT: ***Yes. Let's talk about something we haven't talked about about 10 times already.***

Advisor Fees

The method by which Glenmede and other financial advisory firms are often compensated may have been a motivating factor in not being forthright with the Trust concerning its lack of diligence with the bonds. During the period that the Trust's bonds were illiquid and until Glenmede was fired by the Trust, they continued to collect their full fees on these bonds, as confirmed by Kiep at trial:

[Kiep (emphasis added)]

*Q. - **Now, sir, the fees that Glenmede received were based on the value of the assets, correct?***
*A - **Yes.***
*Q. - **and that included the auction rate securities for Jefferson County and Munro County, isn't that correct?***
*A - **Yes.***
*Q - **And that was so during the entire relationship; isn't that right?***
A - Yes.
*Q - **Even after the markets froze for auction rate securities in March or April of '08?***
*A - **Yes.***

Failure to Communicate!

Discovery revealed that Glenmede employees responsible for managing the Trust account often did not communicate with each other concerning important issues. Robert Kiep was a Glenmede Vice President and Relationship Manager for the Trust. Kiep helped create the Investment Policy Statement (ISP) for the Trust that not only included the legal framework for managing a client's portfolio, but also states the client's investment goals and objectives.

Kiep testified that Glenmede used a team approach for managing the Trust's account. This team included Robert Kiep, Laura LaRosa, Scott McGough, Rich Gale, and Dave Schwartz. However, according to testimony, only LaRosa and Gale were aware of the bonds' problems and neither communicated these issues to Kiep or Schwartz, let alone to the Trust, until after the markets had frozen up, 14 months after Glenmede began having problems trading the bonds.

Kiep Deposition (emphasis added)]

Q. - Were you the person at Glenmede who was the primary contact with Mr. Markowitz?

A. - Yes.

*Q. - **Did you ever advise Mr. Markowitz that all of, that there was any problems with obtaining assets from Wachovia, other than the April of '08 meeting that you've already described?***
*A. - **No.***

[Kiep Deposition (emphasis added)]

*Q. - **Did you ever inform the trust that there were some, there were some problems with anything in regard to the accounts**, any of the investments that the trust held?*

A. - I think it was April of '08.

[Kiep Deposition]

Q. - Does an account, for lack of a better, have a team associated with it?

A. - Yes.

Q. - Has the team changed on the Markowitz trust over time at Glenmede?

A. - No.

Q. - Who is on that team, please?

A. - Well, myself and the fixed income department, people at the fixed income department that the Markowitz have talked to are Laura LaRosa, Scott McGough, Rich Gale, and Dave Schwartz is the trust administrator on the relationship.

[Kiep Deposition (emphasis added)]

*Q. - **So you just learned of it just prior to the April of '08 meeting?***

*A. -**Yes**.*

Schwartz testified in deposition that he was unaware of any issue or problems relating to Trust assets he brought into Glenmede until early 2009, approximately 10 months after they became illiquid.

[Schwartz (emphasis added)]

*Q. - Okay. Now, from this time on, from, I believe the date is January 22nd of '07, from that time onward, what, **when was, when was the first time you were informed by anyone there were any problems in regard to the Jefferson County and Mobile bonds?***
*A. - **Early in 2009 I learned there was some problem with something.***
Q. - And who told you that?
A. - Bob Kiep.

It is hard to understand why bond traders Gale and LaRosa did not inform Kiep of the problems given his responsibility to communicate with the Trust. It is also difficult to understand why Schwartz was not informed of the problem, given Gale's testimony at trial that that he understood Schwartz was responsible for bringing in the Trust bonds to Glenmede.

[Gale (emphasis added)]

Q - Okay. Now, who was responsible for bringing the assets over from Wachovia within Glenmede?
A - The physical request or the person that would coordinate the transfer?
Q - Both.
A - Well, we have operations personnel that put through the paperwork and track the securities from the previous investment manager.
*Q - **Okay. And was Mr. Schwartz overall in charge of bringing those assets over?***
*A - **I think so**.*

A remarkable example of poor internal communications leading to incompetent client service is confirmed by the fact that problems within the Auction Rate Securities market were actually discussed within Glenmede during the fourth quarter of 2007, months before the market froze up and the Trust's bonds became illiquid. However, Glenmede employees responsible for managing its Auction Rate Securities were unaware of the problems or even that these relevant internal discussions had occurred.

Glenmede's James Belanger testified at deposition and trial that problems within the Auction Rate Security market were discussed at a Glenmede employee meeting during the fourth quarter of 2007.

[Belanger Deposition (emphasis added)]

*Q. - **When did you first become aware of auction rate securities?***
*A. - **Fourth quarter of 2007.***
Q. - And how did you become aware of them at that time?
*A. - **I recall there being a discussion about the auction rate securities market having difficulties.***
Q. - Okay. This had nothing to do with the investments in the Markowitz Trust?
A. - No.
Q. - Did it, did you testify you didn't really know anything about the Markowitz Trust until May of '08, did you tell us?
A. - Yes.
Q. - Okay. What was in the discussion in the fourth quarter of '07, that you can recall?
*A. - **There was a general concern about fixed income securities and their, the fixed income securities market and its continuing functioning. ….***
Fourth quarter of -- '07. I'm sorry.
Q. - Do you remember who discussed that, where you heard this discussion and who was involved?

*A.- **There is a Monday morning investment meeting that's open to all employees of the company** where general market conditions are discussed. And it was at that meeting.*

[Belanger Deposition (emphasis added)]

*Q. - **Well, whether it was a report or discussions, there was knowledge at Glenmede in the fourth quarter of '07; we can agree on that, can't we?***
*A. -**We can agree that there was -- we can agree that there was concern about all fixed income investments, including auction rate securities, in the fourth quarter of 2007.***
*Q. - **Why didn't Glenmede tell the Trust, the trustees about these difficulties knowing that the Trust had auction rate securities?***
*A. - **I don't know.***

[Belanger Trial (emphasis added)]

*Q - **Mr. Belanger, you were aware, were you not, that the auction rate security market was having difficulties in the fourth quarter of** '07?*
*A - **I previously testified during my deposition Belanger-that I recalled a meeting during, sometime during the fourth quarter of 2007 where concerns about the auction rate securities market was mentioned.***
Q - Right. And you also were here when both Mr. Gale and Ms., Ms. LaRosa said they knew nothing about that, correct?
A - I believe they testified that they recalled nothing like that.
Q - Okay. But you said it was a general employee meeting of Glenmede?
A - I recall it being a Monday morning meeting which is open to all employees, but it's mostly staff or attended by portfolio managers or relationship managers entrusted and anyone else who may be interested.

While Belanger recalled the Q4 2007 Glenmede meeting discussing the Auction Rate Securities' problems, Richard Gale and his supervisor Laura LaRosa both testified at trial that they did not recall the meeting or discussions of the problems during 2007. At best this testimony can be accounted for by poor internal communications.

[Gale (emphasis added)]

*Q - **Were you at the meeting in the fourth quarter in '07 at Glenmede where it was discussed the auction rate securities market was having difficulties?***
*A - **I don't recall that meeting.***
Q - Did anyone tell you in February of '07 -- I'm sorry. ***In the fourth quarter of 2007, did anybody at Glenmede tell you that the auction rate market was having difficulties?***
*A - **I don't recall hearing that.***

Q - Did you recall hearing that from anyone outside of Glenmede?
A - I don't recall hearing that.
Q - Now, sir, were auction rate securities, did they come within your department, the fixed ~~ was it fixed income department?
A - Correct.
Q. - Did they come within your department?
A - When you say, "come within," do you mean, were they under our review?
Q - I'm sorry. Yes.
A - Yes.
Q - ***Would you have expected if there was someone at Glenmede with some knowledge of some difficulties in the auction rate market that it would have been communicated to you?***
A - ***We probably would have been the ones communicating that there was difficulties****.*

[LaRosa Trial (emphasis added)]

Q - ***Do you remember a discussion in the final LaRosa – Direct quarter of 2007 concerning problems in the-difficulties in the auction rate security market?***
A - ***I do not.*** *I thought about that the other times that you've asked that question. I don't believe there were problems in the auction rate securities market until 2008, but I may be wrong on my recollection of that.*
Q - ***So the fact that it's been admitted by Glenmede, that there were discussions in meetings at Glenmede in the final quarter of 2007 about difficulties in the auction rate security market, you don't recall that?***
A - ***I don't know who would have said that, and I don't remember that.***

[LaRosa Trial (emphasis added)]

Q - ***And given that it was admittedly discussed in the fourth quarter of '07 in a Glenmede meeting open to all employees that there were difficulties in that market, don't you think you should have been told about that?***
A - ***Sir, I don't know who said it.*** *Do you know who said it? Because I don't know who said it.*
Q - Ma'am, ***it's been admitted by Glenmede*** *that it was discussed in a meeting.*
A - Okay.
Q - ***Isn't that kind, the kind of information you would expect your department to know during the fourth quarter of 2007?***
A - ***I --I don't-- yes. Absolutely****. If it was disseminated in a meeting, I would know about it. I don't believe there was trouble in the auction rate securities market until 2008. I've said that many times and I'm pretty sure that's correct.*

Robert Kiep, who also was involved with managing Trust assets, testified at trial that he did not recall the Q4 2007 Glenmede meeting when problems in the Auction Rate Securities market were discussed.

[Kiep (emphasis added)]

Q - ***Mr. Kiep, were you aware of any difficulties in the auction rate security market in the fourth quarter of 2007****?*
A - ***I don't recall that****.*
Q - ***Do you, do you attend regular meetings at Glenmede where market conditions are discussed?***
A - ***Yes****.*
Q - ***Do you remember a meeting in the fourth quarter of 2007 where it was discussed that the auction rate security market was in trouble?***
A - ***I don't recall.***
Q - ***Did anyone at Glenmede tell you during the fourth quarter of 2007 or in early 2008, for that matter, that the auction rate security market was in trouble?***
A - ***I -- I don't recall.***
Q - Sir, you had at least one account, the Markowitz Trust, that had auction rate securities in it, correct?
A - Yes.
Q - Did you have others -- do you know? Can you recall?-- at that time?
A - I don't recall. 9
Q - ***Sir, if there was knowledge within Glenmede that there was a problem with the auction rate security market, do you expect that someone would have communicated that to you because one of your accounts had auction rate securities in it?***
A - ***Sure. But I'm not sure if there was an obligation to do it or not. I don't know.***
Q - But you would have expected someone would have told you, wouldn't you?
A - Yes.

In order to put a nail into this coffin, during the first day of the trial the Trust read into the record Admissions 15 and 16 where Glenmede admitted as incontrovertible fact that it was aware of problems in the Auction Rate Securities market and that they had a meeting open to employees on this issue during the fourth quarter of 2007.

Admissions # 15 and 16 (Emphasis added)

15. **Glenmede was aware of problems in the ARC market in the fourth quarter of 2007.**

Objection and Response: Glenmede objects to this request because it does not know what Petitioners mean by "problems in the ARC market" or to whom they are referring when they say "Glenmede was aware .... " **Subject to, and without waiving, these objections, it is admitted that individuals at Glenmede were aware that the auction rate securities market was having difficulties.**

16. **The problems in the ARC market were discussed in a Glenmede meeting open to Glenmede employees in 2007.**

Objection and Response: Glenmede objects to this request because it does not know what Petitioners mean by "problems in the ARC market." Subject to, and without waiving, this objection**, it is admitted that individuals at Glenmede discussed in a meeting open to employees in the fourth quarter of 2007 that the auction rate securities market was having difficulties.**

After all of this evidence, it was mind-boggling that the trial Judge found that Glenmede was not aware of the problems in the Auction Rate Security market until the markets froze up in March 2008, as will be discussed later in this book.

False Information

The first instance of Glenmede supplying the Trust incorrect information about the bonds actually occurred during the first week of February 2007, approximately five weeks after taking over management of the account. The fact that this false information was supplied out of ignorance does not obviate Glenmede's responsibility to a client. This inaccurate information stopped the Trust from intervening before the bonds became illiquid.

Schwartz incorrectly informed the Trust during the first week of February 2007 that all of its Wachovia-based assets were received at Glenmede, as he confirmed in deposition.

[Schwartz (emphasis added)]

Q. - I'm sorry, the front page.
A. - Okay.
Q. - And what did you say to Roe Rauser in that e-mail?
*A. **- I believe this is everything.***
*Q. - **What were you referring to?***
*A. - **That the items listed on the statements from Wachovia had been transferred to Glenmede.***

[Schwartz (emphasis added)]

*Q. - **Schwartz 9, this purports to be an e-mail dated February 1 of '07 to Mr. Markowitz indicating you had received a check for $180.95 from Cornerstone, so now we have everything here.** Would your answer be the same as to this, you got the information from the securities transfer department?*
A. - That the items listed on the Schwab account had each come to Glenmede.
*Q. - **And now according to, you understood and were conveying that this was the, this completed the funding of the Markowitz Trust account At Glenmede. Correct?***
*A. - **Yes.***
*Q. -**And in fact, that's the subject of your e-mail, isn't it, funding of trust complete, correct?***
*A. - **Yes.***

This false information was critical as it confirmed to me that all Wachovia-based assets were now at Glenmede, ending any concerns I might have had on the issue. Glenmede would not inform the Trust that Schwartz's statement was false for approximately 14 months, even though its bond trading department knew the information was not correct for at least a year. But by then the bonds had become illiquid.

During his first deposition, Belanger testified that he did not know if Schwartz had informed the Trust that Glenmede had received everything relating to the assets transfer. Belanger also testified that it would have been reasonable for Schwartz to correct this with the Trust if his information was not accurate. However, since Schwartz testified that he was not informed of the problem until after the Trust sued Glenmede and he did not even know what an auction rate security was, obviously he could not properly inform the Trust of the problem.

[Belanger (emphasis added)]

*Q. - **Okay. Do you know if he** **[Schwartz]** **ever told Mr. Markowitz that it wasn't everything, that there were still things they needed?***
*A. - **I don't know.***
*Q. - Okay. **You agree that he should have told Mr. Markowitz if, in fact, everything wasn't received, do you not?***
*A. - **I believe that would have been reasonable**.*

During his second deposition Belanger finally confirmed that Schwartz was wrong when he informed the Trust that everything relating to its assets had been transferred in from Wachovia.

[Belanger (emphasis added)]

*Q. - **So Mr. Schwartz was wrong when he said that everything had been received; is that correct?***
*A. - **He was incorrect in the context that the auction rights** had not been transferred to Glenmede's name at that time, correct.*

Belanger testified during his second deposition what was obvious, that the Trust, its client, should have been able to rely on Glenmede's written communications. This was remarkable given the false information Glenmede sent to the Trust in writing authored by Schwartz that was never corrected until they were sued, even though Gale, LaRosa and ultimately Belanger knew that statement it to be untrue. Instead, Glenmede concocted the false story about Wachovia's lack of cooperation that ultimately resulted in the Trust suing Wachovia.

Further, after supplying the Trust with false information, Glenmede had the gall to then blame the Trust for not managing Glenmede properly.

[Belanger Deposition (emphasis added)]

*Q. - **During the time that Glenmede was engaged by the Trust, was it reasonable for the Trust and the trustee to rely on written communications from Glenmede as being accurate?***
*A - **I believe so.***

It was evident that Glenmede was serving its own interests and not that of its client, the Trust. While its own lack of diligence resulted in the Trust's bonds becoming illiquid, it created the false story concerning Wachovia's lack of cooperation in an effort to place blame elsewhere.

Chapter 10

The Cover Up

Glenmede's cover up began on April 3, 2008 when it first informed me of the false story that it was Wachovia's lack of cooperation in obtaining the auction rights that caused the Trust's ARS bonds to become illiquid. Glenmede maintained this false story even after the Trust initiated a lawsuit against Wachovia. Individually, any Glenmede action of cover up is problematic. When viewed as a whole they raise more serious implications.

Discovery and testimony during trial proved that Glenmede completely misrepresented its efforts with Wachovia and Wachovia's lack of cooperation. Placing a nail in the coffin of this cover up, the following Glenmede Admissions were read into the record at trial.

Admissions # 59 and 60 (emphasis added)

59. **Between February of 2007 and March of 2008, Glenmede did not send one written communication to Wachovia concerning the ARS.**

    Glenmede response - Objection and Response: Glenmede objects to this request because it does not know what Petitioners mean by "between February of 2007 and March of 2008." Subject to, and without waiving, this objection, and assuming that "between February of 2007 and March of 2008" means the period from March 2007 through February 2008, **this request is admitted**.

60. **Between February of 2007 and March of 2008, Glenmede did not make one call to anyone At Wachovia Bank concerning the ARS.**

    Glenmede response - Objection and Response: Glenmede objects to this request because it does not know what Petitioners mean by "between February of 2007 and March of 2008." Subject to, and without waiving, this objection, and assuming that "between February of 2007 and March of 2008" means the period from March 1, 2007 through February 29, 2008, **this request is admitted**.

In these Admissions Glenmede confirmed that its representations to the Trust concerning the many contacts to Wachovia in both writing and on the telephone were false without question.

While Glenmede made the decision by February 2007 to sell the Trust's Auction Rate Securities, between February 2007 and March 2008 they made no contact with Wachovia to further that effort. At trial, Gale claimed that this lack of contact was not Glenmede's "standard practice". This response begs the question as to why they represented otherwise to the Trust. The answer is obvious: To hide Glenmede's complicity in not selling the bonds that became illiquid.

[Gale Trial (emphasis added]

*Q. - **In January, February of '07, did you make any communication at all with Wachovia between January, February of '07 and March of '08?***
*A - **I --I don't think that we did. It's not standard practice.***

Almost immediately after being introduced to the Trust, James Belanger, Glenmede's Corporate Council, ghost-wrote a threatening letter for me to send to Wachovia. During his first deposition Belanger indicated that he believed the information included in that letter was correct when penned, including the claim that Wachovia was uncooperative. It should be noted that the deposition was taken in September 2009 after Glenmede was made a codefendant in the litigation, approximately 15 months after Glenmede's cover up with the Trust was initiated.

[Belanger (emphasis added)]

Q. - Let's look at Belanger 4. This purports to be an e-mail dated May 9 of '08 from yourself to Mr. Markowitz, copy to LaRosa and Kiep -- do you see that? -- and a blank copy to Gale?
A. - I do.
Q. - Do you recall sending this?
A. - Yes.
Q. - What was the purpose of sending it?
*A. - **The purpose was to give Mr. Markowitz a draft that could articulate the points that were expressed to me in a manner that would be clear and direct.***
*Q. - Now, you refer to a draft letter. **Did you prepare a draft letter for Mr. Markowitz to send to Miss Pearson?***
*A. - **Yes.***
Q. - Now, the information contained in there in items one through three, that's based on information you received from whom?
A. - Could you repeat the question?
*Q. - Yeah. **Who gave you the information contained in items one through three?***
*A. - Mr. Markowitz, **Laura LaRosa.***
*Q. - **Item two, which says Wachovia has been unresponsive, this may be***

their normal standard, but it is, has been so egregious as to be a liability to them, what are you referring to there? How is, how were you saying that Wachovia had been unresponsive?
*A.- **I was referring to the transfer of the auction rights.***
Q. - And stating, and you believed that Wachovia was unresponsive in transferring the auction rights?
A. - Repeat the question?
Q. - You believed Wachovia was responsive in regard to transferring the auction rights?
A. - Currently?
Q. - No. At the time you wrote this.
*A. - **That was my belief.***
*Q. - **At that time?***
*A. - **Yes.***
*Q. - **Is that your belief today?***
*A. -**Yes.***

However, later in that same deposition, Belanger testified that up until the time of that deposition he did not even check on the number of contacts Glenmede made to Wachovia to obtain the auction rights.

[Belanger (emphasis added)]

*Q. **- Have you subsequently reviewed the attempts made to contact Wachovia regarding the transfer rights subsequent to May 9 of '08? Have you reviewed that?***
*A. - **No.***

[Belanger (emphasis added)]

*Q - **Do you know as you sit here today what steps Glenmede took between January of '07 and January of '08 to liquidate Mobile and Jefferson?***
*A - **Not specifically.***

[Belanger (emphasis added)]

Q. - Do you recognize Belanger 5?
A. - Yes.
Q. - What is that?
*A. - **It is a letter to Miss Pearson. I believe it's the draft e-mail that I sent to Mr. Markowitz.***
*Q. - Okay. **When you wrote this, did you believe it to be accurate?***
*A. - **I was unsure.***
Q. - What were you unsure about?
A. - The first sentence says, I received your letter by e-mail and to say that I

am disappointed would be mild. I was unsure whether that was accurate or not, given the fact that it was a letter from Mr. Markowitz to sign.
Q. - Okay. What else?
A. - The third paragraph, third line, I've been advised this amounts to gross negligence exhibited by Wachovia. I'm not sure that was true either.
Q. - Why did you write it, then?
A. - Because it was a draft, and it was intended to prompt either acceptance or rejection by Mr. Markowitz.

It is shocking that some 15 months after being made a defendant, Belanger still wasn't sure if the claims he made in the letter that he penned for me were truthful. How could this lack of diligence that occurred before Glenmede was fired by the Trust be considered serving the client's interest?

Belanger later in that deposition indicated that he was not sure if Gale's claim of the numerous emails to Wachovia was accurate. In other words, before writing the letter to Wachovia for the Trust, he seemingly took no steps to verify the accuracy of facts included in it.

[Belanger (emphasis added)]

Q. - Okay. Did Mr. Gale tell you there were numerous e-mail and written requests to Wachovia as of May 9 of '08*?*
A. - Again, as to e-mail requests, yes. As to written requests, I don't recall.
Q.- Okay. Mr. Gale had told you as of that time that there were numerous e-mail requests to Wachovia for the rights to sell the securities. Is that right?
*A. - **Yes.***
Q. - Is that, in fact, correct?
Q. - As you sit here today, do you know if that's an accurate statement or not?
*A. - **I don't know.***

When asked during his first deposition whether he was representing the Trust or Glenmede when he penned the Pearson (Wachovia) letter, Belanger incredibly said neither. He also referred to the problems with the bonds as being "perceived" by the Trust. Given the strength of the accusations he made against Wachovia in the letter, this explanation is not credible.

[Belanger's (emphasis added)]

Q. - Now, at the time you wrote this letter, this draft that we are looking at, Belanger 5, did you believe you were representing the trust, or Glenmede?
A. - Neither, in the context of a legal representation.
Q. - Okay. You were simply making a recommendation to a Glenmede client?
A. - No.

Q. - No?
A. - No.
Q. - Well, what was your role in doing this?
A. ***- I was trying to assist the client resolve a perceived problem, and was trying to help the client service team make an unhappy client happy.***

By the time Belanger's second deposition was taken it had become perfectly clear that the story Glenmede created about making many attempts to contact Wachovia was false, as well as the claims that Wachovia was uncooperative. This required Belanger to change his tune in that deposition.

[Belanger (emphasis added)]

Q. - Now, on the first page of the exhibit that you are looking at she states: "This was the first email that we sent out. When we got no response we started calling and we called regularly throughout the whole year with no response to any of our inquiries." *Do you see that?*
A. - I do.
Q. - That was false, wasn't it?
Q. ***- Haven't you admitted in No. 60 that that was false?***
A. - ***In 60****?*
Q. - ***Yes****.*
A. - I believe we have admitted that that is not the case, correct.
Q. - Still looking at that first page, the last sentence that I did not read in that e-mail states: "I will forward the other emails that I have as soon as I come up for air." Do you see that?
A. - I do.
Q. And that was false too, isn't that correct, because there were no other e-mails?
A. - I can't -- I --
Q. - Isn't that what you admitted in 12 No. 59?
A. - I don't know that it's false, in the context of it doesn't assert a fact.
Q. - ***All right. Look at the next page of that exhibit, she says: "Constant phone calls after that" -- referring to February 8 of '07 -- "yielded nothing." Do you see that?***
A. - Correct, I see that.
Q. - ***There were not constant phone calls, were there?***
A. - ***I don't believe that there were constant phone calls.***
Q. - In fact, she goes on to state there: ***"The only real reason that they" -- meaning Wachovia -- "finally helped us is when I mentioned the Jefferson Hills and I told them I would report to the Markowitz' that they knew the bond was going into default and did nothing to help."*** *Do you see that?*

A. - I see that statement.
Q. - ***Well, doesn't that indicate that at least Laura LaRosa thought that Mr. Markowitz' knowledge might have helped?***
A. - ***I don't know.***

Blaming it on Us!

Glenmede came up with a novel defense after being made a defendant. They turned around and blamed me, the Trustee, for not being diligent in managing Glenmede's actions relating to the problematic bonds. Part of this defense was based on the fact that I received monthly statements from Glenmede that listed the problematic bonds. Glenmede contended, therefore, that I should have taken steps to ensure that Glenmede did its job in selling the bonds. This incredible defense begs the question as to why Glenmede was being compensated by the Trust, if not to properly manage its assets.

However, even this tenuous defense depended on information being included in the monthly statements that would have informed me of problems. While the bonds were listed, there was no indication that they risked losing value or becoming illiquid.

During his second deposition, Belanger clarified Glenmede's position on this preposterous position.

[Belanger (emphasis added)]

Q. - ***You also state in your response that the Trustees' (including Petitioner Steven Markowitz) own breaches of fiduciary duty resulted in loss to the trust****; do you see that?*
A. - I do.
Q. - What specific fiduciary duties are you talking about?
A. - ***Duty to supervise.***
Q. - ***Supervise Glenmede****?*
A. - ***And Wachovia****.*

It is telling that Robert Kiep testified at trial that even he could not determine who purchased, or even if the bonds had any issues, by reading the monthly statements. How then, could the Trustee possibly determine this?

[Kiep (emphasis added)]

Q - ***But there's nothing, as far as the assets that had been held prior to that month, it doesn't tell you when they were purchased, does it not?***
A - ***No.***

*Q - **And does it tell you whether the bond -- whether the bonds were purchased by Glenmede or had been brought in from someone else, i.e., Wachovia in the case of the Trust?***
*A - **No.***
*Q - **Does the statement discuss liquidity issues**, if any, of the securities?*
*A - I'm not sure if it's in the disclosure or not; but not individually, **I don't think it does**.*
Q - Okay. Is there anything in the statement that tells you how long the investment horizons are of the various bonds?
A - Investment horizons. Maturities?
Q - I'm ...
A - Maturities?
Q - Yes.
A - It does state maturities.
*Q - **Is there anything in that March 2008 statement that alerts someone to any problem with any of those securities, of any kind**?*
*A - **Not that I see**.*

Kiep also testified in deposition that I questioned him about potential issues with Trust investments, acknowledging my diligence as trustee. He also testified that had he known of any issues with the Trust investments he would have informed me.

[Kiep (emphasis added)]

*Q. - Okay. **Mr. Markowitz questioned whether Glenmede had any exposure rating to the type of investments he had mentioned including CLOs and risking derivatives.** Do you see that?*
*A. - **Yes.***
Q. - Did you respond to that request, that question?
A. - I believe we talked about it at the meeting.
Q. - Okay. And if there would have been an issue with that, you would have told Mr. Markowitz, correct?
A. - Yes.
*Q. - **Okay. And periodically Mr. Markowitz asked you questions like that, did he not?***
*A. - **Yes**.*
*Q. - **And if there were any, if there were any concerns that Glenmede had in regard to any of these investments, you would tell him, correct?***
*A. - **Yes**.*

Kiep, met with me quarterly to review the status of Trust investments at Glenmede. He testified that he was responsible for informing the Trust of any problems in the account. However, the fact that he was not informed of the problems until April 2008, after the markets froze, made it impossible for Kiep to do his job or serve the Trust properly.

[Kiep Deposition (emphasis added)]

*Q. - **Did you consider it part of your responsibility to inform the trust at these meetings where there were any problems with the account**?*
*A.- **If there were. I suppose, yes**.*

[Kiep Trial (emphasis added)]

*Q - **Well, if there were any issues that came up for any-- for example, any assets of the Trust, would it be your responsibility to bring that up with the trustees and discuss it with them**?*
*A - **Yes**.*

<u>LaRosa's Changing Testimony</u>

Laura LaRosa was in charge of bond trading at Glenmede and was Rich Gale's supervisor. At the end of the first day of trial, LaRosa was testifying on the number of Trust Auction Rate Securities Glenmede was able to liquidate before the April 3, 2008 meeting in Philadelphia when the Trust was first informed of the problem. (All bonds were eventually sold except the two that were the subject of the litigation.) At issue was how diligent Glenmede had been in selling the Trust bonds before the April 3 meeting. The Judge interjected with the following exchange:

*THE COURT: - I think I may have some. **Are you able to tell me how many other securities you sold from when you received them from Wachovia, in this case, in this portfolio, from the time you received them until April of '08, not including the two subject securities that we're here about today?***

*THE WITNESS: **I believe we had 11 and we were down to four by the April 3rd meeting**. And then two others, actually, in the month of April went away, so we were left just with those two.*

[LaRosa (emphasis added)]

*THE COURT - **Now, do you know whether those were sold in 2007 2008 were both?** Do you have an idea of the span of time?*
*THE WITNESS - **I believe the first seven were sold through 2007**. Then the other two, obviously, that were done in April 2008, so...*

LaRosa's testimony on the number of bonds sold before the April 3 meeting was questioned by the Trust's attorney. The Judge ended testimony requesting that this issue be clarified during the next day of trial.

When trial resumed, LaRosa agreed that her previous testimony was incorrect

[LaRosa (emphasis added)]

*Q - **Ms. LaRosa, when we were here last you testified that there were 11 auction rate securities in the Markowitz account, correct?***
A - I thought there were approximately 11.
*Q - Right. **And you also testified that seven of them were sold prior to your meeting with Mr. Markowitz on April 3, 2008;** do you recall that testimony?*
A - I thought that they were.
Q - And you also said, and you told the judge, that there were four unsold At that time, the two in question and two more, correct?
A - What was the date?
Q - April 3, 2008.
A - I --I thought that that was the case, yes.
*Q - **Okay. You now know that isn't the case, correct?***
*A - **I -- yes,** I guess so. I think you're going to show me, right?*

[LaRosa (emphasis added)]

*Q. **You now wish to correct your testimony to say there were six unsold at that time?"***
*A. - **I can correct my testimony now that I see that there were six unsold at that time.***

Supplying inaccurate information seems to be an issue within Glenmede.

Belanger's Changing Testimony

James Belanger, Glenmede's Corporate Council, played a key role in supplying the Trust false information after May 2008. Following are examples of Belanger's changing testimony.

Belanger's second deposition had a conflict with testimony in his first as to whether, had the Trustee been informed of the problems Glenmede had obtaining the bonds' auction rights, it could have affected the outcome of their sale.

[Belanger (emphasis added)]

*Q. - **Are you saying that even if Markowitz had known Glenmede was having trouble selling the auction rate securities, there was nothing he could have done to help sell them?***
*A. - **I am denying that his knowing that we were having problems getting***

the auction rights would have had an impact on our ability to sell them.
*Q. - Look at your prior deposition, please, Page 88, starting at Line 16, I asked you a question: "**Did you believe that there were steps that petitioners could have taken to transfer those auction rights?"** You answered: **"Sure." My question: "What steps?" Your answer: "The petitioners could have followed up on the, with Wachovia as to whether they had had any problems transferring the account. They could have called the Wachovia representatives to make sure that everything had gone smoothly. They could have made inquiries to Glenmede as to whether Glenmede was experiencing any problems and needed any assistance. They could have done any number of hypothetical things to elicit further response from Wachovia or Glenmede as to the status of it."** Do you see that?*
A. - Yes.
*Q. - **Now, do you want to change your response that Mr. Markowitz' knowledge would not have had any impact?***
*A. - **No.***

In a remarkable exchange during his second deposition, Belanger first testified that he did not know that Gale's statement to the Trust about Glenmede's numerous emails to Wachovia's was false. Then, when confronted with Glenmede's Admission that confirmed this numerous contacts claim to be false, he blithely changed his testimony.

[Belanger (emphasis added)]

Q. – I am asking you to look at Belanger Exhibit 3, an e-mail to Mr. Markowitz from LaRosa dated April -- I'm sorry; I am looking at the wrong one. I'm sorry. It's an e-mail to Nathan Eckhart at Allen Organ from Rich Gale dated April 7, '08. Do you see that?
A. - I do.
Q. - And it's copied to a variety of people, including Mr. Markowitz, Mr. Kiep, Mr. Gale -- well, Mr. Gale copied to himself, and to Laura LaRosa, correct?
A. - It looks that way.
Q. - And Nathan Eckhart was a financial person associated with the Markowitz family; isn't that right?
A. - He, according to this, is the vice president of finance at Allen Organ Company.
Q. - Right, which was the Markowitz 'family business, correct?
A. - I believe that's true.
*Q. - **Mr. Gale states in his e-mail: "As a response to this mornings e-mail,***

I am enclosing the following information. I would like you to know that many more verbal communications were had with Wachovia/Evergreen for which no record was maintained. We have not attempted to re-create any of those discussions for which we do not have documentation. *" Do you see that?*
A. - I do.
Q. - ***That wasn't true either, was it****?*
A. ***- I don't know.***
Q. - Well, didn't you admit in No --
A. - I did. No; I --
Q. - ***Do you want to retract your admission in No. 60****?*
A. - No.
Q. - move to amend.
A. - Right.
Q. - Yes, I won't let you retract it that easily.
Q. - ***Which is it, is 60 right or wrong? Which is it?***
A. - ***I think we have made the admission in 60, so we will stick with it****.*

In another example, Belanger almost immediately changed his deposition testimony related to the "gross negligence" he was referring to in the letter to Wachovia he penned for Markowitz.

[Belanger's (emphasis added)]

Q. - Right. ***As you sat, as you composed this on May 9 of '08, did you believe that gross negligence had been exhibited by Wachovia?***
A. - ***Yes.***
Q. - ***And what did you base that on?***
A. - ***It was at that time my understanding that Wachovia had been in receipt of a letter from Mr. Markowitz, and that at least one if not more of the securities were purchased subsequent to their investment authority being taken away.***
Q. - Okay. But isn't that sentence referring to the transfer of the auction rights? That whole paragraph seems to be referring to the transfer of the auction rights.
A. - Could you repeat the question again?
Q. - ***Wouldn't you agree with me that the statement concerning gross negligence appears in a paragraph that only talks about the failure to transfer auction rights and doesn't talk about the purchase of a security after the cessation of the relationship between Markowitz and Wachovia?***
A. - ***I believe that's true.***
Q. - ***So how do you, why do you say that the gross negligence refers to the***

latter rather than the former?
A. - ***I didn't.***
Q. - Didn't you just tell us that?
A. - That wasn't the question I answered.
Q. - ***Okay. Then I'll go back and ask it again, then. What is the gross negligence that you were referring to in the third paragraph?***
A. - ***I was referring to the, I was referring to the repeated ignoring of requests from Glenmede.***

In this exchange during his first deposition, Belanger gave an incorrect answer and then when confronted with a written document, changed the response.

[Belanger (emphasis added)]

Q. - ***You don't know that. In March, on March 3rd of '09, were you aware that there were no auctions, that there were no auctions for those investments?***
A. - ***I don't have firsthand knowledge as to the auction rate market and whether or not there were active, active auctions for those securities at that time.***
Q. - ***You don't have knowledge?***
A. - ***I don't have any firsthand knowledge of that.***
Q. - Okay.
Q. - ***All right. Please look at this e-mail, Belanger 9, which purports to be an e-mail, well, at the top from me to you, and then a response dated March 26th of '09.*** *Do you see that? Actually, I think it was probably the other way around --*
A. - Yes. I see that.
Q. -- I'm sorry.
A. - This purports to be an e-mail from you responding to my e-mail to you.
Q. - Right. Dated, and your e-mail is dated March 26th of '09 at 8:39 a.m. Correct?
A. - Correct.
Q.- ***So as of March 26th of '09, you knew illiquidity was a problem, did you not?***
A. - ***It was my understanding that illiquidity was an issue, yes.***
Q. - So in May of '09, is it fair to say you also knew illiquidity was a problem?
A. - When you say knowledge or belief, it was my understanding based on what was told to me that liquidity was an issue. I did not have any firsthand knowledge about whether or not these bonds could be sold.

Even at trial Belanger changed testimony when confronted with facts. This time it was whether he believed facts in the Pearson penned letter for the Trust were accurate.

Belanger (emphasis added)

Q - Now, sir, in regard to P-56, and specifically the third page, the Pearson letter that you drafted
A - Yes.
Q -- do you remember telling us in your deposition that you didn't know if the facts in that letter were true and correct?
A - ***I had no first-hand knowledge of any of those facts.***
Q - Then why did you say it? Why did you write them?
A - ***Because I believed that they were true.***
Q - ***But didn't you tell us in your deposition that you were unsure if it was true? Would you like to see it?***
A - ***No.***
Q - ***Do you remember stating that?***
A - ***I do.***
Q - Okay. Let's look at the Pearson letter. Now, again, you were writing this for Mr. Markowitz to say, right? To write?
A - Yes.
Q - But there's no argument that you authored this letter, correct?
A - No, I drafted this letter and gave it to Mr. Markowitz for him to adopt.
Q - Okay. In that letter, in the third paragraph, you state-- and I quote-- I did not suggest that ***Wachovia ignore the repeated requests from Glenmede to provide the option rights to these securities. I stated it as a fact. I have been advised that this amounts to gross negligence exhibited by Wachovia. In support of this fact are numerous e-mail and written requests to Wachovia for the necessary rights to sell these securities****, end quote.* ***Were you unsure of those facts that you stated in that, in what I just read?***
A - ***Yes. I was un --~as those --one, two, three, those four sentences,*** *I'm asserting things that-I'm putting words in Mr. Markowitz's mouth, so, yeah, I'm uncertain as to whether or not he can say those things.*
Q - But aren't you telling Mr. Markowitz, by writing that, this is true and correct?
A - I don't know that -- again, I'm putting words, based upon my understanding of the situation and Mr. Markowitz's understanding of the situation, and I'm suggesting a way that he can convey that with as much forcefulness and saber-rattling as possible to try to get Wachovia to settle. That was the purpose of the letter.
Q - Who did the understanding as to the truth of those statements come from? Who had first-hand knowledge, sir?

A - That -- as testified, I believe Rich Gale had first-hand knowledge, along with Laura LaRosa and Bob Kiep, depending upon which facts you're talking about.
Q - Well, let's look specifically at the statement. In support of this fact there are numerous e-mail and written requests to Wachovia. Who told you that?
A - As I believe I said earlier, that was advised to me by Laura LaRosa.
Q - And Glenmede is now admitting in this litigation that that wasn't true, correct?
A - That's what we just agreed to.
Q - Okay. So Laura LaRosa told you false information?
*A - **I believe –I don't know that Laura LaRosa told me false information. I believe she misstated the information**.*

Internal Glenmede Policies Conflict with Federal Regulations

As a National Bank, Glenmede falls under the auspices of certain banking regulations included in the *Code of Federal Regulations*. This Code includes provisions, some of which were relevant to issues in the lawsuit. Had Glenmede followed this Code it is likely that either they would not have accepted the Trust's Auction Rate Securities from Wachovia for management, or would have been more diligent in obtaining the auction rights.

Belanger Trial

*Q - **Sir, Glenmede's a national bank, is it not?***
*A - **We are.***
*Q - **And, as such, you come under the Code of Federal Regulations, do you not?***
*A – **We do.***
Q - Are you familiar with the Code of Federal Regulations?
A - I'm familiar with aspects of the Code of Federal Regulations. It's quite a large document.
Q - Well--
A - If you're talking Part 9 specifically that apply to national banks, yes.
Q - Yes, 12CFR, Part 9?

At trial, Glenmede's CEO Gordon Fowler testified that James Belanger was also Glenmede's Compliance Officer responsible for ensuring the bank's compliance with various regulations. The fact that Belanger was managing damage control for Glenmede relating to the Trust created a conflict of interest situation.

Fowler (emphasis added)

Q - Okay. Well, let's go back to-- we'll come back to that then. Who's the compliance officer at Glenmede?
A - ***Mr. Belanger is the compliance officer****.*
Q - And he-- and what does the compliance officer do?
A - That's, you know, ***he makes sure that we're in compliance with the rules.***

It was also revealed at trial that Glenmede was not following its own internal policies, as required under the *Code of Federal Regulations*.

Fowler (emphasis added)

*Q - P-49, which is entitled, "****Client Complaint Policy.****" Do you see that?*
A - Yes, I do, sir.
Q - And it states in there, quote, ***The Compliance Officer will review all complaints and provide the Relationship Management Committee and the Risk Management Committee with quarterly summaries,*** *end quote; isn't that correct?*
A - That is correct.
Q - Do you know if that was done?
A - In this specific case?
Q - Strike that Do you know if it was done in regard to the Markowitz complaint?
A - Do I know whether it was - do I know whether the --the - this complaint was reviewed by our Complaint Compliance Officer?
Q - Right
A - I do not review all of the -- whether -- whether complaints or compliance, whether complaints are being reviewed by the compliance officer. It is not part of my job.
Q - I'm sorry. I may have misstated the question. ***Do you know whether the Relationship Management Committee or the Risk Management Committee were given quarterly summaries of the complaints of the Markowitz Trust?***
MR. PRIOR: - Objection. He just testified, he's not on the Risk Management Committee.
THE COURT: - Understood. Overruled.
Q - Do you know?
A - ***I do not know****.*
Q - If they were not made, would you agree that it's a violation of your internal policy?
A - If they counted as true complaints. If they counted as true complaints. But, you know, there's a gray area as to when something is a complaint or not.

Q - Sir -
A - Or, what point it becomes a complaint. I'm going to read to you -
Q - You'll have to look with me. Let me see if I marked it. I'm sorry. Interrogatory no. 18, Your Honor. I do not have it identified as an exhibit, but it's in response to an interrogatory. The interrogatory is, ***Did Glenmede's relationship committee receive any reports or summaries relating to complaints coming from or relating to the Markowitz Trust or the auction rate securities that are the subject to this litigation? If the answer is yes, state on what date such reports are received and the subject of the summaries or complaints. "ANSWER: -- Response: No.***
Q - ***Now, sir, you would agree with me that the Relationship Management Committee should be getting reports regarding complaints of the Markowitz Trust, would you not?***
A - ***I would, I would think at a certain point, the Markowitz matter would have been discussed at the Relationship Management Committee and I would have been surprised if it was not discussed at the Relationship Management Committee.***
Q - And, sir, isn't it correct, as has been stated in response to ***Interrogatory No. 16, that the Glenmede Relationship Management Committee had as one of its duties, quote, review the status of any pending threatened and ongoing litigation involving Pennsylvania Orphans' court proceedings and proceedings of similar courts in other jurisdictions?*** *Does that sound correct to you?*
A - Would you repeat that a second?
Q - Well, let me show you the interrogatory. It's number 16 and I was referring to Response 5. (Handing.)
A - (Reviewing), So ... yes.
Q - ***You would expect that the Relationship Management Committee would review any, would have reviewed the Markowitz matter since it is, it is ongoing litigation involving the Pennsylvania Orphans' Court, would you not have?***
A - ***I would expect that it would have and it would not surprise me that it would have.***

Fowler (emphasis added)

Q - Are you, are you familiar with the client relationship management software?
A - The CRM software, I am familiar with that.
Q - What is that?
A - That is a place where we can document conversations or discussions with clients or list e-mail.

*Q - **And isn't it correct that any, any complaints or problems are supposed to be memorialized in that client relationship software?***
*A - **Ideally, that is a place where we memorialize complaints.***
*Q - **And, in fact, it's required under the code of ethics, is it not, that's in front of you, P-50?***
A - At what point is it required --where is that?
*Q - **I'm sorry. P-51, under Complaints.***
*A - **It is.***
Q - And do you know if the Markowitz complaints were memorialized in the CRM software?
A - I do not know whether they were, but I do know they were discussed at management levels.
*Q - Sir, I'm going to show you what's been marked as P-52, which is another part of the internal Glenmede policy. Do you see the statement that, quote, **one of the roles of Glenmede is to identify assets that may be appropriate investments for an account and administer such assets**, end quote. Do you see that?*
A - Which paragraph is this?
Q - Let me look and find it. The second sentence on the page.
A - Okay. Yes, I see that.

Belanger testified at trial that Glenmede had a fiduciary responsibility to the Trust. With this responsibility Glenmede had specific obligations under the Code of Federal Regulations.

Q - Okay. Now back again to (e). Fiduciary capacity means -- and I would go down to the end of the second line-- investment advisor if the bank receives a fee for its investment advice, right?
A - It does.
*Q - **Did Glenmede receive a fee for its investment advice**?*
*A - **We do.***
*Q - **So would you now agree with me that you were acting in a fiduciary capacity?***
*A - **I would agree that we were acting in a fiduciary capacity as defined under Title 9.***

Belanger also testified that Glenmede had responsibility under the Code to determine whether it could properly manage assets for a client. However, the Glenmede employee responsible for bringing in the Trust bonds didn't even know what the Auction Rate Securities were when he brought them into Glenmede. Belanger's rather callous response to this issue at the end of the exchange below is remarkable.

Belanger (emphasis added)

Q - Sir, I'm going to direct your attention back -- do you still have that copy of the ***Code of Federal Regulations*** *up there?*
A - I believe I do. Yes.
Q - Would you look at Section 9.5?
A - Okay.
Q - And could you read the first sentence, please.
A - ***A national bank exercising fiduciary powers shall adopt and follow written policies and procedures adequate to maintain its fiduciary activities in compliance with applicable law.***
Q - Okay. Now, it says that the bank shall adopt and follow, correct?
A - Yes.
Q - And in fact, Glenmede has followed that, correct? It has done that; is that correct?
A - ***Yes. We have adopted and we have written policies and procedures.***
Q - Now, look at 9.6. Section (a). ***Before accepting a fiduciary account, a national bank shall review the prospective account to determine whether it can properly administer the account; do you see that?***
A - Yes.
Q - ***Was that done in this case?***
A - ***I believe so.***
Q - What is involved in properly administering the account? Is that, does that include being able to sell security -- the securities in the account?
A - Well, there are two questions there. What's involved in properly administering an account is fact specific to each account. For instance, an estate administration can involve administering a small business in some cases or disposing of collectibles. In particular, in a-M in the account here, where it is an investment management account, it is can properly manage the account, sure.
Q - ***And is properly managing the account being able to buy and sell the securities in that account?***
A - ***Yes****. Before accepting an account, you should make sure that you understand what type of securities are there and whether or not you can properly administer them. It doesn't always necessarily involve buying and selling securities. Many of our accounts come in with private equity investments and limited partnerships that are, in essence, illiquid but are a vital part of the investment program in that account.*
Q - You said part of that is determining what kind of securities they are, correct?
A - I believe that would be one aspect of it, yes.

*Q - **Does it trouble you that Mr. Schwartz testified that he didn't know what an auction rate security was?***
*A - **No.***

However, during his second deposition on July 15, 2010, nearly 3 ½ years after accepting the Trust's ARS for management from Wachovia, Belanger still did not know whether Glenmede had expertise or knowledge of Auction Rate Securities.

[Belanger (emphasis added)]

*Q. - **Did Glenmede have expertise and knowledge in the field of auction rate securities?***
*A. - **I don't know.***
*Q. - **Do you believe as the chief counsel and senior vice president of Glenmede that Glenmede should take custody of auction rate securities if it didn't have that expertise?***
*A. - **I don't know.***
Q. - You don't know?
A. - I don't know.

Belanger confirmed during trial that Glenmede could have declined to accept the Trust's bonds for management. This would have been appropriate given Glenmede's lack of expertise in this area.

Belanger (emphasis added)

*Q - **Now, it is correct, is it not, that Glenmede can decline any assets if it chooses to, correct?***
*A - **Yes**. And, in fact, we frequently ask clients, new clients, to sell to proprietary mutual funds at Wachovia then send us the proceeds as opposed to having them come in and then have to sell them.*
*Q - **You didn't ask this, the Markowitz Trust, to sell, sell the auction rate securities, right?***
*A - **No, we did not.***

Glenmede's internal policies include sections concerning "Truth and Honesty" and error correction that were not followed with the "mistakes" Glenmede made relating to the Trust bonds. When confronted with the Truth and Honesty section at trial, Belanger made the excuse that this was merely an "honest mistake". This backpedaling is not credible given the multiple false statements Glenmede made to the Trust and its cover up.

Trial (emphasis added)

*Q - Okay. I believe it refers to **Exhibit P-50, which has previously been admitted under truth and honesty on the bottom** there, on the first page.*

A - I'd just point out that Question 25 says, Glenmede's policy under Truth and Honesty -- and it references a Bates stamp number GTC 02360/61 and P-50, which you gave me, is GTC 0260 through 0262. I believe. It's unclear. So ...
Q - It's actually --
A - I'm just, I'm not sure. I believe that these aren't the same things. I'm just noting that you referenced a document that had two pages and you're handing me a document that has three.
Q - Okay. Fair enough.
A - And it's true because the third page is our error correction policy which is separate from the ethical conduct policy which is before it.
*Q - **Okay. Let's forget the interrogatory and just look at the bottom of the page of P-50, please.***
A - Sure.
Q About employees not making deliberately false deceptive statements, et cetera. okay? Was that policy breached when the Trust was told that Glenmede had made numerous e-mail and phone contacts with Wachovia when there really were none during that 14-month period?
*A - **No, I don't believe so. I believe that it was an honest mistake.***

Belanger then testified at trial concerning Glenmede's error correction policy that it ignored relating to the Trust bonds.

Trial (emphasis added)

*Q - Okay. Now, sir, **back to that P-50 again**, item Belanger- Direct three, page three, which I think you referenced a moment ago, the error correction policy?*
A - Yes.
*Q - **And am I correct that it states under error correction policy on the third page, it is the policy of Glenmede to correct any client-account trading error, or other error, which is caused by Glenmede and to promptly return the client account to the same position it would have been had the error not occurred, correct?***
*A - **That is what it says.***
*Q - **Now, did Glenmede attempt to correct this, the mistake that you just referenced?***
*A - **No. Because that, that question is nonsensical in the context of the mistake is the description of the activity that occurred with Wachovia. It was not-- there was, as near as I can tell, no mistake in Mr. Markowitz's account and as a practical matter, there was no loss, either.***
*Q - **Well, a lawsuit was started against Wachovia based on that mistake. wasn't it?***

A - Well, then following your logic, if-- if-- if the premise is that our mistake about the communication to you led you to initiate an action against Wachovia, then the answer to the subsequent question of was the error ever attempted to be fixed is, yes, I did try to enter into settlement negotiations with Wachovia at some point shortly before Mr. Markowitz took his account from us and instituted this particular lawsuit.
Q - Couldn't the problem have been rectified just by buying back the securities?
A - There would have been a number of reasons why that couldn't occur. One is, as you have in front of me, the Code of Federal Regulations. I believe it is 9. --bear with me. It is 9.12(b) that says, In general. A national bank may not lend, sell, or otherwise transfer assets of a fiduciary account for which a national bank has investment discretion to the bank or any of its directors, officers, or employees, or to affiliates of the bank or any of their directors, officers, or employees, or to individuals or organizations with whom there exists an interest that might affect the exercise of the best judgment of the bank. I'll try to remember to slow down. And so, it was my understanding that that prohibited us from buying the bonds from Mr. Markowitz's account. At the same token, Mr. Markowitz had not suffered any loss while his account was with us, so there was no error to fix.
Q - Okay. But, sir, you didn't read the next-- you didn't read the rest of Section (b), specifically (ii) that says -- it's an exception to what you read -- if legal counsel advises the bank in writing that the bank has incurred, in its fiduciary capacity, a contingent or potential liability, in which case the bank, upon the sale or transfer of assets, shall reimburse the fiduciary account in cash at the greater of book or market value-- correct?-- of the assets. You didn't read that part?
A - I did not.
Q - So you, as counsel, could have said, could have said that there was a contingent or potential liability for the error and bought them, correct, bought the securities back?
A - ***I don't know that that's the case.***
Q - ***Okay. Well, regardless, when the Markowitz Trust assets were removed, you no longer had even the problem that you just addressed because the –you no longer had the fiduciary account, correct?***
A - ***Correct.***
Q - ***So that problem went away?***
A - ***It did.***

Glenmede's CEO, Gordon Fowler, testified at trial that Glenmede should correct "obvious errors" that it made. Assuming for a moment that the misinformation given to the Trust about the bonds or Glenmede's lack of diligence concerning obtaining the auction rights was not done out of malice, then these were at least "obvious errors".

Fowler (emphasis added)

*Q - **Do you agree that if inaccurate information is disseminated, Glenmede has an obligation to correct it**?*
*A - If we disseminate information that is inaccurate, we first have to remember there is information that's been disseminated. We disseminate a lot of information over time. And then we, again, have to sort of check to see what the facts and circumstances were around it. **But if there was an obvious error, then we would want to correct that.***

Not before, during, or after the litigation did Glenmede attempt to correct its "errors" relating to the Trust's bonds. In fact, when confronted with their lack of diligence, Glenmede instead went into a circle the wagons approach to protect their own interest. This approach likely led to Glenmede spending more on the litigation then what error correction would have cost the firm. The reason for such illogical business behavior is left to the reader.

Chapter 11

A Bad End to a Bad Business

By third quarter of 2009 the Trust still owned two illiquid bonds, Mobile County, Alabama, in the amount of $350,000 and Jefferson County, Alabama, in the amount of $300,000. This was two and a half years after these assets were transferred from Wachovia to Glenmede and approximately one and one half years after Glenmede informed the Trust of the problem.

The bonds' illiquidity became a more pressing problem because of a potentially large tax obligation upcoming for the Trust. While the Mobile County bond had a reasonable chance of being called (redeemed), there were no guarantees. The Jefferson County bond, on the other hand, was a known basket case with a reasonable chance that the County would default on its bond obligations.

Given the situation with both bonds I asked the then current financial advisor, a local firm I engaged after firing Glenmede, to look into the possibility of selling the illiquid bonds on the secondary market, an option never offered by Glenmede. While I understood this would involve a "haircut" on the value of the bonds, I weighed this downside against the possibility of the bonds being illiquid for many years or even becoming worthless.

I obtained an offer through our advisor to purchase the Jefferson County bond at 30% of par (face value) and the Mobile County bond at 67% of par. The purchaser indicated that they were unwilling to purchase the more problematic Jefferson County bond unless we also sold them the Mobile County bond. Given the potential risk versus reward, and the fact that neither Wachovia nor Glenmede were willing to purchase these bonds from the Trust, I decided to limit the Trust's potential loss and sold them for a total of $324,500, a loss of $325,500. This loss was the amount I asked Glenmede to reimburse the Trust as settlement, but they refused.

Glenmede throughout this period advised the Trust to hold the bonds. Given the misinformation already received from them, I took their advice with a grain of salt. Later, Glenmede would make the argument that the Trust sold the bonds, ignoring their advice, and that somehow made the Trust complicit in the loss.

<u>A Verdict to be Queried</u>

The Trust's lawsuit was litigated in the Court of Common Pleas of Lehigh County, Orphans' Court Division. The Orphans' Court was an appropriate venue since the assets were part of a trust for the benefit of remainders (my siblings and I). The judge was the Honorable J. Brian Johnson. There was no jury.

Prior to the trial the Judge got the parties together to attempt settlement. This is typical in civil litigations with judges trying to avoid trials that are complicated and take significant time.

The settlement conference lasted a couple of hours, but was not productive. The Trust asked that Glenmede make it whole for the loss on the bonds and Glenmede was only willing to offer pennies on the dollar. When the settlement conference broke down, the Judge made a comment similar to: "you never know what will happen at trial." That statement, considering the outcome of trial, turned out to have considerable resonance.

The facts laid out in this book make a compelling case about Glenmede's inability to properly manage the Trust's Auction Rate Securities. The evidence showed that Glenmede not only had the opportunity, but also the responsibility, to not accept assets they could not properly manage.

In addition, testimony showed that Glenmede created a cover-up, blaming Wachovia for being uncooperative when in fact it was Glenmede's lack of diligence that led to the bonds becoming illiquid. Also, the Trust's lawsuit initiated against Wachovia was filed based on false information supplied by Glenmede. Glenmede's cover up was an attempt to protect its own interests above those of the Trust. The cover up placed Glenmede in conflict a position with the Trust. And it was dishonest.

In presenting the facts showing Glenmede's lack of competence and disingenuous behavior, this book relied almost entirely on Glenmede's own testimony and information it supplied in discovery and at trial. Multiple statements on similar issues were included to demonstrate that Glenmede's responses were not open for interpretation. But this clear evidence also serves to demonstrate how poorly the Court did its job.

When an individual uses the judicial system to attempt to redress what they believe is an injustice the outcome is never guaranteed, no matter how strong a case may be. Also, being wronged by another party does not by in itself give one legal recourse. Finally, decisions are made by jury's or judges, which puts uncertainty about capabilities and interpretation into play. While all of this is true, it is difficult to read the facts in this case and to come to a different conclusion than Glenmede should have been held responsible to the Trust for damage to its assets.

While the Judge ultimately found Glenmede partially responsible to the Trust, the Trust was only awarded pennies on the dollar. The Judge's findings show that he was not inclined towards the Trust's position, despite the facts. One can only speculate on the reason, which may include:

- A dislike for the case in general. Many got burnt during the financial meltdown and few bankers were held accountable. Possibly the Judge concluded that investors need to accept losses as part of the "game", no matter how inappropriate the behavior of the financial services industry.
- A "plague on both your houses" mentality. Some judges seem to dislike civil litigations between people who are supposedly knowledgeable. This view will generally hurt the party seeking redress.
- A negative reaction to the personality of the Trust's main witness (me) and/or its attorney.
- Facts presented at trial could have been lost or eclipsed due to long delays between the four days of trial, as well as a lengthy delay in the Court rendering its opinion. The schedule included:
    - Trial Day 1 November 9, 2010
    - Trial Day 2 January 28, 2011
    - Trial Day 3 February 4, 2011
    - Trial Day 4 May 12, 2011
    - Judge's Opinion December 6, 2011

Holding a trial in segments, with parts on four different dates over a six-month period, makes it not only difficult for litigants, but also judges. It is hard to imagine a busy judge managing many cases remembering and connecting complex testimony through such an extended period. The Judge did not issue his decision until December 6, 2011, six months after the last day of trial and over a year after the first day of trial. These delays may indicate either a rejection from early on of the Trust's position or a weak strategy for managing caseloads.

The extended period over which the trial was held may help explain significant discrepancies in the Judge's opinion, which is reviewed in the next section. After receiving that decision, the Trust brought the discrepancies to the Judge's attention, as allowed under a judicial process in Pennsylvania called "Exceptions". While he acknowledged significant discrepancies and changed related portions of his original findings, the Judge did not change the amount of damages awarded the Trust.

The Court's Original Opinion

On December 6, 2011 the Judge issued a 27 page opinion included in total at the end of his book. The opinion includes:

a) On Glenmede's decision to liquidate the Auction Rate Securities:

Page 9 states: "*Gale was not directed by Glenmede or Markowitz to liquidate any of the ARSs.*" Given the wealth of testimony on this issue indicating that Gale decided to sell these bonds by early February 2007, the Court's conclusion is incomprehensible. This finding is also in conflict with what the Judge found in another portion of his opinion on page 24 of the decision (emphasis added):

> "..... *Notwithstanding Markowitz's failure to actively supervise the advancement advisor that he hired to manage the Trust's funds, we agree with Markowitz that Glenmede did a poor job in effectuating its investment decision made in February 2007 to liquidate all of the ARSs that it had received via transfer from Wachovia in January, 2007.*"

b) On Trustee not directing Glenmede to sell the bonds:

Also on page 9, the Judge states (emphasis added): "*Moreover, throughout the entire period of time Glenmede held the ARSs, Markowitz never directed Glenmede to liquidate the ARSs.*"

This conclusion is correct, but it is difficult to see how it was relevant. Glenmede had full discretionary authority (control) for Trust investments, as the Court pointed out on page 17 of the opinion, reprinting the following:

> "***Discretionary Account*** *- Glenmede shall have full discretionary authority to make all investment decisions concerning purchasing, holding or selling the Assets taken into the account the owners investment objectives. ....*"

The testimony showed that Glenmede decided to sell the bonds in early 2007 because they did not like to hold this type of investment for clients. This was completely within their discretion and responsibility. It was their inability to act properly on that decision that should have been at issue.

c) On Glenmede's monthly statements including information about the bonds:

Page 10 of the opinion states: "*All of the investment activity and the maturation date of each bond were reported on Glenmede's monthly statements of account sent to Markowitz. ...*"

Implied in this finding is that I should have taken some action with respect to the bonds. However, trial testimony included in this book shows that it was not possible for anyone looking at the statements to know there was a problem with the bonds or their liquidity. Further, Kiep testified that he had quarterly meetings with me and did not mention any problems concerning the investments. In hindsight this is not surprising since Kiep was not aware of any of the problems with these assets.

d) On the ARS market collapse being unforeseen:

On page 10 of the opinion the Court states (emphasis added): "*In late February 2008, as one of several consequences of the massive and unforeseen collapse of the mortgage backed securities market, the market for auction rate securities became volatile and auctions began to fail.*"

It is hard to understand how the Court could have found this given the dearth of testimony and Admissions concerning the fourth quarter 2007 meeting held at and open to Glenmede employees concerning problems in the Auction Rate Securities market, as detailed earlier in this book.

e) On "bad faith" and "gross negligence" required to recoup losses on the account:

Page 17 of the Judge's opinion quotes from the Trust's Investment Advisory Agreement (IAA):

> **Liability** Glenmede shall not be liable to the owner or any other person except for *losses to the Account resulting from* the willful misfeasance, bad faith or gross negligence on the part of Glenmede in the performance of its duties, or reckless disregard by Glenmede of its obligations and duties, under this agreement. (emphasis supplied)

The opinion goes on to state: "This *clause defines a breach as misfeasance, bad faith, gross negligence in the performance of its contractual duties, or recklessly disregarding its contractual obligations and limits Glenmede's liability therefore to "losses to the account" that are casually related thereto. ...*"

It is hard to interpret Glenmede's actions of falsely informing the Trust about its actions with Wachovia, as well as its lack of diligence in implementing its own decision to sell the bonds long before the market froze up, as not being gross negligence and bad faith.

The Court then went on to say on page 18: "*In order to establish that Glenmede breach the IAA, Markowitz was required to establish that, by failing to inform him until April 2008 of its inability to sell the ARSs that it had received from Wachovia in January, 2007 or by offering Wachovia's lack of cooperation as the reason for its lack of possession of the auction rights when it did so inform him, Glenmede acted in a willful, grossly negligent and untruthful manner and that the account suffered a loss by reason of that conduct.*"

This conclusion seems to ignore the testimony that the markets were operating normally from January 2007 through February 2008. It defies logic to maintain that had Glenmede been truthful with the Trust and informed the Trust that it was having difficulty obtaining auction rights from Wachovia that the Trust would not have acted to protect its interest and work to sell the bonds.

f) On proof of negligence:

On page 19, the opinion states: "*The elements necessary to prove an action in negligence are: (1) the existence of a duty or obligation recognized by law, requiring the actor to conform to a certain standard of conduct; (2) a failure on the part of the defendant to conform to that duty, or a breach thereof; (3) a casual connection between the defendants breach and the resulting injury; and (4) actual loss or damage suffered by the complaint. See Jones V. Levin, 940 A.2d 451, 454 (pa Super. 2007).*"

While this writer is not trained in law, the evidence clearly showed negligence relating to Glenmede's decision to sell the Auction Rate Securities in January 2007 and then not acting on that decision until March 2008, only after the markets froze up. In addition, at trial the Trust presented evidence as to Glenmede's responsibilities under the Federal Code of Conduct, obligations "recognized by law." This Code was not mentioned in the Judge's findings.

g) On lack of expert witnesses:

On page 20 the Court faulted the Trust for not presenting an expert witness to show the standard of care that Glenmede should have used in managing the Trust assets stating: "*….. Therefore, Markowitz's "failure to produce an expert witness as to the standard of care under which [Glenmede] should have conducted [it] self and as to any deviation from that standard that may have occurred makes [Markowitz's] case eff. as a matter of law" and justifies its dismissal. River deck holding Corp. v. U.S. liability insurance Co., ___ A.2d, etc ….*"

The Trust presented testimony from Glenmede's own employees, experts in the field, to define the standard of care that should have been used for Trust assets. This included in testimony from its CEOs Piscopo and Fowler, as well as Gale and LaRosa.

In litigations outside expert witnesses are paid by litigants to offer testimony fitting the paying party's "need". It is hard to understand why the Judge ignored Glenmede's own experts, as well Glenmede's responsibilities under the Code of Federal Regulations. It begs the question as to whether a court needs an expert to confirm that lying to a client is inappropriate behavior.

h) On Glenmede's familiarity with ARS:

On page 21 the Judge states: "….. *The evidence showed that Glenmede was well familiar with ARS assets and Markowitz introduced no evidence in support of his allegations that Glenmede made any express representations to him about its knowledge of ARSs.*"

This statement is hard to comprehend given the trial testimony that indicated David Schwartz, the Executive VP responsible for bringing in the Trust's ARSs, didn't even know what ARSs were when bringing them into Glenmede. In addition, Gale, the Glenmede employee responsible for trading the Trust ARSs testified that attempting to trade these bonds was one of the most difficult things he ever did. If these employees are not Glenmede's agents for its clients, then who is?

As for Glenmede making representations to the Trust about their knowledge in ARS's, the Code of Federal Regulations and written internal Glenmede policies indicate that Glenmede should not accept assets for management if they are not capable of properly managing them. By accepting the ARS's they in essence represented to the Trust they had appropriate knowledge to manage them.

i) On ARS's liquidity:

On page 21 of the opinion, the Judge states: "….. *Markowitz produced no document in which the ARSs were identified as assets that Glenmede was to liquidate immediately upon taking possession or within a specified period of time thereafter. Markowitz knew that the Jefferson ARS and mobile ARS were included in the Trust assets that were transferred from Wachovia to Glenmede in January 2007.*"

This part of the opinion might make one believe that documents are the only evidence presented at trial. Gale and LaRosa both testified that they made the decision to sell the ARSs in late January 2007. Keep in mind that in the same opinion, the Judge found on page 24 "… *we agree that Glenmede did a poor job in effectuating its investment decision made in February 2007 to liquidate all of the ARSs that it had received via transfer from Wachovia in January, 2007.*" (Emphasis added)

The problem was caused by Glenmede not acting on a decision it made, not by any action or lack of it by the Trustee.

j) On breach of fiduciary duty:

On page 22 the Judge states: "…. *Because the majority of ARS holdings were successfully liquidated by Glenmede well within the five (5) year investment horizon articulated in the IPS, despite the delay in obtaining auction rights, the lack of a primary market for the mobile ARS and the Jefferson ARS, which represented slightly more than 6% of the account, there was no failure to meet the liquidity objective contained in the IPS.*"

During trial LaRosa was unequivocal in her testimony that the Trust ARSs were considered the same as money market investments that were fully and nearly immediately liquid and were therefore a part of the liquid portion of the Trust's Glenmede portfolio. The Judge incorrectly placed the ARSs in the longer-term part of the portfolio, ignoring LaRosa's testimony.

<u>k) On breach of fiduciary duty:</u>

Beginning on page 23 the Judge makes a finding that is disconnected with his other findings (emphasis added):

"*The Merrill Lynch case provides an excellent discussion of this issue. Guided thereby, we find that the <u>relevant conduct of Glenmede that arguably constitutes a breach of its fiduciary duty are</u>: <u>1) it did not tell Markowitz that the auction rights for the ARSs had not been transferred and/or that it was having difficulty in obtaining them for fourteen (14) months; 2) it did not diligently attempt to obtain the auction rights for twelve (12) of those fourteen (14) months and 3) it did not tell Markowitz in a timely manner when it learned that the ARS market was about to seize.</u> Notwithstanding Markowitz's failure to actively supervise the advancement advisor that he hired to manage the Trust's funds, <u>we agree with Markowitz that Glenmede did a poor job in effectuating its investment decision made in February 2007 to liquidate all of the ARSs that it had received via transfer from Wachovia in January, 2007</u>.*"

The Judge found Glenmede in breach of its fiduciary duty to the Trust. In addition, he noted that Glenmede made the internal decision to sell the problematic bonds in February 2007. Again, contradicting his finding on page 9 that "*<u>Gale was not directed by Glenmede</u> or Markowitz to liquidate any of the ARSs*." (emphasis added)

Further, the statement included in the middle of this paragraph that: "*Notwithstanding Markowitz's failure to actively supervise the advancement advisor that he hired to manage the Trust's funds, ...*" is telling. While the Trust paid Glenmede significant funds to manage the portfolio, the Judge placed management responsibility back on the Trustee. Should the courts uphold this type of logic it is hard to imagine the legal system holding any financial advisor responsible for incompetent behavior, as long as information about the incompetence was in some obscure way available to the client.

l) On Glenmede being disingenuous with Trust (emphasis added):

On page 24, the opinion states: "*Glenmede knew, by at least February 2008, that the ARS market wasn't dramatic decline such that auctions were failing, but did not share this information with Markowitz for at least another four (4) to six (6) weeks; choosing instead to seek and obtain the necessary auction rights during March, 2008. Further, Glenmede was disingenuous when informed Markowitz in April 2008 that it had been aggressively attempting to obtain the auction rights since January 2007 but did not receive them until March 2008 because Wachovia would not cooperate. While it was true that Wachovia had not included them in the initial transfer or responded to Gale's February 2007 request that Wachovia transfer the auction rights, it was not true that Glenmede had been aggressively attempting to obtain the auction rights for the entire prior fourteen (14) months.*" The Judge went on to state on page 25: "*Glenmede's conduct in this regard falls short of the scrupulous good faith and candor that are the cornerstone of a fiduciary relationship and constitutes a breach of its fiduciary duty.*"

It is hard to understand how the Judge could find Glenmede to have been untruthful, misleading the Trust and also breaching its fiduciary duty, without finding them responsible for damages caused by these actions.

m) On lack of evidence about the ARSs liquidity:

On page 25 of the opinion, the Judge states: "..... *We disagree. Markowitz introduced no evidence regarding whether, or at what price, the Jefferson ARS and mobile IRS could've been sold during the period of February 2007 through March 2008 had Glenmede possess the necessary auction rights. .....*"

This is perhaps the most outrageous error in the Court's original findings. Throughout trial Glenmede's LaRosa and Gale testified on multiple occasions that the ARSs were like money market accounts that could have been converted to cash at 100% par every 35 days. In addition, Glenmede admitted in Admissions 42, 43, and 55 that successful auctions (10) were held before the markets froze up. Given these uncontroverted facts, this finding seems to have been written by one who completely ignored the evidence presented at trial.

*****

With the above findings the Court granted the Trust only miniscule damages in the amount of $11,700, less than 4% of the actual loss for the two problematic bonds. It awarded nothing for attorney fees or the cost the Trust incurred in the lawsuit against Wachovia initiated based on Glenmede's false assertions made to the Trust. There seems to have been a "message" in this meager award.

The Court's Modified Ruling

The previous pages include compelling arguments that the Judge significantly erred in his findings. In fact, the Judge ultimately agreed with this conclusion, but did not alter the token damages awarded.

After the Judge issued his opinion the Trust presented arguments to the Court as to what and why it believed the Court erred and requested corrections. It did so in a filing titled "In Support of the Exceptions" allowed under Pennsylvania legal proceedings. The Judge responded on April 16, 2012. A review of the number of, as well as the significance of the changed findings the Court granted, indicates a disconnect between the Judge's original findings and evidence presented at trial.

Of the 24 Exceptions filed by the Trust, six were granted. The importance of these granted Exceptions go far in validating a significant portion of what has been presented in this book.

Granted Exceptions

Exception 1

1. The Court erred in finding that "Markowitz introduced no evidence regarding whether, or at what price, the Jefferson ARS and the Mobile ARS could have been sold during the period of February, 2007 through March, 2008..."

Court's Response - Exception #1 is granted. The record does contain evidence that the price at which the Jefferson ARS and the mobile ARS could have been sold had the auction rights been included in the transfer from Wachovia was their par value.

Given the wealth of evidence presented at trial it is incomprehensible how the Judge came to his original conclusion. In addition, the Judge used his original finding as a reason for not awarding the Trust greater damages for the problematic bonds.

Left unsaid in the Judge's reversal on this issue is the fact of the many successful auctions that occurred in which the ARS s could have been sold before the markets froze up, as well as Glenmede's responsibility in not selling these bonds at those auctions.

Exception 3

3. The Court erred at page 9 of its Opinion in stating that "During the period February, 2007 through March, 2007, Glenmede liquidated

five (5) ARSs, carried at an aggregate value of $2.4 million." That was incorrect as between February, 2007 and March, 2007, Glenmede in fact liquidated three (3) ARSs with an aggregate value of only $1.2 million. (Joint Exhibit 1).

Court's Response - Exception #3 is granted. Joint Exhibit 1 reflects the parties' stipulation that Glenmede liquidated 3 ARSs during the period, February, 2007 through March, 2007.

This reversal shows an error in a material fact. It relates to the Court's finding on Glenmede's overall diligence with Trust assets. The greater the amount of dollars and number of problematic bonds involved in their delayed selling efforts, the more significant was Glenmede's lack of diligence.

Exception 5

5. The Court erred in finding, at page 11 of its Opinion that "Between May 6 and 21, 2009, Glenmede sold every investment except the Jefferson ARS, the Mobile ARS (which collectively constituted 6.6% of the Account), and another asset that is not at issue." In fact, two (2) of the auction rate securities were called, not sold by Glenmede. (Joint Exhibit 1)

Court's Response - Exception #5 is granted. Joint Exhibit 1 reflects that of the ARSs liquidated by Glenmede during the period May 6, 2009 and May 21, 2009, two of said ARSs were called and were not sold or tendered by Glenmede.

This reversal again demonstrates an error in a material fact and further makes clear that the proportion of Glenmede's lack of diligence to the Trust was greater than the Judge originally acknowledged.

Exceptions 15 and 24

15. The Court erred in repeatedly finding fault with the Trustee, Steven Markowitz, for not knowing that ARSs were in the portfolio when Laura LaRosa, Glenmede's expert in the field, acknowledged that she could not tell by examining the Trust's monthly statements from Glenmede that ARSs were in the portfolio. Further, whether or not Markowitz knew there were ARSs in the Trust's portfolio at Glenmede is not relevant to the claims of the Trust since this part of the portfolio was to be completely liquid. As the Court also found, the ARSs were a permissible class of assets for the Trust, "cash substitutes" like money market accounts" as described in the testimony of Laura LaRosa who also testified that she did not need to know risk tolerance since these

investments were “basically cash.”. The problem was not the asset but the liquidity problems arising from the lack of auction rights which Steven Markowitz could only have known about if told by Glenmede.

24. The Court erred in implying at page 10 of its Opinion that because the maturation dates of the ARSs were noted on each statement, that somehow was notice of the long term of the investment even though Glenmede personnel testified repeatedly that all were cash equivalents. If the ARSs were properly managed by Glenmede, maturation dates were irrelevant because of the regular auctions at which the ARSs could readily be turned into cash

Court’s Response - Exceptions #15 and #24 are granted. The inclusion of maturation dates on the monthly Glenmede account statements that were received by Steven Markowitz was neither an indication that certain investments were ARSs, nor that they were long-term investments.

These reversals are significant since the Judge’s original opinion used the initial incorrect findings to imply that I as Trustee was partially culpable in not properly supervising Glenmede’s management of Trust assets.

******

While the Court’s corrections were significant changes to its original findings, <u>the Judge did not change the amount awarded to the Trust by one penny</u>. This is hard to comprehend.

<u>Denied Exceptions</u>

It is also informative to review some of the Exceptions that were denied by the Judge in light of the evidence presented at trial. They demonstrate conflicts between the decision and incontrovertible facts.

<u>Exceptions 2, 16 and 20</u>

Court’s Response - <u>Exceptions #2, #16 and #20 are denied</u>. The plan formulated by Richard Gale and Laura LaRosa to eventually eliminate the ARS that had been transferred to Glenmede by Wachovia in February 2007, was not a **direction** from either their employer, Glenmede, (See N.T. 5/12/2011 at pp. 99-100) to tender them by a date certain, which was intentionally disregarded. Thus, it is not evidence of gross negligence and a breach of the parties’ contract. The particular breach of fiduciary duty found by the court was not Glenmede’s failure to obtain the auction rights for 14 months, but its choice not to tell Markowitz about the lack of auction rights in February, 2008 when it knew auctions had begun to fail, because it had not yet obtained the auction rights.

These denied Exceptions seem in direct conflict with one of the original findings by the Judge that stated:

> *"Notwithstanding Markowitz's failure to actively supervise the advancement advisor that he hired to manage the Trust's funds, we agree with Markowitz that Glenmede did a poor job in effectuating its investment decision made in February 2007 to liquidate all of the ARSs that it had received via transfer from Wachovia in January, 2007."*

Given that Glenmede's Gale decided to sell the bonds in February 2007, it is hard to imagine how that can be interpreted as anything else but a decision or direction from Glenmede, which had fiduciary responsibility and the discretion to sell the Trust bonds.

> Exceptions 4 and 17 (emphasis added)
>
> **Court's Response** - Exceptions #4 and #17 are denied. The record evidence did not establish whether or what "difficulties" in the ARS market were "openly discussed" at Glenmede during the 4th Quarter of 2008. The testimony that unspecified "difficulties" may have been mentioned at an in-house meeting of Glenmede personnel held sometime in the last quarter of 2007 is not sufficient to establish that Glenmede knew or should have foreseen at that time that auctions would begin to fail. Rather, we found persuasive the testimony that the collapse of the auction rate securities market that began in February, 2008 was unprecedented; constituting an unforeseen consequence of the massive dislocation of the **mortgage** market which began in mid-2007 (See, N.T. 11/9/2010 at p. 131; 145; 170 152N.T.5/12/2011 at pp. 105-106; 109-110; 125). Markowitz presented no expert testimony to prove otherwise.

It is hard to understand the Judge's refusal to reverse this finding given the testimony of James Belanger, who indicated that he was aware of the fourth-quarter meeting and the problems of the ARS market. More significantly, Glenmede admitted to the following Admissions that were read into the trial record:

> 15. Glenmede was aware of problems in the ARC market in the fourth quarter of 2007 (emphasis added).
>
> **Objection and Response:** Glenmede objects to this request because it does not know what Petitioners mean by "problems in the ARC market" or to whom they are referring when they say "Glenmede was aware .... " **Subject to, and without waiving, these objections, it is admitted that individuals at Glenmede were aware that the auction rate securities market was having difficulties.**

16. The problems in the ARC market were discussed in a Glenmede meeting open to Glenmede employees in 2007.

Objection and Response: Glenmede objects to this request because it does not know what Petitioners mean by "problems in the ARC market." Subject to, and without waiving, this objection**, it is admitted that individuals at Glenmede discussed in a meeting open to employees in the fourth quarter of 2007 that the auction rate securities market was having difficulties**.

Glenmede's Admissions 15 and 16 are quite clear concerning its understanding of the problems in the ARSs market in late 2007. This market was "having difficulties" and these difficulties were "discussed in a meeting open to employees in the fourth quarter of 2007". Given these Admissions the Judge's refusal to reverse his initial finding is hard to comprehend. Further, it is curious that the Court would demand expert testimony on facts stipulated to by both parties.

****

The Judge's reversal of important portions of his initial findings is significant. However, the Court's unwillingness to modify Glenmede's culpability and the damages awarded is hard to reconcile. This outcome should be a warning to those looking to the legal system to correct wrongs of the financial services industry.

Chapter 12

Getting Justice with Financial Advisors

In February 2012, crime writer Patricia Cornwell won a $50 million award in a lawsuit against her financial advisory firm, the New York-based Anchin, Block & Anchin. This victory, however large in size, was not significant in terms of litigation against financial advisors in the U.S. In general, it's very difficult to win a case against one's financial advisor, and the case law generated by these cases supports the financial services industry more than the cause of justice in America.

It took Cornwell four years to win her battle, even though, in her case, the breach of trust on the part of the advisor was monstrous, and one of the principals has since been convicted of a felony in relation to those activities. Cornwell described what happened in an article:

"What sounds like the plot in one of my own novels began with discovery of a $5,000 check for a "Bat Mitzvah gift," made out to (Evan) Snapper, (principal at Anchin) and supposedly from me for his daughter Lydia, whom I've never spoken to or met… He (Snapper) had simply helped himself to $5,000 of my money.[1]" The firm, Cornwell said in her lawsuit, also simply paid itself $1 million in fees without providing any justification.

"Maybe it's time to hold financial institutions accountable for their greed and questionable practices instead of bailing them out and abandoning those they've financially ruined," Cornwell suggests.[2]

The problem, insofar as getting justice when you feel your trust has been abused by financial advisors, is that the abuse is not usually as egregious as it was in Cornwell's case. More often, the situation is like this:

"Do I have a case against my financial advisor who never took out required minimum distribution from an inherited IRA for 10 years? The financial adviser who handles the account never told me about the 5 year rule or took out any RMDs. I was told to hire a CPA to figure out the taxes. The financial advisor has been sending me statements for 10 years (he was my father's broker and so I trusted him to know what to do with the IRA). What do I do?"

An attorney's answer would likely be: "If you have an advisor that services the account and with whom you've worked with regularly, you may (emphasize may) have something. You will have to consult with a securities attorney to review your documents, emails and the like to ascertain what remedies may be available.[3]"

The "may have," is a great big 'maybe.' Essentially, financial advisors are careful to protect themselves from litigation. Your advisor will tell you that he or she is 'your trusted partner, ready to help with everything,' but the contracts you sign when engaging the advisor's services will say something different. Then, even if you can prove that the advisor was at fault under the terms of the contract, getting back money lost will require proving under strict case law that you have a right to that reimbursement.

On average, investors claim $2 billion annually in losses due to their Financial Advisor's malfeasance or fraud every year in the U.S., according to statistics from the Financial Industry Regulatory Authority (FINRA). Of this amount, awards to investors amount to less than $200 million in an average year – the verdict with an award the size Cornell received is quite rare.

A good example is the award that I received for what the Judge called "a breach of fiduciary duty," was only pennies on the dollars that I lost. The Judge made it clear that Glenmede was at fault finding (emphasis added):

"Glenmede was more concerned with positioning itself favorably vis a vis responsibility for the delay in its receipt of auction rights, than passing along the relevant market information. Glenmede's conduct in this regard falls short of the scrupulous good faith and candor that are the cornerstones of a fiduciary relationship and **constitutes a breach of the fiduciary duty."** (Trial Ruling, p.22)

At least, in this respect, Glenmede was found to be at fault, and this ruling was upheld on appeal.

We demanded reimbursement of our $325,500 loss. The Judge simply stated: "I disagree," and cited as precedent *Rosenfeld 29 Fiduc. Rep. 2d 27, 280 (O.C. Phila 2006).*

The case in question is: TRUST ESTATE OF EMANUEL ROSENFELD, SETTLOR. Appeal of: LESTER ROSENFELD and ROBERT ROSENFELD, No. 2324 EDA 2006. At issue, in this case, is the management of the perpetual charitable trust known as the Mary and Emanuel Rosenfeld Foundation, created by Emanuel Rosenfeld, one of the founders of the Pep Boys company. For the first forty-five years of its existence, the Trust consisted almost entirely of Pep Boys stock. As of April 2002, when the litigation started, the Rosenfeld Trust held 396,900 shares of Pep Boys stock worth $7,600,635. Pep Boys stock regularly outperformed the S&P index over the years, but, at times, performed worse than the index.

The litigation arose out of a demand by one of the managers of trust funds, which were used largely for charitable donations, for diversification of the Trust's assets. The litigant claimed that the Trustees had "breached their fiduciary duty," in not diversifying away from the Pep Boys stock.

Initially, the litigant won the demand in Orphan's Court in Philadelphia. But the decision was reversed on appeal. The issue here is the size of the surcharge given breach of fiduciary trust.

The Appellate Court ruling states: "The Orphans' Court's imposition of a surcharge against the Rosenfelds also must be reversed because, even if they breached some supposed duty to diversify the Trust's investments, there is no basis in the record for calculating damages or for concluding that the Rosenfelds' breach of duty damaged the Trust. In the absence of loss there can be no surcharge, and therefore the Orphans' Court's surcharge must be reversed."

At issue in the case is the value of Pep Boys stock at a given time. The Court stated that clear evidence of that loss must be shown. "Moreover, the evidence that Mrs. Stein introduced in the Orphans' Court to establish a loss to the Rosenfeld Trust was, as the Orphans' Court itself later recognized, entirely insufficient to prove any loss, even on an interim basis."

How do the issues in this case compare with those in my case against Glenmede? In the Rosenfeld case, expert witnesses were produced on both sides, although the Appellate judge found neither side's evidence conclusive. But the testimony of the expert witnesses was absolutely necessary, the judge felt.

The Judge, in my case, insisted on the importance of the expert witness. He claimed that I "produced no evidence" about how the bonds at issue in my case could have been sold without loss. Another case law reference, to *Pew Estate, 440 Pa. Super, 195 at 240, 521 at 543 (1994)* is cited relative to the "propriety of an investment."

Here is the context of *Pew* (We meet an old friend in the case, emphasis added):

In their sixth issue on appeal, the appellants maintain that the co-successor trustee, the **<u>Glenmede Trust Company</u>**, had a conflict of interest and breached their fiduciary duty during the period covered by the supplement to the Third and Final Account of the Mary C. Pew Trust, Sur Trust for Walter C. Pew, by selling off large blocks of Oryx and Sun Company common stock on behalf of other trusts, funds, estates and accounts that it managed and advising certain of its favored clients to sell the Oryx and Sun Company common stocks while failing to sell the Oryx and Sun Company common stocks held by the Mary C. Pew Trust before the value of these stocks declined. Therefore, the appellants argue that the co-successor trustees should be surcharged in excess of $3,053,000.00 to cover the diminution of the value of the stock which occurred during the time period covered by the supplement to the Third and Final Account plus interest and costs, including reasonable attorney fees. Additionally, the appellants assert that the trial court erred by denying their petition for allowance to conduct discovery upon the Glenmede Trust Company, Ann Pew Curran, Sun Company, and Oryx to determine to what extent the Glenmede Trust Company's decision to sell the Sun Company and Oryx common stocks in other trusts it administered while retaining the same stocks in the Mary C. Pew Trust injured the remaindermen.

A trustee cannot be surcharged for a breach of duty unless the breach caused a loss to the trust. *In re Mendenhall,* 484 Pa. 77, 82 n. 3, 398 A.2d 951, 954 n. 3 (1979). One who seeks to surcharge the trustee for breach of trust must bear the burden of proving the particulars of the trustee's wrongful conduct. *Estate of Stetson* 463 Pa. 64, 84, 345 A.2d 679, 690 (1975). *In re Estate of Feinstein,* 364 Pa.Super. 221, 230,527 A.2d 1034, 1038 (1987). The propriety of an investment by a trustee must be judged as it appeared at the time it was made and not as viewed in the light of subsequent events. *In re Glauser's Estate,* 350 Pa. 192, 202, 38 A.2d 64, 69 (1944); *In re Saeger's Estate, supra* 340 Pa. at 75-76, 16 A.2d at 21. The mere retention of stocks which the trustee received from the settlor is not, in itself, negligence. *In re Clabby's Estate,* 338 Pa. 305, 314, 12 A.2d 71, 75 (1940). Especially when such stocks have produced a high rate of return for the trust over an extended number of years. *Id.* at 314, 12 A.2d at 75. Hindsight is not the test of liability for surcharge. *Estate of Knipp, supra* 489 Pa. at 512, 414 A.2d at1008. *Mereto Estate,* 373 Pa. 466, 469, 96 A.2d 115, 116 (1953). To make after-sight the sole judge of the trustee's prudence would be manifestly unfair. *In re Clabby's Estate, supra* 338 Pa. at 315, 12 A.2d at 75.

From ESTATE OF PEW
440 Pa.Super. 195 (1994)
655 A.2d 521

In fact, in my case against Glenmede, a vast amount of evidence was produced to show how the loss could have been avoided. The issue was not the "propriety" of the investment; the issue was that proper communication was not maintained by Glenmede. But the Judge, with the support of the Appellate Court, maintains that a specific argument should have addressed to this issue, with reliance on an expert witness. The pressure of case law is brought to bear, without due consideration of the simple facts of the case.

The Judge, in fact, placed considerable pressure on me in the consideration of the case. It is noteworthy that he towards the beginning of his opinion points out that I was a "sophisticated investor" stating:

"Markowitz is a sophisticated investor, experienced fiduciary, and follower of the financial markets." (Trial Ruling, p.3).

This is a critical determination and it will be a part of the Judge's logic throughout the ruling. A "sophisticated investor," under U.S. law, belongs to a very special category – when signing up for an online investment site, one of the first questions asked is "are you a sophisticated, or qualified investor?" An investment advisor has a much greater duty of care under law with regard to an investor who is not "sophisticated." A considerable number of financial products may be offered to a "sophisticated" investor and many may not be offered to others. This is because such an investor is assumed to have the experience and know-how to make complex investment decisions.

By qualifying me as such a sophisticated investor, the Judge begins building a case against me for not adequately supervising my investments. Yet, the issue of my being a "sophisticated investor," (or not) should have been irrelevant. No matter what my level of knowledge, I could not act because I did not know that the bonds were troubled, and Glenmede kept me from knowing this crucial information. What's more, the Trust was paying Glenmede to take proper care of the Trust's investments – why is there no mention of any case law, in the entire opinion, that treats their responsibility to me and the Trust?

The Judge continues to make his case against me, citing case law to show that I failed to provide the required level of proof.

"The type of relationship between the parties, that of investor and investment advisor, and the associated work, is not elementary and non-technical, requiring only simple common sense." (Trial Ruling, p. 20).

The particular case law cited here is *Himmelreich vs. Adams Abstract Assoc. 59 D&C 4th 382 (Adams Co. 2002)*. In this case, the issue was whether insurance covered damages. The question was: Does common sense apply? As so often in law, the answer is negative:

Is this an elementary and non-technical transaction which requires only simple common sense . . . [In this case,] whether [the insurance broker] failed to exercise a reasonable degree of care and skill related to common professional practice in [obtaining sufficient insurance] is a question of fact outside the normal range of the ordinary experience of laypersons.

I had supposed that the joint testimony of Glenmede's employees, experts, would be sufficient to cover this matter. It would also have been a simple task to look up sales of the bonds at issue during the period in question to see what price they fetched. But this case law is cited as to show that this would not have been sufficient.

But none of this, according to the Judge, constitutes "proof of loss." The case law cited in this regard is "A trustee cannot be surcharged for a breach of his duty unless the breach caused a loss." In re Inter Vivos Trust of Mendenhall, 484 Pa. 77, 82 n. 3, 398 A.2d 951, 954 n. 3 (1979). The case places the burden of proof of loss very significantly on my shoulders. After all, the value of an investment is not necessarily easy to ascertain, the Judge claims.

This view makes it easy for financial advisors to hide behind the law. If you hire an expert who says the advisor cost you money by mishandling your investments, the advisory firm will hire another expert who says it didn't. The courts routinely take time deciding which expert is right, but they often rule that one cancels out the other one. In fact, the Trust had our then current advisor testify at trial as an expert. However, the Judge rejected much of his testimony.

What about the legal fees? Here there is specific precedent in:

LAVELLE v. KOCH
532 Pa. 631 (1992)
617 A.2d 319

This case was brought by President Judge Lavelle to compel the three County Commissioners sitting as members of the Carbon County Salary Board to provide funds to run the Carbon County Court. The details are complex, and don't concern us except in regard to the determination of reimbursing legal fees.

Pennsylvania is particularly tough in this area. "*We have consistently reaffirmed in this Commonwealth, a litigant cannot recover counsel fees from an adverse party unless there is express statutory authorization, a clear agreement of the parties, or some other exception,*"" the case law says. Again, the burden of proof is placed on me requiring a specific argument to address this case law.

But perhaps the most challenging element in the Judge's case against me is his demand that I prove "gross negligence," "willful malfeasance," or "bad faith." A very long list of cases is cited in the Trial Ruling (p.17-p.21) regarding this issue. The conclusion the Judge comes to is that a very high level of proof is required to show "gross negligence" and that I didn't prove it. The result is that my demands for awards under Torts law – which would have demanded greater reimbursement

– were denied. Not being a lawyer, the evaluation of this argument is beyond my scope here. But surely it raises questions about the legal evaluation of financial-advisor conduct?

On the one hand, the Judge agreed that the advisor has a fiduciary duty to the client. On the other hand, client compensation is only awarded if the client can prove "gross negligence?" Doesn't this place too considerable a burden on the client? Doesn't this give enormous latitude to the financial advisor? Is this congruent with the rule of fiduciary responsibility? Does it seem fair? Granted, what is legal and what is fair are not necessarily the same thing. But do we want to run our economy based on this kind of law?

---

1 "Stranger than Fiction," The Huffington Post, October 2, 2012

2 "Stranger than Fiction," The Huffington Post, October 2, 2012

3 Cited from legal research website Avvo, http://www.avvo.com/legal-answers/do-i-have-a-case-against-my-financial-advisor-who--1203318.html

Chapter 13

Bad Debt and Politics: Why our Economy has Gone Sour

While the issues discussed in this book focus on problems associated with bad debt and the financial services industry in the private sector, the discussion would be incomplete without reference to government debt and the policies of the Federal Reserve Bank (Fed). While greed and incompetence from the financial services industry in the private sector exists irrespective of governmental policies, an irresponsible swelling of the money supply and the maintenance of interest rates at dangerous low levels have caused imbalances throughout the economy.

There is nothing morally wrong with debt, and there is nothing intrinsically wrong with a government running at a budget deficit. A balanced budget is not sacred and does not necessarily lead to lower taxes or a stronger economy. The more crucial issue is how governmental funds are spent. If used to improve economic efficiency and activity, government spending can lower long-term deficits by increasing tax revenues. Unfortunately, as often occurs in the private sector, deficit spending by the government is wasted on goals that are not worthwhile.

Government spending is a necessity; that is a substantial reason for governments to exist. We elect our presidents and the Congress to decide on spending to promote the overall good of the country

There are always competing interests for government spending, which is a huge portion of the overall economy. For 2012 this spending was approximately 22% of GDP or $3.6 trillion dollars.[1] This competition should require trade-offs between various interest groups to keep the deficit under control. However, because the government can in essence print money and has injected funds into the money supply in order to increase spending, deficit spending has become unchecked. This has perverted the normal government spending process by creating the illusion that government spending has no real cost. Excessive levels of government deficit spending and easy money policies historically have led to high inflation and also produced other economic crises. For example, they have incited high-yield seeking within the financial community irrespective of risk and have led to bubbles and irresponsible lending. This bad-debt environment was a major cause of the 2008 financial crisis whose negative effects continue to this day.

---

[1] "Federal Spending by the numbers," The Heritage Foundation

While the people suffer – all too often the banks and financial advisors don't.

The History of the Bad Debt Environment – The Eisenhower Years

It is widely thought that President Eisenhower, in the Fifties, presided over a balanced budget throughout his administration. This is, in fact, not true.[2] One priority for the Eisenhower administration was combating the Cold War with money lavishly spent on defense against the Communist threat outside our borders. In addition, his administration financed education and social programs, in part, as a means to move the less affluent to support other governmental programs. Eisenhower positioned his administration as "moderate" Republicans and he continued to support New Deal legislation. In 1954, Eisenhower signed legislation that increased the size of the social security program and increased funding for education.[3]

In addition to these social measures, Eisenhower maintained 3.5 million men at arms (various branches of the service) and participation in the arms race with the Soviet Union, which required deficit spending. In 1959, his administration ran a deficit of $12.4 billion, which is paltry by today's standards, but was a significant amount at the time, particularly as the value of the dollar was much greater then. It was equivalent to 2.5 percent of GDP at the time.[4]

The Eisenhower deficits during the 1950s did not have major negative impacts on the overall economy. From 1944 to 1960, the U.S. economy expanded at the gradual rate of 2.1 percent per year. There was a slight period of sharper growth from 1947 to 1953, when GDP increased 4.6 per year.[5] However, this use of deficit spending during a period that included no catastrophic economic or war event set the country sliding down a slippery slope. The slide down into ever-greater excess would continue.

Inflation was an issue following World War II. Two major waves of inflationary conditions swept the country in the wake of the war. The first followed the end of WWII and the second at the onset of the Korean War in 1950. The cause of this inflation has been attributed to increased consumer demand while consumer goods productivity did not keep pace. The service sector experienced the biggest price increases due to the removal of price controls after the war. The Federal

---

2 Please see *A People and A Nation, A History of the United States since 1865, Vol. II* (Wadsworth, Boston, 2012)

3 *A People and A Nation, A History of the United States since 1865, Vol. II* (Wadsworth, Boston, 2012)

4 "Eisenhower and the Budget: Neustadtian 'Amateur' or Machiavellian 'Professional'" Iwan Morgan, Institute for the Study of the Americas, 2010 American Politics Group conference (Jan. 9, 2010)

5 "Current Population Report," U.S. Census, 1989

Reserve Bank worked to control inflation using quantitative devices of credit control-the discount rate, open market operations and changes in the reserve ratios. In fact, the Fed of the 1950s displayed a sophisticated handling of inflation control:

"Inflation, measured using the GDP deflator, averaged less than 2.0 percent per year between 1952 and 1960, and never went above 3.3 percent in a single year. Real GDP over the same eight-year period grew at an average rate of 2.9 percent per year and the unemployment rate averaged 4.7 percent. While the two recessions during this decade, that in 1954 was exceedingly mild and that in 1958 was sharp, but very brief. And, even in the worst year of the decade, 1958, the unemployment rate was just 6.8 percent.[6]"

In other words, although the government ran deficits, the then truly independent Fed was still able to control inflation. Economic growth was steady, if slow. This is why most of us who studied or remember the Fifties see it as a period of prosperity.

Kennedy Cuts Taxes

It is not often remembered that John F. Kennedy was elected in 1960 partly on a platform of speeding up economic growth. In addition, he railed against the supposed "missile gap" between the US and the Soviet Union and promised increased spending in this area.

Kennedy also supported a series of tax cuts, for business and individuals, and these were eventually passed into law in 1964 (after his assassination). The cuts were combined with liberal political programs that included increasing the minimum wage, expanding unemployment benefits, increasing Social Security benefits, and infrastructure spending. At a macro level, these policies worked with economic growth jumping to 6.6 percent in 1966. Unemployment declined and investment on the stock market increased sharply.[7]

Not all economists attribute the economic upturn during this period to government policy, however. There is considerable debate over the role of the Federal Reserve in the economy's growth at this time.[8]

William McChesney Martin Jr. was the governor of the Federal Reserve during the Kennedy administration and continued under Lyndon Baines Johnson. Martin

---

6 "A REHABILITATION OF MONETARY POLICY IN THE 1950S," National Bureau of Economic Research, February 2002

7 "JFK's lasting economic legacy," NPR, November 14, 2013

8 "William McChesney Martin Jr.: A Reevaluation," Federal Reserve, Region Focus, 2006

set Fed policies to keep interest rates higher despite pressure from the Kennedy administration to reduce them in an effort to stimulate growth, without regard for the inflation a looser policy would bring on.

On the other hand, Martin was not immune to presidential pressure. "The administration persuaded Martin (despite dissents at the Fed) to nudge short-term rates upward while keeping long-term rates low. Operation Nudge turned into Operation Twist, which would involve vigorous actions to reduce long rates.[9]" This was a historic reversal of Fed policy, and one that sent the country in a dangerous direction under LBJ.

There is also debate about the increase in the money supply under Martin at the Fed. Statistics would seem to show that M2 grew significantly over the years of the Kennedy and Johnson administrations – a change that also arguably helped cause the inflation of the Seventies. Again, economists differ widely about this issue. But it is clear that the Kennedy administration paved the way for a historic change that took place after the assassination.

LBJ and the Great Sea Change

The assassination of JFK and then the presidency of LBJ brought a sea change to American government and to American history. We are all aware of the great social changes that took place during this period, but the economic ones are less well known.

One tends to perceive this period through the social aspects, especially if one was a 'Baby Boomer,' growing up at the time that was dominated by the Civil Rights movement and the Vietnam War. As a teenager, I understood the basic issues. President Lyndon Johnson was determined through his expansive and expensive Great Society programs to eliminate poverty. He was also determined to win a widening war in Vietnam, both very expensive propositions.

Prior to Vietnam, when the United States went to war, Americans were asked to sacrifice for the effort. President Johnson took a different approach. He not only did not ask for sacrifice, but continued his Great Society programs, an approach that became known as "guns and butter."

Under Johnson, the federal government's intrusion into economic life swelled enormously. In little more than two years after LBJ took office, Congress enacted over two hundred major bills and at least a dozen landmark measures [10]. The ferment rivalled that of Roosevelt's New Deal. Major events included enactment of the Civil Rights Act of 1964, the Economic Opportunity Act of

---

[9] "William McChesney Martin Jr.: A Reevaluation," Federal Reserve, Region Focus, 2006

[10] Paul K. Conkin, *Big Daddy from the Pedernales: Lyndon Baines Johnson.* Boston: Twayne Publishers, 1986)

1964, the Food Stamp Act of 1964, the Elementary and Secondary Education Act of 1965, and the Social Security Amendments of 1965 (creating Medicare and Medicaid), as well as establishment of the Office of Economic Opportunity (to oversee programs such as VISTA, Job Corps, Community Action Program, and Head Start), hundreds of Community Action Agencies, and many other bureaus intended to promote poor people's health, education, job training, and welfare.

In addition, during Johnson's presidency, broad-gauge economic regulatory measures were adopted in connection with traffic safety, coal-mine safety, consumer-products safety, age discrimination in employment, truth in lending, and other areas. In five years the American government approximately doubled its regulatory role and at least doubled the scope of transfer payments[11]. All of this was accomplished at the same time the Vietnam War was costing increasing amounts of money.

Most would agree with hindsight that the Vietnam War did more damage to America than any benefit it brought to the world. The debate over the success or failure of the Great Society programs is not relevant here. What is important is that Johnson's choices had vast economic consequences. "As we have pointed out, this conversion was a gradual one, extending over the several decades, but 1964-1965 offers the historical watershed. Before this date, the fiscal politics of America was at least partially "pre-Keynesian" in both rhetoric and reality. After 1965, the fiscal politics became definitely "post-Keynesian" in reality, although elements of the old-time religion remained in the political argument. "[12]

"The results are on record for all to see. After 1964, the United States embarked on a course of fiscal irresponsibility matched by no other period in its two-century history. A record-setting deficit of $25 billion in 1968 generated a temporary obeisance to the old-fashioned verities in 1969, the first Nixon year. But following this, the federal government's budget swept onward and upward toward explosive heights, financed increasingly and disproportionately by deficits. Deficits of more than $23 billion were recorded in each of the 1971 and 1972 fiscal years. This provided the setting for Nixon's putative 1974 "battle of the budget," his last pre-Watergate scandal effort to bring spending into line with revenues. Fiscal 1973 saw the deficit reduced to plausibly acceptable limits, only to become dangerously large in fiscal 1975 and 1976, when a two-year deficit of more than $100 billion was accumulated.[13]"

---

11 Paul K. Conkin, *Big Daddy from the Pedernales: Lyndon Baines Johnson.* Boston: Twayne Publishers, 1986)

12 Buchanan, James M. and Richard E. Wagner, *Democracy in Deficit: The Political Legacy of Lord Keynes* (Liberty Fund, 1999, Indianapolis)

13 Buchanan, James M. and Richard E. Wagner, *Democracy in Deficit: The Political Legacy of Lord Keynes* (Liberty Fund, 1999, Indianapolis)

Under Johnson, the money supply grew, inflation rose, and bad debt got worse.

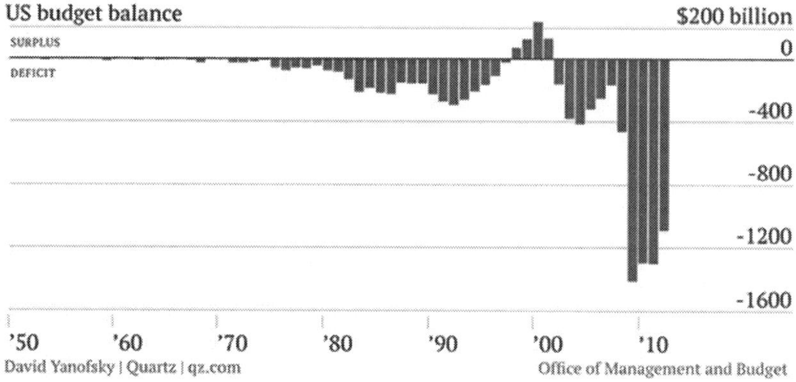

Nixon and the Gold Standard

While President Richard Nixon did take steps to battle spending, he took the dangerous step of decoupling the US dollar from the gold standard. Again, there is nothing moral or magical about the gold standard, and vast amounts of hot air are blown about its importance. However, any significant change in fiscal or monetary policies for a country has consequences.

The decoupling with gold made the dollar worth less against foreign currencies, and thus drove prices higher in the U.S. –adding to inflation. Since that decoupling, the value of an American dollar has fallen by 70 percent against the euro (and its predecessor currencies) and the Japanese yen.[14]

Nixon repeatedly pushed then Fed chairman Arthur Burns to increase the money supply in an attempt to juice up the economy. "An aide asked Nixon: But that will leave you with a larger inflation if you do get re-elected. And he said, "Well, we'll worry about that after we get re-elected." On 19 March 1971, Nixon urged Burns "We've got to think of goosing it [the money supply] . . . late summer and fall of this year [1971] and next year [1972]. As you know, there's a hell of a lag".[15]

Burns caved in to Nixon's wishes, a dangerous precedent for the supposedly independent Fed. The result was a costly inflationary boom-bust cycle. "The eventual elimination of wage and price controls in 1973 and the excessively aggressive monetary policy of 1971-72 produced an inflationary boom. The inflation rate measured by the change in Consumer Price Index in 1973 was

[14] "Nixon's Colossal Monetary Error," Forbes, August 15, 2011

[15] "How Richard Nixon pressured Arthur Burns," Journal of Economic Perspectives, Fall 2006

9.6 percent. In response to the post-election Federal Reserve tightening, the economy swung into a recession in November 1973, one year after the election. The recession lasted until March 1975, but even this recession was insufficient to stop inflationary pressures leading to a relatively new economic malady called stagflation. The inflation rate for 1975 was 6.7 percent. It was not until Paul Volcker became chairman of the Fed in 1979, and the subsequent recession in 1980, that things began to change."[16]

It is impossible to put the genie back into the bottle. But it is worth noting that Nixon's decoupling of the dollar and gold, along with the Fed's acquiescence to White House pressure contributed to long-term economic damage. The dollar's depreciation led to a currency war between various countries in the 1970s and inhibited economic growth worldwide. Jimmy Carter's administration took the brunt of the resulting economic malaise.

The Volcker Federal Reserve

During the 1970s inflation became a regular feature of American life, with yearly increases in the consumer price index (CPI) regularly exceeding 10 percent. This marked the most sustained period of peacetime inflation in U.S. history. A key contributor to this inflation was the oil supply shock of the early 1970s, but as we have seen, the increasing government spending and increases to the money supply of the 1960s also played key roles in driving up wages and prices.

Presidents Nixon experimented with wage and price controls to manage inflation, but they were ineffective and likely counterproductive.

During Paul Volcker's tenure as its Chairman (1979-1987) the U.S. Federal Reserve limited the rate of growth in the U.S. money supply and increased short-term interest rates. These policies significantly brought down inflation and helped to create the conditions for the lengthy period of prosperity that followed.

Soon after taking office in August 1979 Volcker instituted a policy of monetary targeting in which the Federal Reserve focused on directly limiting the amount of money in circulation through tighter control over private bank reserves. This marked an important shift in Fed strategy, which to that point had largely concentrated on raising or lowering interest rates through its open market operations. The policy was not painless and triggered two years of deep recession, from 1980 to 1981, but it finally, and definitively, brought inflation down.

The country paid a price for Volcker's intervention. Unemployment rose, and

---

[16] "How Richard Nixon pressured Arthur Burns," Journal of Economic Perspectives, Fall 2006

GDP contracted. But President Reagan was on board for such a move. The result was that the inflationary breach in the economy was healed, and the bad-debt/lose money environment was sealed off for a time. Money once again had real value and the economy operated in a stable environment[17]. But this would change in the future as politics and greed brought back the bad debt policies and lose money.

Volcker and Reagan

Much credit is given to President Reagan for taming inflation and improving the economy, and he deserves some of it. Although markets and consumer sentiment had been ravaged by ongoing inflation, the toll that the tight money policy required to stop it would add to that negative sentiment. Housing and auto sales collapsed. Unemployment rose to 10.8 percent. However, Reagan maintained a sense of order and optimism throughout the recessions of 1980 and 1981. "No other possible president at the time, Democrat or Republican, would have so steadfastly supported Volcker. Reagan faced enormous pressure from both Republicans and Democrats to push the Fed to relent. He was vilified in the press; his approval rating fell to 35 percent. Reagan and Volcker, though lacking a close personal relationship, did share a common conviction: America could not thrive with high inflation. If the Fed had relaxed prematurely, inflation would almost certainly have revived and exceeded its previous peaks.[18]"

On the other hand, it is not true, as is often implied, that Reagan reduced government spending. In 1980, federal spending was 21.7 percent of GDP; in 1988, it was 21.3 percent. The safety net was not shredded, and entitlements (Social Security, Medicare) were not reduced. Instead, the deficit increased, as the chart shows. But Reagan and Volcker created the conditions for the period of prosperity that the country enjoyed, especially under President Clinton.

The Greenspan Fed

Federal Reserve chairpersons since Volcker, Greenspan and Bernanke, have taken a different view of the Fed's role in the economy. Instead of focusing on a stable money supply and low inflation, they have intervened in efforts to stop economic downturns, and their actions not only allowed, but fostered the financial services industry's ability to create the bad-debt environment in the private sector that led to subsequent crises. In addition, by hindering downturns that are a natural

---

[17] "The real Reagan legacy," Robert Samuelson, Real Clear Politics, February 11, 2011

[18] "The real Reagan legacy," Robert Samuelson, Real Clear Politics, February 11, 2011

part of economic activity, the Fed inhibited the market's ability to balance supply and demand. This added to bubble creation and increased the severity of the inevitable downturns. It also led to huge profits for the financial services industry.

One of the consequences of the Volcker regime at the Fed was to genuinely release it from presidential pressure – at least for a time. Alan Greenspan was able to run the country's money supply quite independent of the Clinton administration and Congress.[19]

The Greenspan Fed presided over a prolonged period of economic growth. It was the Fed's policy during that period to keep interest rates low, and to resist pressure to raise them. Allied with this policy was the financial services industry that thrived in a climate of self-regulation. During the period of prosperity, Greenspan was treated as a prophetic figure, one almost beyond criticism[20]. Since the 2008 crisis hit, he has been vilified, and there was even talk of legal action against him.[21]

It is possible to distinguish between the good and the bad of Greenspan's policies. Clearly, his maintenance of low interest rates drove economic growth. Robert Reich, who was a member of the Clinton administration, admits that Greenspan contributed as much as his president to American prosperity in the 1990s: "The smart thing was to keep interest rates low in the 1990s when standard economic models at that time instructed otherwise. By the spring of 1996 the U.S. economy was growing quickly, at an annual rate of 6 percent, and unemployment had dropped to well below 5.5 percent. According to textbook economics, these circumstances called for higher interest rates to slow the economy and avoid inflation. But Greenspan saw the American economy in a new light. He believed that globalisation and rapid technological change allowed faster growth without inflation. Companies could easily expand production by outsourcing abroad or subcontracting, thereby avoiding inflationary pressures. In addition, foreign competition inhibited companies' abilities to raise prices.

So Greenspan kept interest rates relatively low. He was right, to a point. Unemployment in the late 1990s eventually dropped to 4 percent in the U.S., without igniting inflation. And as demand picked up for unskilled workers, inequality temporarily narrowed. Bill Clinton is usually credited with the 1990s boom, but it was really a product of Greenspan's willingness to reject the old economic models in favour of new realities, and let the economy roar.[22]"

---

19 "The questionable legacy of Alan Greenspan," Thomas Palley Challenge, November –December 2005

20 "Fed chairman virtually deified," Star-News, February 21, 2000

21 "Could US officials be charged for causing the financial crisis?" Foreign Policy, September 30, 2010

22 "Alan Greenspan," Robert Reich, The Guardian, January 17, 2009

But there were consequences, as there always are, prophetically enumerated by Thomas Palley in 2005 (emphasis added):

"The [Greenspan] regime has momentous consequences. In the real economy, it has meant that full employment, robust real-wage growth, and a healthy manufacturing sector are no longer explicit policy priorities. In the financial sector, it has created a moral hazard among investors that generates asset price inflation. Since investors increasingly realize that the stability of the system is configured around asset prices, they realize that the Fed cannot afford to let asset prices go to hell in a hand basket and they have an incentive to put everything in stocks and other such assets. Moreover, this incentive also encourages debt bubbles, since economic agents have an incentive to finance their asset purchases with debt, thereby maximizing their gain from asset-price inflation. Finally, the new regime may have had collateral effects on the social attitude toward risk sharing..."[23] (This essay by Thomas Palley in *Challenge* is a truly extraordinary prediction of just about everything that went wrong in 2008).

To look at Greenspan's interventions in crises, is to see Palley's worst fears fulfilled. The Asian monetary crisis, which began in 1997 with the fall of the baht against major currencies, was caused, at least in part, by the high levels of private debt in the rapidly developing "Tiger" nations, and this was supported by cheap money. The failure of the governments involved to maintain the necessary levels of reserves was due to the idea that money would be cheaply and readily available. It was all part of the kind of "social attitude toward risk sharing," that Palley invokes.

Similarly, the "encouragement of debt bubbles," along with the "incentive to put everything in stocks," drove the Dotcom and Datacom bubbles of the late 1990s. Between late 1996 and 1999 the Dow Jones Industrial Average climbed from 6,437 points to 9,355 points, a 45 percent gain. The Nasdaq Composite improved more, growing from just over 1,300 points to 2,400 points, an 85 percent gain. The tech-heavy NASDAQ continued to 4,760 a year later, only to plunge back to 1,100 by 2002.[24] Companies did IPO's based on little more than business plans in PowerPoint and financed by debt. When it was over, Greenspan raised interest rates slightly, but the environment and consequences did not change.

Worst of all was the housing bubble. I cite Robert Reich, who was, after all, Greenspan's close associate: "Greenspan's worst move was to contribute to the giant housing bubble and the worst worldwide crash since the Great Depression. In 2004 he lowered interest rates to 1 percent, enabling banks to borrow money for free, adjusted for inflation. Naturally, the banks wanted to borrow as much as

23 "The Questionable Legacy of Alan Greenspan," Challenge, November-December 2005

24 "DotCom bubble burst 10 years later, " BBC News, March 9, 2010

they possibly could, then lend it out, earning nice profits. The situation screamed for government oversight of lending institutions, lest the banks lend to unfit borrowers. He refused, trusting the market to weed out bad credit risks. It did not.

Years earlier Greenspan had urged Congress to dismantle the wall separating investment and commercial banking, thereby allowing investment banks to become lightly regulated financial behemoths that sold their shares to the public, borrowed to the hilt, and invested wildly. Greenspan was also against regulating the "derivatives" they invested in - securities derived from making bets on the future prices of real assets, such as those tied to rising home values.

The result was to magnify the housing bubble many times over. When it burst, the entire global financial system went down with it. There's no single culprit for the mess we're in, but Alan Greenspan comes closest.[25]"

The Bernanke Fed

Federal Reserve Chairman Benjamin Bernanke pursued policies very similar to those of his predecessor. In an effort to stimulate the economy, he kept interest rates at record low levels and injected large amounts of money into the economy. Unemployment has come down slightly, at this writing; growth has been low.

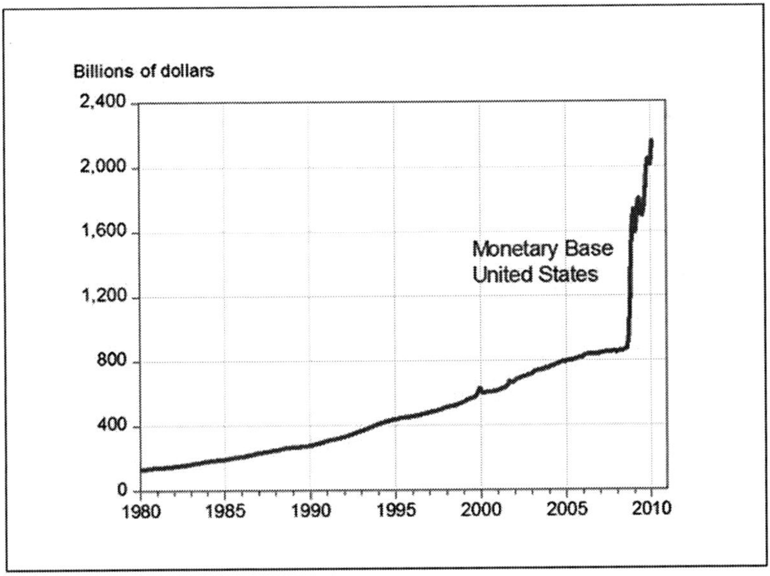

[25] "Alan Greenspan," Robert Reich, The Guardian, January 17, 2009

Presidents George W. Bush and Barack Obama have spent billions on economic stimulus, which, along with our defense spending, has driven the deficit to unprecedented levels. The pressure of financing the deficit is becoming a significant force on the American economy, not to mention on its political life. When the cost of financing this debt increases, as it inevitably will, the financial pressures could become unbearable. Given this, it is likely that the Fed will be pressured into continuing the low interest rate policies long into the future. The consequences will also play out in the future.

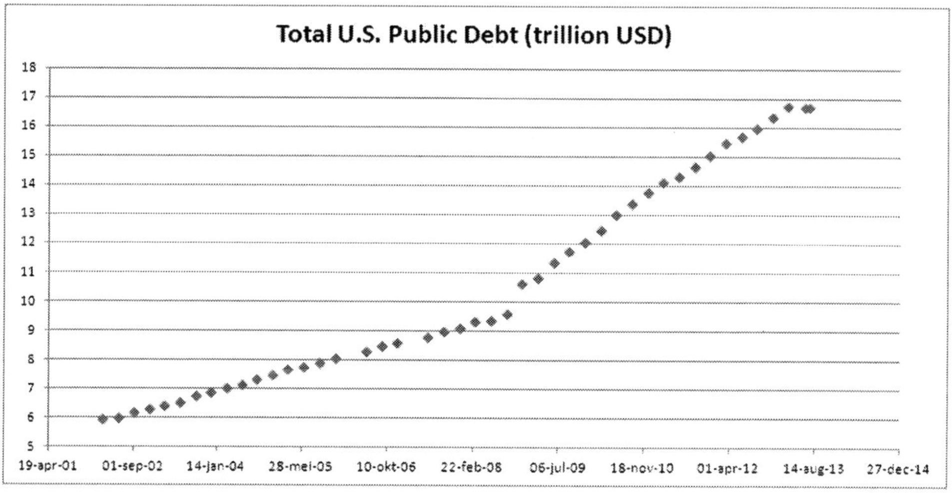

Nearly 6 years after the financial crisis occurred, we are all still waiting to see if the easy money, cheap debt policy of Bernanke and Obama will lead us out of "recession". While this recession officially ended four years ago, it is been the most anaemic recovery in modern US history. That raises the obvious question as to whether the Fed's policies themselves played a role in the ongoing economic malaise.

The Bad-Debt Government: From Johnson to Reagan to Clinton to Obama

The decision to bail out the biggest banks, the very actors who created the financial crisis, and to reward the system that caused so much misery to so many Americans, was made essentially by Bernanke and the Federal Reserve, along with then Treasury Secretary Henry Paulson under the Bush administration in September 2008.[26] That these actors had to be supported through the crisis, in order to save the world banking system, is defensible (although the related decision not to support Lehman Bros. is reprehensible under the circumstances). However, it is hard to justify providing these banks with support that has made

26 "There is vast literature, but for quick and specific reference, please see "Paulson, Bernanke strained for consensus on bailout," Wall Street Journal, November 10, 2008.

them so profitable while many other businesses struggle. There is also no reason why the bankers who created the crisis should still be at the helm of these institutions. And it is impossible to justify allowing bonuses to be paid to these bankers after the bailouts.

Further, the policy of "stimulating" the economy with cheap funds has done nothing to bring back growth. It has, however, provided the financial services industry with cheap money for trading – an action unrelated to productive economic activity. Investment in such productive activities is at an all-time low.[27] Why not. Under current Fed and governmental policies productive activities take longer to reap rewards. Financial speculation, on the other, only requires risk and it is often funded with other people's money.

We as a country could have made very different policy choices. We still can, but that requires political will. There is time to take our economy back to the path set by Volcker, to raise interest rates, and to make the dollar a valued currency again. This would make investing in creative industry in the U.S. worthwhile once more and less in the potential profitability of speculation. The Fed's policies of low interest rates and easy money have not allowed the economy to prosper. Continuing the same policies will not lead to different results. Instead, we should think in terms of long-term value and creativity; two attributes that allowed this country to grow and prosper for most of its history. However, that road is first covered with the reality of economic hardship, similar to the early days of the Reagan administration and Volcker's tough love economic medicine.

As the country's total debt has increased, the cost to finance it under normal economic circumstances also increases. However, the government, through an unholy alliance with the supposedly independent Fed has been able to drive interest rates down to historic lows. Governments that have spent too much have also sponsored a cheap money policy that has artificially constrained the country's overall debt cost, and that has added to a bad-debt environment in the country and for the greater economy.

The choice is clear. Do we continue to depend on financial manipulation and trickery, or do we look for creativity and productivity to create economic growth? Those who indicate both approaches can coexist are disingenuous.

---

27 "Whither U.S. Manufacturing?" Reuters, November 27, 2013

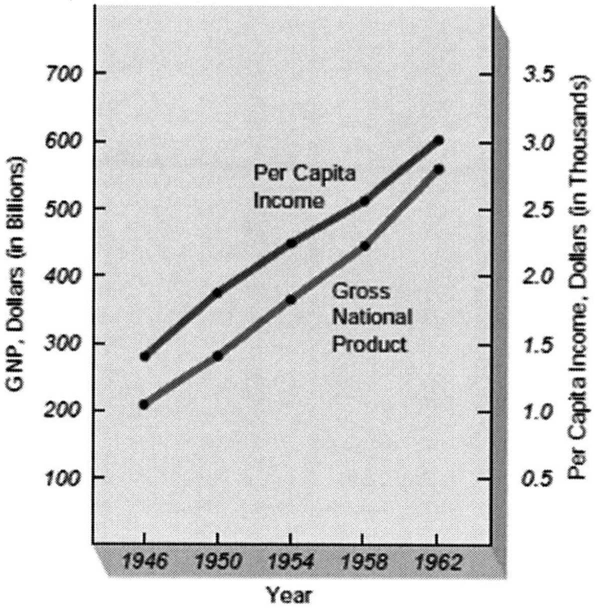

Gross National Product and Per Capita Income, 1946–1962

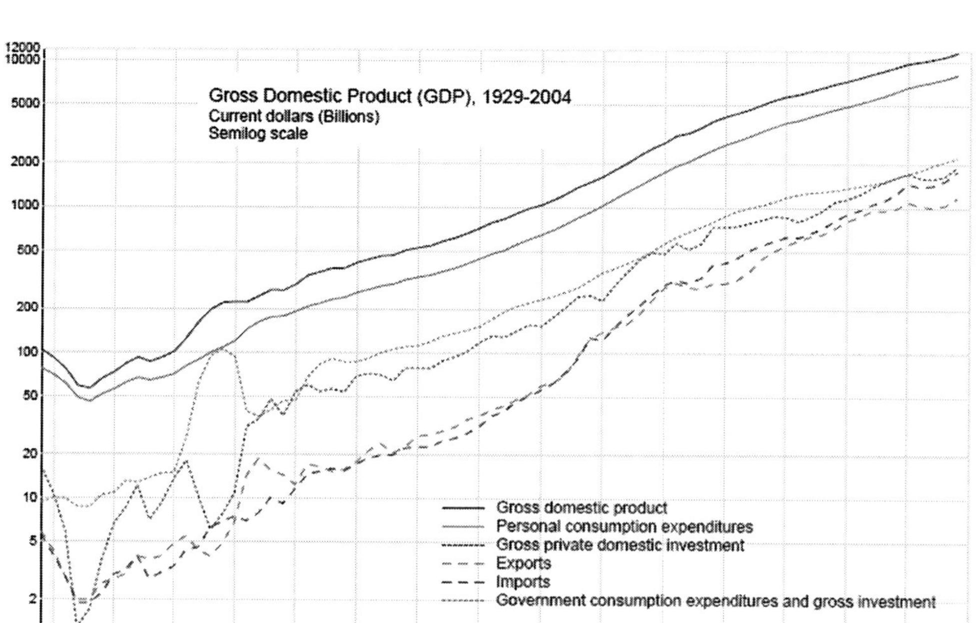

Chapter 14

Conclusion – Investing, In the Future

This book compares two different approaches to finance and investing.

One is the speculative and frenzied search for yield, without regard to those that suffer in the wake of this approach; one that prevails in the financial services industry. It has destroyed companies like Nortel Networks and many others that failed after the Dot-com and Datacom bubbles burst. This approach, promoted by the financial services industry, overloads companies with debt and in general promotes risky behavior with other people's money. It caused, as we have seen, thousands of investors to lose their lifesavings because they had bought into the market for CDOs, which was not under proper supervision by the ratings agencies.

Government intervention in banking and finance has only led to a proliferation of government agencies – more government jobs for the politicians who rule by patronage. We have a wave of new regulations – but very little change in the way the financial services industry operates.

Compared with this approach, we have seen how my family and I grew and financed businesses using a more conservative approach to investment, one that is viewed with disdain by many within the financial services industry. We built and continue to build businesses that we believe in, based on value creation. We take risks in building businesses, providing them with funds for innovative projects, and supporting them through periods of challenge.

But we do this because we have a vision for the companies based on their know-how and on the characters and skills of those who run them. When we take risks on these companies and finance them, we do it through cash flow and from accumulated assets, not by loading them up with debt so that they are dependent on good fortune in the future to get them out of trouble. That is, effectively, in opposite of what the bankers who focus on yield do.

Yes, we have had some failures. However, because these failures are conservatively and internally financed, not through debt, they were not catastrophic to the investors.

My father, Jerome Markowitz, built a successful company based on a product he invented. He then took a considerable risk on another new technology, digital sound, that he helped develop – but, using funds the Company had in hand. And then that new technology helped propel the company with additional success.

I continued to grow that Company according to the same conservative principles. When the opportunity came, I expanded into new technologies, Datacom, but again using funds our Company had already generated. And that approach succeeded again, even though we had to survive the serious challenges of a major correction in the industry.

We stuck to our vision. We kept our companies running and out of debt. We succeeded, where many others failed. And we accomplished this because we did not indulge in excessive speculation, nor did we, the manager-owners of the company, attempt to profit at the expense of the business itself, as so many managers did during the ill-fated LBO trend of the late 1980s and the Dot. com and Data Com bubbles. We ran our companies in a way that enabled all stakeholders – managers, employees, shareholders, suppliers and our community – to earn a reasonable level of profit.

Yes, even the communities where our companies are located profited by this philosophy. We have kept our manufacturing company in the US, despite the considerable economic pressure to relocate it to Asia. We have kept our employees in jobs – sometimes for over fifty years! And we have paid plenty of taxes that supported the local communities.

Because of changes in governmental regulations regarding reporting for publicly held companies, we took our Company private after being public for decades. In doing so this made significant changes for our family trust. Therefore, I placed its funds under the management of two different financial advisors. I made this choice because it seemed part of my responsibility as trust executive, part of my fiduciary responsibility.

I believed that the advisors engaged would behave with the best interests of the Trust. I believed that they would exercise fiduciary responsibility. We've seen just how wrong I was. Both advisors thought more about earning fees from our account than about protecting it from loss, or even taking measures to limit losses when they should have.

The financial advisors I chose were supposed to be there to assist us. They were supposed to be part of our extended family that built companies to create value and earn profit through skills. Instead, there was betrayal. They acted with a disregard for basic business and ethical standards. They did not manage carefully the funds that were entrusted to them. Then one tried to avoid blame by either shifting it to others or by simply not being honest with the Trust, their client. In short, they completely failed to maintain the fiduciary standard that they were committed to upholding

Ironically, everyone lost out as a result of the advisors' behavior and decisions. We spent a large sum on litigation and received only pennies on the dollar as compensation for losses caused by the financial advisors' negligence. The advisors themselves were obliged to also spend large sums on litigation, which gained them nothing – indeed, it only made public their lack of professionalism and standards.

Yet, when we sought remedy for the advisor's actions in court, proving our case served no purpose. The legal system protected the financial services industry, even though there was no doubt about their negligence.

All of this leaves me with a series of questions about the future of investing in the United States. Under the legislation that is unfolding today there is nothing to prevent bankers, financial advisors, and others charged with managing money that belongs to others, from engaging in what can only be called irresponsible behavior and speculation.

There are various legislative proposals that tend in a positive direction. For example, it is proposed that Congress bring back the "Glass-Steagall" Act that forced banks to separate speculative trading activities from retail banking activities – funds deposited by clients for management would not be available for trading. However, banks will find ways around legislation – most easily by grouping retail banking and trading under a holding company, and then doing the speculation at the holding level.

Banks have and will always find ways around restrictive legislation. Similarly, financial advisors, who are to be held to the fiduciary standard under recent legislation, will find ways around it too. The standard itself has too vague a legal basis for enforcement, as we have seen.

Ultimately, the creative capacity of those in the financial services industry will always surpass the ability of regulators to control it. It is already well beyond the ability of the legal system to enforce the regulations that currently exist.

We cannot count on the government or the law to protect us when we entrust bankers and advisors with investments. What can we do?

The only real way to work with bankers and advisors is to gauge their character and decide if they can be trusted. We have to oblige these people, who want to use our money, to prove that they should be entrusted with it.

Before agreeing to work with a financial advisor, we must to spend significant time with him or her and get to know them. We should not only hear their ideas about finance, but they should also show us that they understand who we are, what we need, and why we need it. We should have the sense that they are willing to become part of the greater community, in the same way that my family/ company has with our community.

A few words of caution: Those who work in the financial services industry require sales skills to be successful. They should be viewed as any salesperson attempting to sell a product; with jaundice. It is important not only for them to understand the investor's needs and risk tolerance, but also for investors to understand how the financial services company is compensated. This compensation issue will play a significant role on how investor funds are put to work.

The negative experience I suffered with the financial services industry reinforced the jaundiced view of it I had prior to the occurrence. While I currently use a local financial advisory firm, it is for a small portion of my investing activity and those funds are very conservatively invested. My major focus remains on the organ and assemblies manufacturing businesses, as well as investing in growing technology companies.

I avoid investing in public companies since I feel small investors are at an informational disadvantage versus mega investors who ultimately dictate market direction. Instead, I invest directly in private companies after doing significant due diligence through Goldin Ventures. While this approach does not guarantee success, I feel comfortable that these investments are made with appropriate information to judge the potential risks and rewards, placing me on a level playing field.

To do the financial industry justice, a growing number of financial advisors perceive the need for change as well. There is increasing pressure within the industry for advisors to forge long-term viable relationships with clients and change the way they are compensated. But this is only a trend; it is not a legal guarantee of reliability.

Perhaps in the future, it will become a norm. For now, we can only hope that more and more people will choose the kind of philosophy that my family has hewn to throughout its life in America.

Acknowledgments

The business experience and economic philosophy shared in this book were developed over a significant time period. I formulated the theories included long before deciding to write a book. However, given that this was my first effort at authoring a book, I found the task daunting. This book would not have been possible without the assistance of others.

In gathering historical financial data for Allen Organ Company, I relied on my associate and the company's Vice President of Finance, Margaret Bova. Mike Doyle, my long-term associate who previously managed the Company's Datacom division, gathered the historical data required to for the chapters relating to that subsidiary's history. He also assisted in the editing those chapters.

Another associate, Barry Holben, Allen Organ Company's VP of Sales, has also been a longtime personal friend. Over the years we have had many lengthy discussions on the issues relating to and the dangers of excessive debt at all levels of society. Those discussions played a role in firming up my conclusions concerning the problems of excessive debt discussed in this book.

There are too many "thank yous" owed to my father, Jerome Markowitz. I regret that this can only be done posthumously. Without my father's guidance, it is likely that my business acumen and values would have gone in a different direction, as well as other significant issues in my life. He left his family and the Allen Organ Company's shareholders a healthy company that was debt-free though it reduced his own personal gain. That focus on the future became a main theme of this book.

Realizing that writing and publishing a book would require significant effort and time from my already crowded obligations, I wrestled with the decision to go forward. I have to thank my wife, Ann Marie, for encouraging me. Over the years I often discussed with her the topics included in this book, undoubtedly to the point of excess. She understood my passion behind the issues and coaxed me to go forward. However, that is but a small part of the gratitude I owe Ann Marie on so many levels. Without her encouragement, support and willingness to successfully manage the "home-front" at the expense of her own career, I could not have dedicated the time needed for my business life.

Appendix A

Materials Related to the Litigation with Glenmede

The reader will find in this Appendix documents from the litigation between the Glenmede Trust Company and the Jerome Markowitz Trust. These documents are referred to at various points in the book.

IN THE COURT OF COMMON PLEAS OF LEHIGH COUNTY, PENNSYLVANIA
ORPHANS' COURT DIVISION

In re: JEROME MARKOWITZ TRUST B, under Agreement dated October 6, 1983, as amended February 19, 1985	: : :	File No. . 1991-0304A

****

Appearances:

Steven A. Bergstein, Esquire
For Petitioners,
Steven A. Markowitz, Trustee of the
Jerome Markowitz Trust B
and
Steven A. Markowitz, Marc Markowitz, Sandra Goldstein
and Judy Roberts, Remaindermen of the Jerome Markowitz Trust B

Karl Prior, Esquire
For Respondent, Glenmede Trust Company, N.A.

****

OPINION

J. Brian Johnson, Judge

I. INTRODUCTION

Before the Court for consideration is the *Second Amended Petition Seeking Reimbursement Of Investment Funds And Other Relief From Glenmede Trust Company, N.A.* filed November 6, 2009 ("*Markowitz's Petition*") by Petitioner, Steven A. Markowitz, ("Markowitz") seeking relief from Glenmede Trust Company, N.A. ("Glenmede") in relation to services Glenmede provided or failed to provide as the investment advisor, custodian and agent for the Jerome Markowitz Irrevocable Trust under agreement dated October 6, 1983 as amended

February 19, 1985 ("Trust"). A Hearing was held on November 9, 2010, January 28, 2011, February 4, 2011 and May 12, 2011.

Glenmede's arguments that the Orphans' Court Division lacks jurisdiction, that some of the claims in *Markowitz's Petition* are barred by the statute of limitations and that all or some of the claims in *Markowitz's Petition* are precluded because Markowitz has unclean hands are rejected.

II. DISCUSSION

The Petitioner is Steven A. Markowitz ("Markowitz"), an adult individual residing at 1125 Treeline Drive, Allentown, Lehigh County, Pennsylvania. Although *Markowitz's Petition* identifies the Petitioner only as Steven A. Markowitz individually and not in his fiduciary capacity as Trustee of the Trust, the parties conducted the hearing as though Markowitz brought this action in his capacity as Trustee. Therefore, we find that *Markowitz's Petition* was brought in Markowitz's fiduciary capacity and all references herein to "Markowitz," refer to Steven Markowitz as Trustee. By Order dated March 16, 2010, (approximately two months after the death of the life income beneficiary and co-trustee, Martha Markowitz on January 29, 2010), Steven Markowitz, Marc Markowitz, Sandra Goldstein and Judy Roberts (the remaindermen of the Markowitz Trust) were added as individual petitioners. The Respondent is The Glenmede Trust Company, N.A., a corporation having its principal place of business at 1650 Market Street, Suite 1200, Philadelphia, Pennsylvania ("Glenmede").

Markowitz has been responsible for, and has managed, all financial aspects of the Trust since 1991. This included investments, distributions, disbursements and responsibility for tax returns. It also included the selection of, and interaction with, investment managers or advisors for the Trust. Markowitz is a sophisticated investor, experienced fiduciary and follower of the financial markets. Since 1992, Markowitz has served as the sole trustee of Allen Organ's $20 million pension fund and has had sole responsibility for making the pension fund's investment decisions. He also has served and continues to serve as Trustee of other Trusts. Markowitz has been assisted in his role as Trustee of the Trust and in connection with Allen Organ corporate affairs and the Allen Organ pension fund by Allen Organ's Chief Financial Officer, Nathan Eckhart ("Eckhart"). Eckhart, a Certified Public Accountant, has provided accounting services to the Trust. Eckhart maintained Trust records and accounts, prepared Trust tax returns, reviewed monthly Trust statements, discussed Trust investment decisions with Markowitz, participated in the selection of Trust investment advisors, communicated with Trust investment advisors on behalf of the Trust and attended and participated in every quarterly meeting between Glenmede and Markowitz.

The Trust was a majority shareholder in the Allen Organ Company. In 2006, in anticipation of the Trust's receipt of proceeds from the conversion of Allen Organ from a publicly held corporation to a closely held corporation, Markowitz sought to hire an investment advisor. On August 16, 2006, he hired Wachovia Bank, N.A. ("Wachovia") to hold the proceeds from the privatization of Allen Organ in its Short Term Investment Management ("STIM") product while the Trust explored long-term investment strategies. Wachovia's STIM portfolio at that time included Auction Rate Securities ("ARSs"). An auction rate security ("ARS") typically refers to corporate or municipal bonds with a long-term nominal maturation date and for which the interest rate is regularly reset through an auction. Auctions are held usually every 7, 28, or 35 days and interest on ARSs is paid at the end of each auction period. To participate in an auction, the owner of an ARS must possess the auction rights for that ARS. Auction rights are normally memorialized by a written document or are acknowledged by a remarketing agent. At all times relevant to this dispute, most ARSs were AAA rated and insured. In the event of a failure at auction, ARSs typically pay an increased interest rate to the ARS owner.

On August 31, 2006, the Trust (defined as "Client") entered into an Investment Management Agreement with Wachovia ("Wachovia Agreement"). Of significance to the present matter are Paragraphs 9, which provides that Wachovia "shall distribute Assets from the Account in accordance with the Client's written instructions" and Paragraph 13, which provides that, upon termination, "the assets then held by [Wachovia] shall be delivered as the Client may direct in writing and [Wachovia] shall have no further responsibility for the Account."

On September 28, 2006, Markowitz and Eckhart met with Wachovia representatives to discuss investment issues and Markowitz directed Wachovia to place $9 million of Trust funds in the STIM. The Trust deposited $9 million of Trust funds into the Trust's Wachovia Bank account ("Wachovia Account") on October 4, 2006.

By October 31, 2006, the Wachovia Account was invested 99.9% in fixed income tax exempt investment grade securities made in the ARS market. The Trust's ARS investments at the end of October 2006 included a $400,000 investment in Mobile County, Alabama Limited Obligation Warrants (Cusip # 607341AA2) ("Mobile ARS"). The Mobile ARS then had a Moody's Aaa rating and an AAA rating from Standard & Poor's Rating Services, meaning that it was investment grade and that there was little or no risk of default. Payment of the principal and interest on the Mobile ARS when due was also insured by a financial guaranty insurance policy issued by AMBAC Assurance Corporation. AMBAC's bond insurance business had an AAA rating from Standard & Poor's Rating Services as of October 2006 and held that rating until June 2008.

During the period that Wachovia served as temporary investment adviser, Markowitz continued to meet with other candidates to serve as the Trust's long-term investment advisor. By late October 2006, Markowitz had contacted Glenmede for this purpose. On October 30, November 16 and November 27, 2006, Markowitz and Eckhart met with Glenmede representatives to discuss Glenmede's products and services and to review Glenmede's operations. On December 11, 2006, Markowitz decided to retain Glenmede as an investment advisor for the Trust and notified Wachovia that the Trust assets would be moved to another manager; Wachovia acknowledged receipt of this notification on the same date.

On December 12, 2006, Markowitz and Martha, as co-trustees of the Trust identified as "Owner," and Glenmede, identified as "Glenmede" executed an Investment Advisory Agreement ("IAA") establishing a contractual relationship between Glenmede and the Trust in which Glenmede agreed establish an investment advisory account ("Account") in the Trust's name and to serve as the Trust's investment advisor, custodian and agent, hold assets of the Trust and provide investment management of the assets. The IAA does not contain any clause that mentions an investment policy statement or any reference to the IPS, it does not indicate that the IAA is conditioned on the parties completing an investment policy statement and it states that the IAA, along with Glenmede's *Disclosure and Statement of Policy,* is the entire agreement between the parties and requires that any amendment thereto be signed by the party affected by the amendment.

On December 13, 2006, Glenmede mailed a letter of authorization to Markowitz with directions that it be signed by Markowitz and Martha as the first step in effectuating the transfer of Trust assets from Wachovia to Glenmede. On December 14, 2006, Markowitz agreed to an "in-kind" transfer of the investments in the Wachovia Account to Glenmede, but indicated that the transfer not occur until January 2007. On December 15, 2006, Wachovia representative Sharon Malia prepared an Account Closing Request for the Trust assets held in the Wachovia Account. On December 27, 2006, Glenmede sent a letter to Wachovia, via Federal Express for delivery on December 28, 2006, instructing Wachovia to transfer Trust assets "in kind" to Glenmede.

Unbeknownst to Markowitz or Glenmede, and despite having received and acknowledged notice of its removal as investment advisor on December 11, 2006, Wachovia, through it's investment officer continued to engage in purchases after that date, most significantly, on December 27, 2006, when it purchased a $300,000 investment in Jefferson County, Alabama Sewer Revenue Warrants (Cusip # 472682NH2) ("Jefferson ARS"). Like the Mobile ARS, the Jefferson ARS then had a Moody's Aaa rating and an AAA rating from Standard & Poor's Rating Services, was considered investment grade and was also insured by Financial Guaranty Insurance Corporation which had a Fitch AAA rating as of December of 2006 and held that rating until January of 2008. On December 28, 2006, the day after the purchase of the Jefferson ARS, Wachovia received the December 27, 2006 Federal Express letter instructing it to transfer all Trust assets to Glenmede.

The December 27, 2006 purchase of the Jefferson ARS was reflected on the December 2006 Wachovia Account statement which also included the Mobile ARS and fourteen (14) other ARSs. Markowitz received and reviewed a copy of the December 2006 Wachovia Account statement on or about its issue date, and did not question the December 27, 2006 purchase of the Jefferson ARS or the investment suitability of fourteen (14) other ARSs identified therein.

On January 4, 2007, Markowitz and Glenmede jointly created an Investment Policy Statement ("IPS"), the purpose of which was "to provide a clear understanding of the Trust's goals, objectives, expectations and constraints applicable to the management of the investment portfolio." It specified that the "most important objectives for the account are preservation of capital, real growth after inflation, liquidity and minimizing taxes." The IPS further set forth four (4) particularly relevant items as follows:

1.) "Portfolio Size: $12,280,000"
2.) "Permissible Asset Classes" included Cash, Fixed Income, Equities and Alternative Assets. The Fixed Income class included Investment Grade Bonds.
2.) "Term: The investment time horizon is less than 5 years."
3.) "Liquidity Needs: For liquidity, the client would like to maintain cash reserves as dictated by Glenmede policy."
4.) "Investment Authority: Glenmede has sole investment authority."
5.) "Other: Cash includes $3,000,000 for outside private investment by trustee."
6.) The Asset Allocation Target for Fixed Income was between 22% and 42%.

The IPS listed investment grade bonds as a permissible class of asset for the fixed income portfolio. As of January 2007, ARSs were considered investment grade bonds. The IPS does not indicate that it is an amendment, addendum or supplement to the IAA, does not refer to the IAA in any way and was not executed by either of the parties.

On January 4, 2007, Wachovia notified its personnel that the Trust relationship had been terminated and that Trust assets were to be sent, in kind, to Glenmede. Glenmede notified Markowitz that the transfer had not occurred as of January 17, 2007. On that date, Eckhart, on behalf of Markowitz, contacted Wachovia and requested that it complete the transfer as soon as possible. By January 18, 2007, Wachovia had agreed to expedite the transfer process.

On January 22, 2007, Wachovia transferred to Glenmede the majority of Trust assets in its possession, comprised of sixteen (16) investments, eleven (11) of which were ARSs, the Jefferson ARS and the Mobile ARS among them. However, Wachovia's January 22, 2007 transfer of the eleven (11) ARSs, failed to include the auction rights associated with each ARS. On or about, February, 2007, when it realized that Wachovia had failed to transfer the auction rights and/or to notify remarketing agents, Glenmede instructed its employee, Richard Gale ("Gale"), to obtain the auction rights for the ARSs. Glenmede did not inform Markowitz that it had not received the auction rights from Wachovia. Gale was not directed by Glenmede or Markowitz to liquidate any of the ARSs.

Glenmede mailed, and Markowitz received, a Statement of Account dated January 31, 2007, which identified all assets held by Glenmede as of that date, including the ARSs that Wachovia had transferred to Glenmede on January 22, 2007.

At no time relevant to this dispute has Glenmede had a policy against ARS investments or a standing direction that ARSs must be liquidated. As investment grade holdings, the bonds were permissible investments and fell within the class of assets that Markowitz selected when he characterized the Account as "Growth with Income." Moreover, throughout the entire period of time Glenmede held the ARSs, Markowitz never directed Glenmede to liquidate the ARSs. Nonetheless, Glenmede preferred not to invest in ARS, so it decided to attempt to sell the ARSs at auction.

By early February 2007, Gale had spoken with Wachovia's Sharon Malia regarding the ARSs. Gale also contacted various Wachovia Securities personnel whom he knew to enlist their help in obtaining auction rights. Through Gale's efforts, Glenmede was able to obtain auction rights for some, but not all ARSs, and to successfully liquidate certain ARSs without auction rights. During the period February, 2007 through March, 2007, Glenmede liquidated five (5) ARSs, carried at an aggregate value of $2.4 million. Each of the ARSs retained in the account generated interest income on a monthly basis. On April 9, 2007, although Glenmede was not able to auction the Mobile ARS, that ARS was partially called and the Trust received $25,000 in cash, leaving the Trust with $375,000 in that ARS. (Because of a subsequent partial call in

March 2008, the carrying value of the Mobile ARS at the time the Account was transferred was $350,000).

All of the investment activity and the maturation date of each bond were reported on Glenmede's monthly Statements of Account sent to Markowitz. In addition, Glenmede made presentations to Markowitz on or about April 11, 2007, July 11, 2007, October 5, 2007, December 12, 2007, January 29, 2008 and April 3, 2008. At each presentation, Markowitz received a spiral-bound presentation document which included a tab for "Asset Class Summary" and within that tab a then current Asset List. The Asset List included a Fixed Income component. The Fixed Income component contained a complete list of the municipal bonds held by the Trust. During this same period, Glenmede also had email communication with Markowitz and/or Eckhart related to Trustee fees, investment allocation, and investment strategy.

Glenmede produced no documentation of any efforts it made to obtain the auction rights for the ARSs that remained in the Account during the period March, 2007 to March, 2008. In contrast to its actions in January 2007 when it informed Markowitz that Wachovia was slow to transfer the investments to Glenmede which prompted Eckert to contact Wachovia to "expedite" the transfer, Glenmede chose not to inform Markowitz that it was having difficulty obtaining the auction rights for the ARSs.

In late February 2008, as one of several consequences of the massive and unforeseen collapse of the mortgage-backed securities market, the market for auction rate securities became volatile and auctions began to fail. In February, 2008, when Glenmede was confronted with this unprecedented market instability it resumed its efforts to obtain auction rights for the ARS. Through a series of March 2008 communications with Wachovia, Glenmede successfully obtained auction rights for all of the ARSs still held by the Trust.

On April 3, 2008, Glenmede held a quarterly presentation with Markowitz and discussed the seizure of the ARS market and its efforts to obtain auction rights for the ARSs and to liquidate the ARSs. This was the first time Glenmede informed Markowitz of the ARS market problems and the fact that it had not obtained auction rights for all of the ARSs in the Account.

Glenmede continued to liquidate the ARSs and, by May 27, 2008, Glenmede had liquidated all ARSs but the Mobile ARS and the Jefferson ARS. All of the investment activity was reflected in the monthly Statements of Account provided to Markowitz .

On October 13, 2008, the Trust sued Wachovia for its handling of the ARSs. (That litigation was settled in August, 2010). On April 20, 2009, the Trust instituted this action against Glenmede for its handling of the ARSs (though the Second Amended Petition was not filed until November 6, 2009).

In May 2009, the Trust formally terminated its relationship with Glenmede. Accordingly, between May 6 and 21, 2009, Glenmede sold every investment except the Jefferson ARS, the Mobile ARS (which collectively constituted 6.6% of the Account), and another asset that is not at issue. On May 21, 2009, Glenmede delivered $8.9 million cash and the Jefferson ARS and Mobile ARS in-kind, at values of $300,000 and $350,000 respectively, to BNY-Mellon, the custodian for Markowitz's new investment advisor, thereby emptying the Trust's Glenmede Account as of May 21, 2009. The Jefferson ARS and the Mobile ARS were received by BNY-Mellon at the values of $300,000 and $350,000 in May, 2009. Approximately two weeks after Markowitz terminated his contract with Glenmede, he calculated and paid himself Trustee commissions as a percentage of the Trust's gross assets that included the par values of both the Jefferson ARS, ($300,000) and the Mobile ARS, ($350,000).

The Mobile ARS had been issued as part of the Limited Obligation School Warrants, Series 2003, issued by Mobile County, Alabama ("Series 2003 Warrants"). On or about August 25, 2009, the Public Educational Building Authority of the City of Mobile, Alabama issued an Official Statement in which it declared that it would be issuing Limited Obligation School Bonds, Series 2009-A ("Series 2009-A Bonds") and stated that the purpose of the issuance of the Series 2009-A Bonds was to raise money that would be used to retire, or redeem, the Series 2003 Warrants.

In an email sent to Markowitz's counsel on October 8, 2009, Glenmede forwarded the Official Statement to the Trustees and encouraged them to investigate its application to the Mobile ARS, now held by BNY-Mellon. On October 9, 2009, the Trustees, by counsel, stated that they had concluded that there was little likelihood that the Mobile ARS would be covered by the Official Statement issued on or about August 25, 2009. In response, Glenmede, through counsel, advised the Trustees that Glenmede had researched the issue, believed the Official Statement applied to the Mobile ARS and was confident that the Mobile ARS would be redeemed at full face value.

Before selling the Mobile ARS, neither the Trustees nor their agents contacted the Public Educational Building Authority of the City of Mobile, Alabama, bond counsel, Haskell Slaughter Young & Rediker, LLC of Birmingham, Alabama or the bond underwriter or did anything to investigate and determine whether the Mobile ARS would be redeemed as a result of issuance of the Series 2009-A Bonds. Markowitz directed that BNY-Mellon sell the Mobile ARS, and on October 30, 2009, the Mobile ARS was sold for $234,500 which represented 67% of its $350,000 par value. Slightly more than a month later, on December 9, 2009, the Series 2003

Warrants were redeemed at full par value. Had it not been sold by Markowitz, the Trust would have realized no loss.

On October 30, 2009, also at Markowitz's direction, the Jefferson ARS was sold and the Trust realized $90,000, which represented 30% of its $300,000 par value. As of the final day of the hearing, May 12, 2011, the Jefferson ARS had not been declared in default and continued to pay all ARS holders increased interest.

III. LEGAL ANALYSIS

Markowitz asserts that Glenmede's conduct regarding the Jefferson ARS and the Mobile ARS constitutes a breach of contract (Count I), Misrepresentation, (Count II), Breach of Fiduciary Duty (Count III), Willful Malfeasance, Deceit, and Violation of Duty of Fair Dealing, (Count V) and Gross Negligence and Reckless Disregard (Count VI). The conduct of Glenmede that is the basis for each Count is comprised of the following:

1. Glenmede misrepresented its expertise and did not do enough soon enough to obtain the auction rights for the Mobile ARS and the Jefferson ARS after receiving those two investments from Wachovia on or about January 22, 2007.
2. Glenmede did not inform all of the Glenmede personnel who were involved with the Markowitz Account until on or about February 2008, and did not inform Markowitz until April 2008 that the auction rights to the Mobile ARS and the Jefferson ARS had not been included in Wachovia's transfer of those investments to Glenmede that occurred on January 22, 2007.
3. Glenmede intentionally misled Markowitz in April 2008 when it informed him that the auction rights for the Jefferson ARS and the Mobile ARS had not been received until March 2008 because of Wachovia's lack of cooperation.

The relief he seeks from Glenmede is as follows:

1. Reimbursement of $325,500.00, the difference between the par values of the Jefferson ARS and the Mobile ARS and the proceeds from Markowitz's sale thereof in October 2009;

2. Reimbursement of the compensation paid to Glenmede in the amount of $161,549.42;

3. Payment of in an amount equal to the legal fees he expended in connection with the litigation against Wachovia and in connection with this litigation, the amounts of which are unspecified.

For the reasons set forth below, Count I is denied and dismissed for failure to prove breach of contract, and accordingly, Counts II, V and VI are denied and dismissed because they are barred by the "gist of the action" doctrine. Count III is sustained. The claims for reimbursement of the loss realized by Markowitz on his sale of the Jefferson ARS and the Mobile ARS is denied, the claim for reimbursement of compensation paid to Glenmede is granted in part, and the claim for legal fees is denied.

A. Contract and Tort Claims Distinguished

Pennsylvania law recognizes a conceptual distinction between breach of contract claims and tort claims. *See generally Bash v. Bell Tel. Co.*, 411 Pa. Super. 347, 355-56, 601 A.2d 825, 829 (1992) (citing *Iron Mountain Sec. Storage Corp. v. American Specialty Foods, Inc.*, 457 F. Supp. 1158, 1165 (E.D. Pa. 1978)), *superseded by rule as stated in Keefer v. Keefer*, 741 A.2d 808 (Pa. Super. 1999). Whereas a tort action lies for a breach of a duty imposed by law as a matter of social policy such as a duty of care, a breach of contract claim arises solely from the obligations imposed by private agreements between particular individuals or entities. *eToll, Inc. v. Elias/Savion Advertising, Inc.*, 811 A.2d 10, 14 (Pa. Super. 2002) (citing *Bash*, 411 Pa. Super. at 355-56, 601 A.2d at 829). The "gist of the action" doctrine is intended to preclude a plaintiff from "recasting ordinary breach of contract claims as tort claims." *Id.* (citing *Bash*, 411 Pa. Super. at 355-56, 601 A.2d at 829). If the allegedly tortious conduct forms the heart of the plaintiff's claim, with the contract being only collateral, only then can the tort claim survive.

See, e.g., Bash, 411 Pa. Super. at 355-56, 601 A.2d at 829 (citing *Closed Circuit Corp. v. Jerrold Electronics Corp.*, 426 F.Supp. 361, 364 (E.D. Pa. 1977)). On the other hand, where the "gist of the action" is that the defendant did not perform its contractual duties, the plaintiff must seek a remedy under contract law, and tort claims should be dismissed. *Id.* Therefore, Pennsylvania "courts have held that the doctrine bars tort claims: (1) arising solely from a contract between the parties; (2) where the duties allegedly breached were created and grounded in the contract itself; (3) where the liability stems from a contract; or (4) where the tort claim essentially duplicates a breach of contract claim or the success of which is wholly dependent on the terms of a contract." *Reed v. Dupuis*, 920 A.2d 861, 864 (Pa. Super. 2007) (quoting *Hart v. Arnold*, 884 A.2d 316, 339-40 (Pa. Super. 2005)

In Pennsylvania, the Courts treat the torts of fraud, deceit, fraudulent misrepresentation and intentional misrepresentation as identical claims. *Wilson,* 410 Pa. Super. at 40-41, 598 A.2d at 1315. Moreover, the Pennsylvania Supreme Court has equated the elements of "fraudulent misrepresentation" and "deceit." *See Scaife Co. v. Rockwell-Standard Corp.*, 446 Pa. 280, 285, 285 A.2d 451, 454 (1971).. Furthermore, Pennsylvania does not recognize a separate cause of action for "Violation of Duty of Good Faith and Fair Dealing." Pennsylvania Courts follow Section 205 of the Restatement (Second) of Contracts, which provides: "Every contract imposes upon each party a duty of good faith and fair dealing in its performance." *See, e.g., Germantown Mfg. Co. v. Rawlinson,* 341 Pa. Super. 42, 61, 491 A.2d 138, 148 (1985) (citing Restatement (Second) of Contracts § 205 (1981)). As such, violations of the duty of good faith and/or the duty of fair dealing arise under the law of contracts, not tort. *See, e.g., Creeger Brick and Bldg. Supply Inc. v. Mid-State Bank and Trust Co.*, 385 Pa. Super. 30, 35, 560 A.2d 151, 153 (1989); *AM/PM Franchise Ass'n v. Atlantic Richfield Co.*, 373 Pa. Super. 572, 579-80, 542 A.2d 90, 94

(1988), *reversed in part on other grounds* (both citing RESTATEMENT (SECOND) OF CONTRACTS § 205 (1981)). Therefore, "a breach of the covenant of good faith is nothing more than a breach of contract claim and ... separate causes of action cannot be maintained for each, even in the alternative." *Philips Bros. Elec. Contractors, Inc. v. School Dist. of Phila.*, 3 Pa. D. & C.5th 562, 565-66 (C.C.P. Phila. 2008) (citations omitted).

On the basis of the foregoing, we find that the "gist of the action" doctrine bars Markowitz's separate tort claims alleged in Counts II, V and VI because they essentially duplicate the breach of contract claim. *Reed v. Dupuis*, 920 A 2d 861, 864, (Pa Super 207); *Hart v Arnold* 884 A. 2d 316, 339-340 (Pa. Super. 205). In other words, if Markowitz had proven willful misfeasance or bad faith as required to sustain his breach of contract claim, he would also have proven the several fraud-based tort claims raised by Counts II and V. Similarly, if he had proven gross negligence and/or reckless disregard sufficient to sustain the breach of contract claim he would have also have proven the several tort claims of which gross negligence is an element that are raised by Count VI.

B. Breach of Contract

We reject Markowitz's contention that the IPS is part of the IAA. The IAA was dated December 12, 2006. It does not contain any clause that mentions an investment policy statement or an express reference to the IPS that was not even created by Markowitz and Glenmede until January, 2007. The IAA does not state that it is conditioned upon the parties completing an investment policy statement. Rather, at Paragraph 19, the IAA expressly states that "This Agreement, with Glenmede's Disclosure and Statement of Policy, *represents the entire agreement between the parties...*" and requires that any modification or amendment must be in writing be signed by the party affected by the amendment. (emphasis supplied) Accordingly, we must look to the IAA for its delineation of the contractual obligations assumed by Glenmede as well as the scope of its liability and the measure of damages for any breach thereof.

The IAA sets forth the duties that Markowitz (defined as "Owner") delegated to Glenmede, and characterizes the nature of their relationship with each other at ¶3A.

> **Discretionary Account** - *Glenmede shall have full discretionary authority to make all investment decisions concerning purchasing, holding or selling the Assets taking into account the Owner's investment objectives.* Consistent with Owner's investment objectives, and subject to any restrictions Owner may impose in writing, Glenmede will invest in securities of any kind, including , but not limited to, investing in mutual funds or investment companies that are managed by Glenmede. *The Owner hereby grants to Glenmede, and confirms that Glenmede has, the authority to act as the Owner's agent and attorney in fact with respect to the Assets in the Account.* This authorization is a continuing one and shall remain in full force and effect until limited or terminated by Owner by written notification to Glenmede. *In buying, selling, or trading in securities or other assets on behalf of the Owner, Glenmede shall act in its sole discretion and shall have no responsibility to consult with, or receive approval from, the Owner prior to any such transactions.* (emphasis supplied)

At paragraph 18, the IAA defines what constitutes a breach of any contractual obligation:

> **Liability** Glenmede shall not be liable to the Owner or any other person except for *losses to the Account resulting from* the willful misfeasance, bad faith or gross negligence on the part of Glenmede in the performance of its duties, or reckless disregard by Glenmede of it obligations and duties, under this Agreement. (emphasis supplied)

This clause defines a breach as misfeasance, bad faith, gross negligence in the performance of its contractual duties, or recklessly disregarding its contractual obligations and limits Glenmede's liability therefor to "losses to the Account" that are causally related thereto. The IAA defines "Account" as the investment advisory account held by Glenmede. Thus, if

Glenmede breached any of its contractual duties, the IAA limits its liability to losses sustained to the assets of the Trust while in the possession of Glenmede that were caused by the breach.

In order to establish that Glenmede breached the IAA, Markowitz was required to establish that, by failing to inform him until April 2008 of its inability to sell the ARSs that it had received from Wachovia in January, 2007 or by offering Wachovia's lack of cooperation as the reason for its lack of possession of the auction rights when it did so inform him, Glenmede acted in a willful, grossly negligent and untruthful manner and that the Account suffered a loss by reason of that conduct.

We find that the terms willful misfeasance and reckless disregard contained in the IAA are the equivalent of gross negligence. Accordingly, Markowitz must prove conduct by Glenmede that is more egregious than ordinary negligence but does not rise to the level of intentional indifference to the consequences of one's acts. *In re Scheidmantel,* 868 A.2d 464, 485 (Pa. Super. 2005) (quoting *Ratti v. Wheeling Pittsburgh Steel Corp.*, 758 A.2d 695, 703 (Pa. Super. 2000)). Gross negligence has also been defined as "a lack of slight diligence or care comprising a conscious, voluntary act or omission in 'reckless disregard' of a legal duty and of the consequences to another party." *Ratti,* 758 A.2d at 704-05 (citing BLACK'S LAW DICTIONARY 1057 (7th Ed. 1999)). "The words 'willful misconduct' and 'gross negligence' not only differ in degree from 'ordinary negligence,' but also connote a more reckless and uncaring mind than that of the tortfeasor who is simply careless." *Hall v. Dreszer,* 43 Pa. D. & C.3d 442, 447 (CCP Luz. 1985). Gross negligence is the "omission of care which even the most inattentive and thoughtless men take of their own concerns." *Ferrick Excavating v. Senger Trucking,* 506 Pa. 181, 189, 484 A.2d 744, 748 (1984) (quoting *First Nat'l Bank of Carlisle v. Graham,* 79 Pa. 106, 116 (1875)).

The elements necessary to prove an action in negligence are: (1) the existence of a duty or obligation recognized by law, requiring the actor to conform to a certain standard of conduct; (2) a failure on the part of the defendant to conform to that duty, or a breach thereof; (3) a causal connection between the defendant's breach and the resulting injury; and (4) actual loss or damage suffered by the complainant. *See Jones v. Levin*, 940 A.2d 451, 454 (Pa. Super. 2007).

We find that the term "bad faith" is akin to fraud and thus consists of the following elements: (1) a material misrepresentation of fact; (2) a fraudulent utterance thereof; (3) the maker was aware of its falsity or recklessness as to whether it was true or false; (4) the statement was made or omitted with the intent of misleading or inducing the Plaintiff into relying on it; (5) justifiable reliance by the plaintiff on the misrepresentation; and (6) damages to the plaintiff as a proximate result of reliance on the misrepresentation. *Shapiro v. UJB Fin. Corp.*, 964 F.2d 272, 284 (3d Cir. 1992); *Gibbs v. Ernst*, 538 Pa. 193, 207, 647 A.2d 882, 889 (1994); *Bortz v. Noon*, 556 Pa. 489, 499, 729 A.2d 555, 560 (1999); *see also Smith v. The Windsor Group*, 750 A.2d 304, 307 (Pa. Super. 2000). Accordingly, to succeed on his breach of contract claim, Markowitz has the burden of proving the same by clear and convincing evidence. *Moser v. DeSetta*, 527 Pa. 157, 163, 589 A.2d 679, 682 (1991) (citing *Estate of Bosico*, 488 Pa. 274, 278, 412 A.2d 505, 506 (1980)). Clear and convincing evidence is the highest burden in civil trials, requiring the witnesses to be credible, the facts distinctly remembered, the details narrated exactly and in due order, so as to be clear, direct and convincing, enabling the fact finder to come to a clear conviction, *without hesitancy*, of the truth of the precise facts at issue. *In re LaRocca Trust Estate*, 411 Pa. 633, 640, 192 A.2d 409, 413 (1963) (quoting *Broida v. Travelers Ins. Co.*, 316 Pa. 444, 448, 175 A. 492, 494 (1924).

Given that investing, investment advice and management are subjects that require specialized knowledge, skill, education or experience, expert testimony as to standard of care is required in order to establish any claim of willful misfeasance, gross negligence or fraud. The relationship between the parties is a professional one. Glenmede's work requires specialized education, training, experience, skill and/or knowledge that is not within the normal range of knowledge or experience of laypersons. The type of relationship between the parties, one of investor and investment advisor, and the associated work, is not elementary and non-technical, requiring only simple common sense. *River Deck Holding Corp. v. U.S. Liability Ins. Co.*,___ A.2d ___, 2004 WL 594069, Pa.Com.Pl., 2004; *Storm v. Golden*, 371 Pa.Super. 368, 377, 538 A.2d 61, 65 (1988). *See also Himmelreich v. Adams Abstract Assoc.*, 59 D & C 4th 382 (Adams Co.2002) (expert report required to establish duty and breach of duty of title insurance agent). Markowitz did not provide testimony from an industry expert. The closest Markowitz came to presenting standard of care evidence was the testimony of Kevin Karpuk of Cornerstone, the Trust's current investment advisor. He purported to be an expert, but provided only general information about investments and did not provide standard of care testimony. In any event, we do not find his testimony credible or useful to this case. Therefore, Markowitz's "failure to produce an expert witness as to the standard of care under which [Glenmede] should have conducted [it]self and as to any deviation from that standard that may have occurred makes [Markowitz's] case defective as a matter of law" and justifies its dismissal. *River Deck Holding Corp. v. U.S. Liability Ins. Co.*, ___ A.2d ___, 2004 WL 594069, Pa.Com.Pl., 2004; *Storm v. Golden*, 371 Pa.Super. 368, 378, 538 A.2d 61, 65 (1988). *See also Al's Café, Inc. v. Sanders Insurance Agency*, 820 A.2d 745, 752 (Pa.Super.2003)

Markowitz's claim that Glenmede represented to him that it had expertise in ARSs but, in fact, it did not, and that such conduct constitutes willful misfeasance, we find to be without merit. The evidence showed that Glenmede was well familiar with ARSs and Markowitz introduced no evidence in support of his allegation that Glenmede made any express representations to him about its knowledge of ARSs.

We are similarly unpersuaded by Markowitz's claim that Glenmede had a contractual obligation to inform him that it had not received the auction rights as soon as it became aware of this fact. Because Markowitz selected the *Discretionary Account* option in the IAA rather than the *Non-Discretionary Account*, he delegated sole discretion regarding investments to Glenmede. Because Markowitz did not produce the requisite expert evidence that the "freeze" of the bond market that occurred in March 2008 was foreseeable in January 2007, we find that the fact that Glenmede was without the auction rights for the ARSs received via transfer from Wachovia in January, 2007, was, at that time, not so much noteworthy as bothersome. This is especially true in light of the express language of the IAA that, in carrying out its investment duties for Markowitz, Glenmede "...shall have not responsibility to consult with or receive approval from [Markowitz] prior to any such transactions."

Although Markowitz asserts that a key objective of the investment strategy for the Trust was liquidity, that objective is only mentioned in a general sense and not with respect to any particular asset or type of investment. Markowitz produced no document in which the ARSs were identified as assets that Glenmede was to liquidate immediately upon taking possession or within a specified period of time thereafter. Markowitz knew that the Jefferson ARS and the Mobile ARS were included in the Trust assets that were transferred from Wachovia to Glenmede in January 2007. The Jefferson ARS and the Mobile ARS were listed on every Glenmede

Statement of Account that he received over the course of 2007 and 2008. Markowitz never directed Glenmede to liquidate the ARSs or even inquired why they remained unliquidated. Because the majority of the ARS holdings were successfully liquidated by Glenmede well within the five (5) year investment horizon articulated in the IPS, despite the delay in obtaining auction rights, the lack of a primary market for the Mobile ARS and the Jefferson ARS, which represented slightly more than 6% of the Account, there was no failure to meet the liquidity objective contained in the IPS.

For all of the foregoing reasons, Counts I, II, V and VI are denied and dismissed.

C. Breach of Fiduciary Duty

Markowitz has pled that Glenmede had a fiduciary duty to the Trust and that its "fiduciary responsibility was to provide investment management and administration consistent with the client's investment objectives and any written constraints." Second Amended Petition at paragraph 24. Glenmede argues that this alleged fiduciary responsibility is nothing more than the duty identified in the IAA and that it is thus barred by the "gist of the action" doctrine. We disagree because fiduciary obligations are imposed by law as a matter of social policy and are not contractual. *See, eToll, Inc. v. Elias/Savion Advertising, Inc.*, 811 A.2d 10, 14 (Pa. Super. 2002) (citing *Bash,* 411 Pa. Super. at 355-56, 601 A.2d at 829). "Fiduciary duty" is defined by Black's Law Dictionary as: "A duty to act for someone else's benefit, while subordinating one's personal interests to that of the other person. *It is the highest standard of duty implied by the law.*"([emphasis supplied)

Pennsylvania recognizes a fiduciary duty from an investment broker to his customer. Pennsylvania has adopted the Restatement (Second) of Torts. At Section 874, Violation Of

Fiduciary Duty, it states, in pertinent part, that, "[o]ne standing in a fiduciary relation with another is subject to liability to the other for harm resulting from a breach of *duty imposed by the relation.*" (emphasis supplied) Further, the comment to that section states:

> A fiduciary relation exists between two persons when one of them is under a duty to act for or to give advice for the benefit of another upon matters within the scope of the relation. A fiduciary who commits a breach of his duty as a fiduciary is guilty of tortious conduct to the person for whom he should act.... the beneficiary is entitled to tort damages for harm caused by the breach of duty arising from the relation... Further, when there is a contract between the parties or when there has been an assumption of duty by a trustee, guardian or executor, the beneficiary may be entitled to what the fiduciary should have made in the prosecution of his duties. The same underlying principles apply to the liability of other fiduciaries, such as administrators and guardians; *the liability is not dependent solely upon an agreement or contractual relation between the fiduciary and the beneficiary but results from the relation.* (emphasis supplied)

"The relationship between a broker and his customer is one of principal and agent by virtue of which the broker is subject to certain fiduciary obligations to his client." *Merrill Lynch, Pierce, Fenner & Smith v. Perelle*, 356 Pa.Super. 165, 514 A.2d 552 (1986). In this case, the IAA expressly stated that Glenmede was acting as Markowitz's "...agent and attorney in fact with respect to the Assets in the Account." One of essential duties of a fiduciary is the duty to communicate, defined in Section 381 of the Restatement (Second) of Agency. *Id.* at 182. "Unless otherwise agreed, an agent is subject to a duty to use reasonable efforts to give his principal information which is relevant to affairs entrusted to him and which, as the agent has notice, the principal would desire to have and which can be communicated without violating a superior duty to a third person." *Id.* at 183.

The *Merrill Lynch* case provides an excellent discussion of this issue. Guided thereby, we find that the relevant conduct of Glenmede that arguably constitutes a breach of its fiduciary duty are: 1) it did not tell Markowitz that the auction rights for the ARSs had not been transferred and/or that it was having difficulty obtaining them for fourteen (14) months; 2) it did not diligently attempt to obtain the auction rights for twelve (12) of those fourteen (14) months; and 3) it did not tell Markowitz in a timely manner when it learned that the ARS market was about to seize. Notwithstanding Markowitz's failure to actively supervise the investment advisor that he hired to manage the Trust's funds, we agree with Markowitz that Glenmede did a poor job in effectuating its investment decision made in February 2007 to liquidate all of the ARSs that it had received via transfer from Wachovia in January, 2007. By doing virtually nothing to obtain the auction rights for twelve (12) months, it placed itself in the position of being unable to sell the ARSs at the most opportune time. Glenmede knew, by at least February 2008, that the ARS market was in dramatic decline such that auctions were failing, but did not share this information with Markowitz for at least another four (4) to six (6) weeks; choosing instead to seek and obtain the necessary auction rights during March, 2008. Furthermore, Glenmede was disingenuous when it informed Markowitz in April 2008 that it had been aggressively attempting to obtain the auction rights since January 2007 but did not receive them until March 2008 because Wachovia would not cooperate. While it was true that Wachovia had not included them in the initial transfer or responded to Gale's February 2007 request that Wachovia transfer the auction rights, it was not true that Glenmede had been aggressively attempting to obtain the auction rights for the entire prior fourteen (14) months.

We find that Glenmede's decision to defer informing Markowitz of the seizing of the bond market until after it acquired the auction rights, is indicative both of its recognition that this unprecedented bond market volatility was "... information... relevant to affairs entrusted to [it] and which...the principal would desire to have" (Section 381 of the Restatement (Second) of

Agency. *Id.* at 182), and, that Glenmede was more concerned with positioning itself favorably *vis a vis* responsibility for the delay in its receipt of auction rights, than passing along the relevant market information. Glenmede's conduct in this regard falls short of the scrupulous good faith and candor that are the cornerstone of a fiduciary relationship and constitutes a breach of its fiduciary duty.

In Orphans' Court, a surcharge is the penalty imposed for a breach of fiduciary duty. *Rosenfeld Trust* 29 Fiduc. Rep. 2d 27, 280 (O.C. Phila. 2006). Markowitz contends that Glenmede should be ordered to "reimburse" him a sum equal to the loss he realized on his sale of the Jefferson ARS and the Mobile ARS in October 2009, or $325,500. We disagree. Markowitz introduced no evidence regarding whether, or at what price, the Jefferson ARS and the Mobile ARS could have been sold during the period of February 2007 through March 2008 had Glenmede possessed the necessary auction rights. "The propriety of an investment ...must be judged as it appeared at the time it was made and not as viewed in the light of subsequent events." *Pew Estate,* 440 Pa.Super. 195 at 240, 655 A. 2d 521 at 543 (1994). By April 2008, the ARS market had frozen, so there was no decision to be made regarding the ARSs, except whether to sell them at a discount or hold them and continue to earn interest and possibly sell them later. Glenmede's April 2008 disclosure did not cause a loss to the Trust or cause Markowitz to do anything other than to sue Wachovia. As of May 21, 2009, the last day the Glenmede Account held the Trust assets, no loss had been realized. Indeed, Markowitz shortly thereafter paid himself a commission calculated on the full par value of those two (2) investments. It is also significant that Markowitz sold the Mobile ARS in October 2009, notwithstanding his receipt of information from Glenmede in August 2009 that it was reasonably likely that the Mobile ARS would be redeemed at par within several months, without adequately investigating the reliability of the information and Glenmede's assessment. Had he not sold the Mobile ARS in October 2009, he would not have realized any loss on that investment. Under Pennsylvania law, an essential element of surcharge is proof of loss. *In re Mendenhall,* 484 Pa. 77, 82, 398 A.2d 951,954 (1959) For these reasons, we find that the loss Markowitz realized on his sale of the Jefferson ARS and the Mobile ARS is not the proper measure of a surcharge for Glenmede's breach of its fiduciary duty.

We are similarly unpersuaded that denial of any compensation to Glenmede for its approximately twenty-nine (29) month tenure as investment advisor is an appropriate surcharge. Neither party produced evidence regarding the method of calculation of the $161,549.42 fee paid to Glenmede. Thus, we are left to simple arithmetic and discretion. The fee paid to Glenmede ($161,549.42) represents 1.8% of the Trust assets that it was given to invest ($9 million). Applying that percentage to the aggregate $650,000 carrying value of the Mobile ARS and the Jefferson ARS (which is the value at which those assets were reflected on receipt and upon transfer by Glenmede), reveals that the amount of compensation attributable to those two investments is $11,700.00. Accordingly, we sustain Count III and impose a surcharge upon Glenmede in the amount of $11,700.00 for breach of its fiduciary duty.

D. Attorneys Fees

A litigant cannot recover counsel fees from an adverse party unless there is (a) express statutory authorization; (b) a clear agreement of the parties; or (c) some other established exception. *See, e.g., Mosaica Academy Charter School v. Com. Dept. of Ed.,* 572 Pa. 191, 206-07, 813 A.2d 813, 822 (2002) (citing *LaVelle v. Koch,* 532 Pa. 631, 638, 617 A.2d 319, 323

(1992). The statutory authority is found at 42 Pa.C.S.A. § 2503, which provides in pertinent part as follows:

> The following participants shall be entitled to a reasonable counsel fee as part of the taxable costs of the matter:
>
> ...
>
> (6) Any participant who is awarded counsel fees as a sanction against another participant for violation of any general rule which expressly prescribes the award of counsel fees as a sanction of dilatory, obdurate or vexatious conduct during the pendency of any matter.
>
> (7) Any participant who is awarded counsel fees as a sanction against another participant for dilatory, obdurate or vexatious conduct during the pendency of a matter...
>
> (9) Any participant who is awarded counsel fees because the conduct of another party in commencing the matter or otherwise was arbitrary, vexatious or in bat faith.

Because Markowitz has failed to prove that his claim for the recovery of attorneys' fees falls under any of these categories, it is denied and dismissed.

IV. CONCLUSION

For the reasons set forth above, the *Second Amended Petition Seeking Reimbursement Of Investment Funds And Other Relief From Glenmede Trust Company, N.A.* is denied in part and granted in part, and Glenmede is surcharged in the amount of $11,700.00, which it shall pay to Markowitz within thirty (30) days .

BY THE COURT:

December 6, 2011

J. Brian Johnson, J.

IN THE COURT OF COMMON PLEAS OF LEHIGH COUNTY, PENNSYLVANIA
ORPHANS' COURT DIVISION

In re:	JEROME MARKOWITZ TRUST B,	:	
	under Agreement dated October 6, 1983,	:	File No.: 1991-0304A
	as amended February 19, 1985	:	

ORDER

AND NOW, this 6th day of December, 2011, upon consideration of the Second Amended Petition Seeking Reimbursement Of Investment Funds And Other Relief From Glenmede Trust Company, N.A. filed November 6, 2009, after hearing and for the reasons set forth in the accompanying Opinion;

IT IS ORDERED that the Second Amended Petition Seeking Reimbursement Of Investment Funds And Other Relief From Glenmede Trust Company, N.A. is denied in part and granted in part, and Glenmede is surcharged in the amount of $11,700.00, which it shall pay to Markowitz within thirty (30) days of the date of this Order.

BY THE COURT:

J. Brian Johnson, J.

CLERK OF ORPHANS
COURT DIVISION
LEHIGH COUNTY
2011 DEC -8 A 11:49
COURTHOUSE
ALLENTOWN, PA.

COURT OF COMMON PLEAS OF LEHIGH COUNTY, PENNSYLVANIA
ORPHANS' COURT DIVISION

NO. 1991-0304A

IN RE: JEROME MARKOWITZ TRUST B
UNDER AGREEMENT DATED OCTOBER 6, 1983,
AS AMENDED FEBRUARY 19, 1985

OBJECTIONS AND RESPONSES OF
RESPONDENT THE GLENMEDE TRUST COMPANY, N.A. TO
PETITIONER'S REQUEST FOR ADMISSIONS PURSUANT TO PA. R.C.P. 4014

The Glenmede Trust Company, N.A. ("Glenmede"), by its undersigned attorneys, objects and responds to Petitioner's Request for Admissions pursuant to Pa. R.C.P. 4014 as follows:

GENERAL OBJECTIONS

1. Glenmede objects to each and every request for admission to the extent that it seeks information that is not reasonably calculated to lead to the discovery of admissible evidence and/or is otherwise beyond the proper scope of discovery as set forth in Pa. R.C.P. 4003.1 *et seq.*

2. Glenmede objects to each and every request for admission to the extent that it seeks information protected by the attorney-client privilege, the work product doctrine and/or any other applicable privilege and/or protection.

3. Glenmede objects to each and every request for admission to the extent it is overbroad as to time, oppressive, unduly burdensome and/or would require an unreasonable investigation.

4. Glenmede objects to each and every request for admission to the extent it is duplicative of prior discovery and seeks information that Petitioners have already obtained via

EXHIBIT
P-63

depositions, document production or otherwise. Glenmede further objects because, under the circumstances, the requests constitute harassment.

5. Glenmede objects to the number of requests for admission as being oppressive, unduly burdensome and harassing.

SPECIFIC OBJECTIONS AND RESPONSES

1. In late 2009, the Markowitz Trust, through its attorney, Steven A. Bergstein, offered to sell Glenmede its Mobile County ARC at a discount.

Objection and Response: Glenmede objects to this request because it is not reasonably calculated to lead to the discovery of admissible evidence. Subject to, and without waiver of this objection, it is admitted that by letter dated September 23, 2009, the Markowitz Trust, through its attorney, offered, under false pretenses, Glenmede and Wachovia the opportunity to match an alleged verbal offer the Markowitz Trust had received to sell the Mobile County ARC to Glenmede "for 80¢ on the dollar." Counsel for the Markowitz Trust and Petitioner Steven Markowitz later acknowledged that the Trust had not received any such offer.

2. Glenmede did not accept the Markowitz Trust's offer to purchase the Mobile County bond at a discounted price.

Objection and Response: Glenmede objects to this request because it is not reasonably calculated to lead to the discovery of admissible evidence. Subject to, and without waiver of this objection, this request is admitted.

3. Had Glenmede purchased the Mobile County bond from the Markowitz Trust it could have since redeemed it at full par value, $350,000.

Objection and Response: Glenmede objects to this request because it is not reasonably calculated to lead to the discovery of admissible evidence. Subject to, and without waiver of this objection, it is admitted that any person or entity (including the Markowitz Trust) that owned the Mobile County bond would have received full par value upon redemption of the bond. Glenmede encouraged the Markowitz Trust on October 8 and October 9, 2009 to investigate the possibility of full redemption, which ultimately occurred on December 9, 2009, so as to mitigate any claim for damages with respect to that bond.

4. Exhibit A, as attached to Defendant's Request for Admissions, sent on December 17, 2009, does not include the terms "auction rights", "bidding rights" or "trading rights".

Objections: Glenmede objects to this request because it is not reasonably calculated to lead to the discovery of admissible evidence; because it is oppressive, burdensome and intended to harass; and because it calls for characterization of a document that speaks for itself.

5. Exhibit B, as attached to Defendant's Request for Admissions, sent on December 17, 2009, does not include the terms "auction rights", "bidding rights" or "trading rights".

Objections: Glenmede objects to this request because it is not reasonably calculated to lead to the discovery of admissible evidence; because it is oppressive, burdensome and intended to harass; and because it calls for characterization of a document that speaks for itself.

6. Glenmede began having difficulties selling the ARC's that are the subject of this *litigation in January or February of 2007.*

Objection and Response: Glenmede objects to this request because it does not know what Petitioners mean by Glenmede "having difficulty selling the ARC's." Subject to, and without waiving, this objection, and assuming that by "having difficulties" Petitioners mean that Glenmede "was unable to sell the ARCs because it did not have the auctions rights," the request is admitted.

7. Glenmede did not inform the Markowitz Trust of any difficulties selling the ARC's that are the subject of this litigation until April 2008.

Objection and Response: Glenmede objects to this request because it does not know what Petitioners mean by "any difficulties selling the ARC's" or to whom they are referring when they say "Glenmede did not inform... ." Subject to, and without waiving, this objection, and assuming that by "any difficulties" Petitioners mean that Glenmede "was unable to sell the ARCs because it did not have the auctions rights," the request is admitted in part and denied in part. It is admitted that the individuals at Glenmede who were aware that Glenmede was unable to sell the ARCs because it did not have the auctions rights did not inform the Trustees until April 2008. The request is denied in that Glenmede denies as calling for a legal conclusion the implication that it had an obligation to inform the Markowitz Trust that it was unable to sell the ARC's. Moreover, the Trustees breached their fiduciary obligation by apparently failing to review the monthly account statements, which reflected the retention of the ARC's despite the alleged instruction by Trustee Steven Markowitz to sell all assets Glenmede had received from Wachovia.

8. Glenmede did not inform the Markowitz Trust Relationship Manager and Trust Investment Officer, Robert Kiep, of any difficulties selling the ARC's that are the subject of this litigation until March or April 2008.

Objections and Response: Glenmede objects to this request because it does not know what Petitioners mean by "any difficulties selling the ARC's" or to whom they are referring when they say "Glenmede did not inform... ." Subject to, and without waiving, these objections, and assuming that by "any difficulties" Petitioners mean that Glenmede "was unable to sell the ARCs because it did not have the auctions rights," it is admitted that the individuals at Glenmede who were aware that Glenmede was unable to sell the ARCs because it did not have the auctions rights did not inform Robert Kiep until March or April 2008.

9. Glenmede did not inform the Markowitz Trust Administrator, David Schwartz, of any difficulties selling the ARC's that are the subject of this litigation until after April 2008.

Objections and Response: Glenmede objects to this request because it does not know what Petitioners mean by "any difficulties selling the ARC's" or to whom they are referring when they say "Glenmede did not inform... ." Subject to, and without waiving, these objections, and assuming that by "any difficulties" Petitioners mean that Glenmede "was unable to sell the ARCs because it did not have the auctions rights," it is admitted that the individuals at Glenmede who were aware that Glenmede was unable to sell the ARCs because it did not have the auctions rights did not inform David Schwartz until after April 2008.

10. David Schwartz and Robert Kiep were the Glenmede employees responsible for communicating with the Markowitz Trust about the transfer of Trust assets from Wachovia to Glenmede including the assets that are the subject of this litigation during 2007.

Response: It is admitted that, to the extent anyone at Glenmede would need to communicate with the Markowitz Trust about the transfer of Trust assets from Wachovia to Glenmede, it would have been David Schwartz or Robert Kiep.

11. Glenmede, through employee David Schwartz, informed the Markowitz Trust in early 2007 that Glenmede had received everything from Wachovia relating to the Trust assets transferred to Glenmede that included the ARC's that are the subject of this litigation.

Response: It is admitted that David Schwartz informed the Markowitz Trust by email dated February 1, 2007 that "we now have everything here," meaning that Glenmede had received custody of all underlying assets that had been in the custody of Wachovia.

12. Robert Kiep was the Glenmede employee responsible for communicating with the Markowitz Trust about its assets and investments during 2007 and through March of 2008.

Response: Admitted.

13. Glenmede had the sole investment authority for the Markowitz Trust while it was the Trust's advisor.

Response: Denied. Glenmede's authority is defined by the Investment Advisory Agreement, which is a document that speaks for itself. Moreover, any investment discretion Glenmede had was always subject to the directions and objectives of the Trustees.

14. Glenmede charged the Markowitz Trust a fee for being its investment advisor that was based on the total value of the assets managed which total included the value of the ARC's that are the subject of this litigation.

Response: Admitted. Similarly, Petitioner Steven Markowitz, in his capacity as Trustee, calculated his Trustee compensation based in part on the total value of the assets managed by Glenmede, which total included the par value of the ARCs that are the subject of this litigation.

15. Glenmede was aware of problems in the ARC market in the fourth quarter of 2007.

Objection and Response: Glenmede objects to this request because it does not know what Petitioners mean by "problems in the ARC market" or to whom they are referring when they say "Glenmede was aware… ." Subject to, and without waiving, these objections, it is admitted that individuals at Glenmede were aware that the auction rate securities market was having difficulties.

16. The problems in the ARC market were discussed in a Glenmede meeting open to Glenmede employees in 2007.

Objection and Response: Glenmede objects to this request because it does not know what Petitioners mean by "problems in the ARC market." Subject to, and without waiving, this objection, it is admitted that individuals at Glenmede discussed in a meeting open to employees in the fourth quarter of 2007 that the auction rate securities market was having difficulties.

17. Glenmede had the obligation to inform Markowitz Trust if it could not follow Trust's instructions.

Objection: Glenmede objects to this request because it calls for a conclusion of law.

18. Glenmede had a fiduciary responsibility to the Markowitz Trust and/or its Trustees from January 2007 when the assets were transferred from Wachovia until the assets were transferred out from Glenmede.

Objection: Glenmede objects to this request because it calls for a conclusion of law.

19. James Belanger, in-house counsel to Glenmede, indicated in an email sent to Steven Markowitz on May 9, 2008 that "Wachovia has been unresponsive. This may be their normal standard, but it has been so egregious as to be a liability to them."

Objections and Response: Glenmede objects to this request because it is not reasonably calculated to lead to the discovery of admissible evidence and because this request calls for a characterization of a document that speaks for itself. Subject to, and without waiving, these objections, it is admitted that the quoted words appear in an email dated May 9, 2008 from James Belanger to Steven Markowitz. It is denied that James Belanger was acting in his capacity as in-house counsel with respect to his communications with Steven Markowitz on May 9, 2008.

20. At the time that Belanger so represented to Mr. Markowitz, he knew this to be untrue.

Objection and Response: Glenmede objects to this request because it is not reasonably calculated to lead to the discovery of admissible evidence. Subject to, and without waiving, this objection, the request is denied.. At the time Mr. Belanger made the statements to Mr. Markowitz, he did not know them to be untrue.

21. The attachment to the email of May 9, 2008 was a proposed draft letter to Pamela Pearson of Wachovia in which Mr. Belanger stated that it was a "fact" that "Wachovia ignored the repeated requests from Glenmede to provide the auction rights to these securities."

Objections and Response: Glenmede objects to this request because it is not reasonably calculated to lead to the discovery of admissible evidence and because this request calls for a characterization of a document that speaks for itself. Subject to, and without waiving, these objections, it is admitted that the quoted words appear in a draft letter that was attached to an email dated May 9, 2008 from James Belanger to Steven Markowitz. However, it is denied that Mr. Belanger was making these statements. The draft letter was a document for Petitioner Steven Markowitz to review and revise as appropriate before Mr. Markowitz sent it to Pamela Pearson.

22. At the time the statements were made, May 9, 2008, Mr. Belanger knew that to be untrue.

Objections and Response: Glenmede objects to this request because it is not reasonably calculated to lead to the discovery of admissible evidence and because Mr. Belanger was not making the statements. The draft letter was a document for Petitioner Steven Markowitz to review and revise as appropriate before Mr. Markowitz sent it to Pamela Pearson. Subject to, and without waiving, these objections, the request is denied. At the time the statements were made, Mr. Belanger did not know them to be untrue.

23. In the attachment to the May 9, 2008 email, Mr. Belanger wrote that there were "numerous email and written requests to Wachovia for the necessary rights to sell these securities."

Objections and Response: Glenmede objects to this request because it is not reasonably calculated to lead to the discovery of admissible evidence and because this request calls for a characterization of a document that speaks for itself. Subject to, and without waiving, these objections, it is admitted that the quoted words appear in a draft letter that was attached to an email dated May 9, 2008 from James Belanger to Steven Markowitz. However, it is denied that Mr. Belanger was making these statements. The draft letter was a document for Petitioner Steven Markowitz to review and revise as appropriate before Mr. Markowitz sent it to Pamela Pearson.

24. At the time the statement in the proceeding request was made, Mr. Belanger knew that were not "numerous email and written requests to Wachovia for the necessary rights to sell these securities."

Objections and Response: Glenmede objects to this request because it is not reasonably calculated to lead to the discovery of admissible evidence and because Mr. Belanger was not making that statement. The draft letter was a document for Petitioner Steven Markowitz to review and revise as appropriate before Mr. Markowitz sent it to Pamela Pearson. Subject to, and without waiving, these objections, the request is denied. At the time the statement was made, Mr. Belanger did not know "that [there] were not 'numerous email and written requests to Wachovia for the necessary rights to sell these securities.'"

25. Glenmede has not been able to point to "numerous email and written requests to Wachovia for the necessary rights to sell these securities."

Objections: Glenmede objects to this request because it presumes Glenmede has been required "to point to 'numerous email and written requests to Wachovia for the necessary rights to sell these securities'" and because Glenmede does not know what Petitioners mean by "point to." In that regard, this request is denied. Moreover, Glenmede objects because the request calls for the characterizations of the voluminous email and other correspondence that have been produced in this litigation, all of which are documents that speak for themselves.

26. In the attachment to his May 9, 2008 email to Steven Markowitz, James Belanger stated that the actions of Wachovia constituted "gross negligence."

Objections and Response: Glenmede objects to this request because it is not reasonably calculated to lead to the discovery of admissible evidence and because this request calls for a characterization of a document that speaks for itself. In fact, the request grossly mischaracterizes the document, which states in relevant part: "I [meaning Steven Markowitz] have been advised that this amounts to gross negligence exhibited by Wachovia." Subject to, and without waiving, this objection, it is denied that Mr. Belanger "stated that the actions of Wachovia constituted 'gross negligence.'" It is denied that Mr. Belanger was making these statements. The draft letter was a document for Petitioner Steven Markowitz to review and revise as appropriate before Mr. Markowitz sent it to Pamela Pearson.

27. At the time this was written by Mr. Belanger, he knew those statements to be untrue.

Objections and Response: Glenmede objects to this request because it is not reasonably calculated to lead to the discovery of admissible evidence; because it calls for a conclusion of law as it relates to Wachovia's conduct; and because Mr. Belanger was not making those statements. The draft letter was a document for Petitioner Steven Markowitz to review and revise as appropriate before Mr. Markowitz sent it to Pamela Pearson. Subject to, and without waiving, these objections, the request is denied. At the time the statements were made, Mr. Belanger did not know those statements to be untrue; in fact, the Court will decide whether Wachovia exhibited gross negligence.

28. Until early April, 2008, no one at Glenmede represented to Steven Markowitz or anyone connected with the Markowitz Trust that Wachovia had been negligent, grossly negligent, or in any way had not cooperated.

Response: Admitted.

29. On January 31, 2007, Glenmede liquidated $600,000 of the $800,000 position in Philadelphia Pa Wtr & Wastewtr.

Response: Admitted.

30. On February 1, 2007, a successful auction was held for the Jefferson County ARS. Glenmede did not liquidate the ARS at that auction.

Response: It is admitted that Glenmede did not liquidate the ARS at that auction, because it could not.

31. On February 8, 2007, Richard Gale of Glenmede sent an email to Wachovia stating, *inter alia*, that "[t]he client has asked us to sell all the positions but the remarketing agents have been unable to verify and transfer the auction rights.... Any help you can provide would be much appreciated." The email attached a list of 11 (out of the 16) transferred ARS as to which Glenmede sought Wachovia's assistance. Included on the list were the Mobile County and Jefferson County ARS.

Objection and Response: Glenmede objects because this request calls for a characterization of a document that speaks for itself. Subject to, and without waiving, this objection, the request is admitted in part and denied in part. It is admitted that on February 8, 2007, Richard Gale sent an email to M. Kennedy at Wachovia that contains the quoted language and that has as an attachment a list of 11 ARS, including the Mobile County and Jefferson County ARS. It is denied that Wachovia transferred 16 ARS to Glenmede.

32. Between February 8, 2007, and February 12, 2007, Mr. Kerr of Wachovia contacted the remarketing agent for each of the 11 listed ARS and advised each remarketing agent that Glenmede held the ARS and associated bidding rights. On February 12, 2007, Ken Kerr of Wachovia confirmed in an email that "[a]ll have been notified."

Objection and Response: Glenmede objects to this request because it asks Glenmede to admit facts that are not within the personal knowledge of anyone at Glenmede. Accordingly, after reasonable inquiry, the information known or readily obtainable by Glenmede is insufficient to enable Glenmede to admit or deny this request.

33. On February 21, 2007, Glenmede liquidated the $400,000 position in Philadelphia Pa Regl Port Auth MBIA.

Response: Admitted.

34. On February 26, 2007, Glenmede liquidated the $400,000 position in Access to Lns for Learning Stu Ln Var.

Response: Admitted.

35. On February 28, 2007, a successful auction was held for the Mobile County ARS. Glenmede did not liquidate the ARS at that auction.

Response: It is admitted that Glenmede did not liquidate the ARS at that auction, because it could not.

36. On March 8, 2007, Glenmede liquidated the $400,000 position in the Phila Pa School Dist. Var Ref B-9

Response: Admitted.

37. On March 8, 2007, a successful auction was held for the Jefferson County ARS. Glenmede did not liquidate the ARS at that auction.

Response: It is admitted that Glenmede did not liquidate the ARS at that auction, because it could not.

38. On April 4, 2007, a successful auction was held for the Mobile County ARS. Glenmede did not liquidate the ARS at that auction.

Response: It is admitted that Glenmede did not liquidate the ARS at that auction, because it could not.

39. On April 9, 2007, the Mobile County ARS was partially called and Glenmede received $25,000 in cash, leaving the Trust with a $375,000 position in that ARS.

Response: Admitted.

40. On April 12, 2007, a successful auction was held for the Jefferson County ARS. Glenmede did not liquidate the ARS at that auction.

Response: It is admitted that Glenmede did not liquidate the ARS at that auction, because it could not.

41. Glenmede's statements of account show no activity with respect to the ARS (other than the payment of interest) for May, June, July, or August of 2007.

Objections and Response: Glenmede objects to this request because it calls for the characterization of documents that speak for themselves, because it does not know what Petitioners mean by "Glenmede's statements of account show no activity" and because it does not know what Petitioners mean by "the ARS." Subject to, and without waiving, these objections, and assuming that "the ARS" means the Mobile County and Jefferson County ARS, and that "Glenmede's statements of account show no activity" means "Glenmede's statements of account do not indicate any sales, purchases or calls," this request is admitted.

42. Successful auctions for the Mobile County ARS were held on May 9, June 13, July 18, August 4, and September 26, 2007. Glenmede did not liquidate the ARS at those auctions.

Response: Admitted that there were five successful auctions for the Mobile County ARS from May to September 2007 and that Glenmede did not liquidate the ARS at those auctions because it could not. For clarification, Glenmede believes the August auction was held on August 22, not August 4.

43. Successful auctions for the Jefferson County ARS were held on May 17, June 21, July 26, and August 30, 2007. Glenmede did not liquidate the ARS at those auctions.

Response: It is admitted that Glenmede did not liquidate the ARS at those auctions, because it could not.

44. Glenmede's statements of account show no activity with respect to the ARS (other than the payment of interest) for October, November, and December of 2007.

Objections and Response: Glenmede objects to this request because it calls for the characterization of documents that speak for themselves, because it does not know what Petitioners mean by "Glenmede's statements of account show no activity" and because it does not know what Petitioners mean by "the ARS." Subject to, and without waiving, these objections, and assuming that "the ARS" means the Mobile County and Jefferson County ARS, and that "Glenmede's statements of account show no activity" means "Glenmede's statements of account do not indicate any sales, purchases or calls," this request is admitted.

45. Successful auctions for the Jefferson County ARS were held on October 4, November 8, and December 13, 2007. Glenmede did not liquidate the ARS at those auctions.

Response: It is admitted that Glenmede did not liquidate the ARS at those auctions, because it could not.

46. Successful auctions for the Mobile County ARS were held on October 31 and December 5, 2007. Glenmede did not liquidate the ARS at those auctions.

Response: It is admitted that Glenmede did not liquidate the ARS at those auctions, because it could not.

47. As of the end of 2007, Glenmede was reporting to the Trust that all the ARS were investment grade. *See* Glenmede 12/07 statement of account.

Objections and Response: Glenmede objects to this request because it calls for the characterization of a document that speaks for itself and because it does not know what Petitioners mean by "the ARS." Subject to, and without waiving, these objections, and assuming that "the ARS" means the Mobile County and Jefferson County ARS, it is admitted that it is reported on the December 2007 statement that the Mobile County and Jefferson County ARS had Aaa ratings.

48. A successful action for the Mobile County ARS was held on January 9, 2008. Glenmede did not liquidate the ARS at that auction.

Response: It is admitted that Glenmede did not liquidate the ARS at that auction, because it could not.

49. A successful action for the Jefferson County ARS was held on January 17, 2008. Glenmede did not liquidate the ARS at that auction.

Response: It is admitted that Glenmede did not liquidate the ARS at that auction, because it could not.

50. On or about January 29, 2008, Glenmede represented to Steven Markowitz that the ARS were all investment grade.

Response: It is admitted that it is reported on the January 2008 statement that the Mobile County and Jefferson County ARS had Aaa ratings.

51. Glenmede's statement of account show no activity with respect to the ARS (other than the payment of interest) for January of 2008. *See* Glenmede 1/08 statement of account.

Objections and Response: Glenmede objects to this request because it calls for the characterization of a document that speaks for itself, because it does not know what Petitioners mean by "Glenmede's statement of account show [sic] no activity" and because it does not know what Petitioners mean by "the ARS." Subject to, and without waiving, these objections, and assuming that "the ARS" means the Mobile County and Jefferson County ARS, and that "Glenmede's statement of account show [sic] no activity" means that "Glenmede's statement of account does not indicate any sales, purchases or calls," this request is admitted.

52. On February 7, 2008, Glenmede liquidated the $400,000 position in Tobacco Settlement Fing Corp N. *See* Glenmede 2/08 statement of account.

Response: Admitted.

53. A successful auction for the Mobile County ARS was held on February 13, 2008. Glenmede did not liquidate the ARS at that auction.

Response: It is admitted that Glenmede did not liquidate the ARS at that auction, because it could not.

54. On February 14, 2008, Glenmede liquidated the $800,000 position in New Garden Gen Auth Pa Var Rate Rev. *See* Glenmede 2/08 statement of account.

Response: Admitted.

55. From February of 2007 through January of 2008, there were 11 successful auctions involving the Mobile County ARS and 11 successful auctions involving the Jefferson County ARS.

Response: It is admitted that during this time period, there were 11 successful auctions involving the Jefferson County ARS. It is denied that there were 11 successful auctions involving the Mobile County ARS; to the contrary, there were 10.

56. There is no credible evidence that Glenmede took any steps to liquidate the Mobile County and Jefferson County ARS at any of those auctions.

Objection: Glenmede objects to this request because it calls for a conclusion of law.

57. If Glenmede had participated in any of the successful auctions involving Mobile County ARS or Jefferson County ARS between February 2007 and January 2008, the Mobile County ARS and/or the Jefferson County ARS could have been sold at par value.

Objections: Glenmede objects because this request is not reasonably calculated to lead to the discovery of admissible evidence and because it calls for a conclusion of law.

58. In late February of 2008, the market for auction rate securities froze as part of the credit market meltdown and auctions began to fail.

Response: Admitted.

59. Between February of 2007 and March of 2008, Glenmede did not send one written communication to Wachovia concerning the ARS.

Objection and Response: Glenmede objects to this request because it does not know what Petitioners mean by "[b]etween February of 2007 and March of 2008." Subject to, and without waiving, this objection, and assuming that "[b]etween February of 2007 and March of 2008" means the period from March 1, 2007 through February 29, 2008, this request is admitted.

60. Between February of 2007 and March of 2008, Glenmede did [not] make one call to anyone at Wachovia Bank concerning the ARS.

Objection and Response: Glenmede objects to this request because it does not know what Petitioners mean by "[b]etween February of 2007 and March of 2008." Subject to, and without waiving, this objection, and assuming that "[b]etween February of 2007 and March of 2008" means the period from March 1, 2007 through February 29, 2008, this request is admitted.

61. Prior to the market freeze, Glenmede never told the Trustees that it was having any difficulty acquiring the bidding rights to the ARS.

Objection and Response: Glenmede objects because it does not know what Petitioners mean by "Prior to the market freeze." Subject to, and without waiving, this objection, and assuming that "Prior to the market freeze" means "Prior to the time when the market for auction rate securities froze as part of the credit market meltdown," this request is admitted.

62. On March 28, 2008, Glenmede sent out a letter to its clients, including the Trust, discussing its approach to municipal bond portfolios and the "market dislocations" of "the past few months." "We did not sell into this unusually weak market. Instead, we were proactive during the two days of market dislocation and added bonds to client portfolios at attractive levels." The Trust's February 2007 statement of account indicates $250,000 in such purchases.

Objections and Response: Glenmede objects to this request because it is not reasonably calculated to lead to the discovery of admissible evidence and because it calls for a characterization of documents that speak for themselves. Subject to, and without waiver of, these objections, it is admitted that the Trust's February 2008 statement indicates $250,000 in bond purchases.

63. Fourteen (14) of the ARS transferred to GM from Wachovia were liquidated or redeemed at par.

Response: Denied. The request presumes that there were 16 auction rate securities transferred from Wachovia to Glenmede; in fact, there were 11. With this factual correction, and assuming that by "GM" Petitioners mean "Glenmede," it is admitted that nine of the ARS transferred to Glenmede from Wachovia were liquidated or redeemed at par.

Adam T. Gusdorff

James F. Mannion (I.D. No. 58951)
Adam T. Gusdorff (I.D. No. 87998)
Mannion Prior, LLP
840 First Avenue, Suite 100
King of Prussia, PA 19406
(610) 265-7800

Counsel for The Glenmede Trust Company, N.A.

Dated: July 1, 2010

VERIFICATION

I, James R. Belanger, verify that I am a Senior Vice President of The Glenmede Trust Company, N.A. and am authorized to execute this Verification on behalf of The Glenmede Trust Company, N.A.; that the responses to the foregoing discovery requests are true and correct to the best of my knowledge, information and belief; and that this Verification is made subject to the penalties of 18 Pa. C.S. § 4904, relating to unsworn falsification to authorities.

THE GLENMEDE TRUST COMPANY, N.A.

By: ______________________
James R. Belanger
Senior Vice President

<u>Certificate of Service</u>

I, Adam T. Gusdorff, certify that on July 1, 2010, I served a true and correct copy of the foregoing Objections and Responses, via first class U.S. Mail, postage prepaid, upon the following:

Steven A. Bergstein, Esquire
Engel, Wiener and Bergstein
825 N. 12th Street
Allentown, PA 18102

Counsel for Steven Markowitz (individually and as Trustee), Marc Markowitz, Sandra Goldstein and Judy Roberts

Henry F. Reichner, Esquire
Reed Smith, LLP
2500 One Liberty Place
1650 Market Street
Philadelphia, PA 19103-7301

Counsel for Wachovia Bank, N.A.

Adam T. Gusdorff

IN THE COURT OF COMMON PLEAS OF LEHIGH COUNTY, PENNSYLVANIA
ORPHANS' COURT DIVISION

IN THE MATTER OF:	)	
	)	FILE NO. 1991-0304 A
JEROME MARKOWITZ TRUST	)	
	)	

EXCEPTIONS OF STEVEN A. MARKOWITZ, TRUSTEE, TO THE ORDER AND OPINION OF THE HONORABLE J. BRIAN JOHNSON FILED ON DECEMBER 8, 2011

AND NOW comes the Trustee of the Jerome Markowitz Trust, Steven A. Markowitz, and files the following exceptions to the Order and Opinion filed in this matter on December 8, 2011. It is requested that the notes of testimony for January 28, 2011, February 4, 2011, and May 11, 2011 be transcribed prior to briefing and argument on these exceptions pursuant to PA Orphans' Court Rule 7.2.

1. The Court erred in finding that "Markowitz introduced no evidence regarding whether, or at what price, the Jefferson ARS and the Mobile ARS could have been sold during the period of February, 2007 through March, 2008..." (Opinion, p. 25) There was substantial evidence in the form of testimony by Glenmede personnel, documentary evidence, and admissions concerning this issue. (See Exhibit P-63, Admissions #42 and #55) Each and every Glenmede Statement during the period listed the "market" price of the Mobile and Jefferson ARSs and Glenmede admitted that there were numerous successful auctions in this market during this time in which Glenmede failed to participate. At any of those auctions, the ARSs could have been sold at market price. Laura LaRosa testified that the problem that developed with the ARSs was that you

"couldn't cash them in." "Cashing in" would have been at market price. The evidence showed that all sales of ARSs before the markets froze were at market price which was the same as par value when the markets were operating normally. (Joint Exhibit 1)

2. The Court erred in finding that "Gale was not directed by Glenmede or Markowitz to liquidate any of the ARSs." (Opinion, p. 9) Gale admittedly was instructed by Laura LaRosa to sell the ARSs, confirmed by both Gale and LaRosa. Gale agreed that as of February 7, 2007, his instructions were to get the ARSs sold. LaRosa admitted that "a determination" was made as did the Court in its Opinion at page 24. That "determination" was never implemented. Richard Gale testified that during February, 2007 "We decided that we were going to try to liquidate the securities to try to get the auction rights, participate in the auctions and move them out of the portfolio." Further, the Court found at page 24 of its decision that "Glenmede did a poor job in effectuating its investment decision made in February, 2007 to liquidate all of the ARSs..." Since Glenmede made the investment decision, and Gale testified that he was told to liquidate the ARSs, the factual statement at page 9 of the Opinion is incorrect.

3. The Court erred at page 9 of its Opinion in stating that "During the period February, 2007 through March, 2007, Glenmede liquidated five (5) ARSs, carried at an aggregate value of $2.4 million." That was incorrect as between February, 2007 and March, 2007, Glenmede in fact liquidated three (3) ARSs with an aggregate value of only $1.2 million. (Joint Exhibit 1).

4. The Court erred on page 24 of its Opinion in failing to find a fact admitted by Glenmede, namely that the difficulties in the auction rate security market were openly discussed at Glenmede during the fourth quarter of 2007 though Glenmede did nothing about it in regard to the Markowitz Trust. (Exhibit P-63, Admissions #15 and #16)

5. The Court erred in finding, at page 11 of its Opinion that "Between May 6 and 21, 2009, Glenmede sold every investment except the Jefferson ARS, the Mobile ARS (which collectively constituted 6.6% of the Account), and another asset that is not at issue." In fact, two (2) of the auction rate securities were called, not sold by Glenmede. (Joint Exhibit 1)

6. The Court erred in finding that the value of the Jefferson ARS was $300,000 and the Mobile ARS $350,000 in May, 2009 when the account was transferred to BNY-Mellon. Those were the par values, not market values. Kevin Karpuk as well as Glenmede personnel acknowledged that the value of those securities at that time was less than par since there was no market for said securities. Further, it was freely admitted at trial by Glenmede that there was no market for these securities, hence no market value, exactly the reason why Glenmede attempted to try to force Wachovia to buy back the securities since no one else would take them.

7. The Court erred at page 12 of its decision in taking into account the subsequent calling of the Mobile ARS after the securities had been liquidated as the Court noted at the time of trial, upon objection, that after-the-fact issue was irrelevant. The propriety of the decision by Steven Markowitz to sell the ARSs at a discount must be judged, if at all, as of the time it was made, not in light of subsequent events. *Pew Estate*,

440 Pa Super 195, 655 A,2d 521,543 (1994), cited by the Court at page 25 of its Opinion. Parenthetically, if subsequent events are relevant, it should be noted that the Jefferson ARSs have become worthless due to Jefferson County's subsequent bankruptcy, one of the largest governmental bankruptcies in history. If Markowitz had not sold the Jefferson ARSs when he did, the loss would have been even greater than it was.

8. The Court erred generally in failing to find not only that liquidity was a requirement of the Trust, acknowledged by Glenmede, but that the reason for the liquidity requirement was also readily acknowledged by Glenmede, namely the advanced age of Martha Markowitz, the Trust's income beneficiary, as well as the fact that she died, making the liquidity requirement even more crucial.

9. The Court erred in finding that the Trustee did not prove its breach of contract claim given that the Court found that Glenmede breached its fiduciary duties and misrepresented and/or concealed various facts to Markowitz (Opinion, p. 24), acting instead in its own self interest, yet did not find that these breaches of fiduciary duty arose to the level of willful, grossly negligent, untruthful conduct, willful malfeasance or reckless disregard. In this regard, the Court also erred in ignoring unrebutted evidence that Glenmede violated its own internal procedures and also its obligations under the Code of Federal Regulations.

10. The Court erred in failing to find gross negligence under the contract despite the fact that one of Glenmede's executives specifically charged with bringing the Trust's auction rate securities into the firm from Wachovia, David Schwartz, testified that at the relevant time he did not even know what an auction rate security was and therefore

could not make a judgment as to whether everything had been received. Despite this lack of knowledge, Mr. Schwartz represented to the Trust that "everything" had been received which Glenmede has acknowledged was untrue.

11. The Court erred in failing to find gross negligence under the contract in light of the fact that Glenmede assigned an individual, Richard Gale, to handle the sale of the Trust's auction rate securities who had serious difficulties accomplishing what Laura LaRosa testified was a simple task, Gale stating that it was the hardest thing he ever had to do, then choosing to do nothing for an extended period of time, compounding the problem by not informing the Trust or anyone at Glenmede of his difficulties.

12. The Court erred in finding that the absence of sufficient standard of care evidence was fatal to the breach of contract claim. Standard of care evidence was not necessary since the Court found that breaches of fiduciary duty were proven and the Defendant actively concealed and misrepresented its actions in an attempt to transfer liability to another party, namely Wachovia Bank. Expert testimony is not needed to show that these actions violated any reasonable standard of care as understanding the wrongful nature of these actions is not beyond the knowledge of the average person. Ordinary experience and comprehension is sufficient to establish that these actions, already found by the Court to violate Glenmede's fiduciary duties, violated the Standard of Care. _Rizzo v. Haines_, 520 Pa. 484, 502, 555 A.2d 58, 66 (1999). [1]Further, the Standard of Care was violated as a matter of law because of Glenmede's breach of its own internal policies and operating procedures and breach of Federal Regulations as acknowledged in testimony.

---

[1]In _Rizzo_, the expert testimony proferred by the Plaintiff was rejected but the Court upheld a claim that the Standard of Care had been violated in a case of legal malpractice without expert testimony.

13. The Court erred in finding, at page 21 of its Opinion, that Glenmede was "well familiar with ARSs." While arguably some people at Glenmede were "well familiar" with ARSs, the two individuals who were charged with acting directly for Glenmede in regard to the ARSs belonging to the Trust, David Schwartz and Richard Gale, did not have expertise and in the case of Schwartz, admittedly did not even know what an auction rate security was. This was a direct violation of 12 C.F.R. §9.6(a) which states "Before accepting a fiduciary account, a national bank shall review the prospective account to determine whether it can properly administer the account." Because Schwartz did not know what an auction rate security was, and he was the person entrusted by Glenmede to review the prospective account, he obviously could not make that determination. The actions of Glenmede rise far above mere negligence as it did not even assign competent people. Richard Gale, the other Glenmede individual involved directly with the Trust's ARSs, stated that ARSs were "one of the more confusing and difficult things" he had ever handled.

14 The Court erred in its opinion on page 21 where it indicated that it was "unpersuaded" by the Claimant that Glenmede had a contractual obligation to inform Markowitz that Glenmede had not received the auction rights. That is a misstatement of the issue. The issue was not whether Glenmede had a contractual obligation to inform the Trust that it had not received the auction rights; the issue was that Glenmede had a contractual and legal obligation to "review the prospective (fiduciary) account to determine whether it can properly administer the account." Even though the ARSs admittedly could not be properly administered because of the lack of auction rights, Glenmede accepted the

ARSs then misrepresented what it had received. David Schwartz's statement that "everything" had been received was clearly false. Given that Glenmede, with a fiduciary and contractual obligation to the Trust, chose to have David Schwartz perform this function, it is submitted that Glenmede failed in its obligation to entrust that function to someone who possessed the appropriate knowledge. Further, having made the investment decision to sell the ARSs, Glenmede had an obligation to at least see to it that Gale carried out that investment decision which Glenmede, in its discretion, decided was in the Trust's best interest.

15. The Court erred in repeatedly finding fault with the Trustee, Steven Markowitz, for not knowing that ARSs were in the portfolio when Laura LaRosa, Glenmede's expert in the field, acknowledged that she could not tell by examining the Trust's monthly statements from Glenmede that ARSs were in the portfolio and David Schwartz was obviously unaware also. Further, whether or not Markowitz knew there were ARSs in the Trust's portfolio at Glenmede is not relevant to the claims of the Trust since this part of the portfolio was to be completely liquid. As the Court also found, the ARSs were a permissible class of assets for the Trust, "cash substitutes. like money market accounts" as described in the testimony of Laura LaRosa who also testified that she did not need to know risk tolerance since these investments were "basically cash." The problem was not the asset but the liquidity problems arising from the lack of auction rights which Steven Markowitz could only have known about if told by Glenmede.

16. The Court erred in finding at page 21 that the discretionary nature of Glenmede's obligations and the contractual provision that Glenmede "shall not have responsibility to consult with or receive approval from Markowitz prior to any such transactions" is dispositive of the issue. Glenmede, in the exercise of its discretion, made the decision to dispose of the auction rate securities in February, 2007 and so instructed Richard Gale. Then, due to the incompetence and/or ignorance of Mr. Gale and Mr. Schwartz, Glenmede failed to carry out this decision. It is not a question of Glenmede's discretion since Glenmede had already made its discretionary decision, a decision which, if carried out, would have prevented the harm. Rather, it is a question of Glenmede's actions in carrying out its discretion. Laura LaRosa stated that a "determination was made (to sell the ARSs in January/February, 2007)" which was never done. Discretion is not an excuse to avoid duty once a decision is made.

17. The Court erred in failing to find that, at least in the fourth quarter of 2007, as admitted by Glenmede (Exhibit P-63, Admission #16), Glenmede was aware of the difficulties in the auction rate security market. This was long before the February, 2008 date used by the Court. To further compound Glenmede's wrongful actions, the individual in charge of that department at Glenmede, Laura LaRosa, testified she did not know of the problems that were admittedly common knowledge at Glenmede at that time. Other Glenmede personnel who could have made use of that important knowledge in protecting the Trust's assets were also not told.

18. The Court erred in finding at page 21 of its Opinion, that Markowitz produced no document in which the auction rate securities were identified as assets that Glenmede was to liquidate immediately upon taking possession or within a specified time thereafter. While there was no document, the evidence clearly showed that Glenmede made that decision, then failed to implement it. There was ample testimony as to the importance of liquidity for all of the assets. In addition, Glenmede personnel testified that the auction rate securities were "cash equivalents" or "a money market-type substitute." Such investments should be readily available, not readily available in 30 years, 30 months, or only if you have the auction rights.

19. The Court erred in finding at page 22 of its Opinion that "Because the majority of the ARS holdings were successfully liquidated by Glenmede well within the five (5) year investment horizon. There was no failure to meet the liquidity objective." The five year horizon did not apply to liquidity as acknowledged by Robert Kiep, among others. The auction rate securities were "cash equivalents" before the markets froze, by Glenmede's own admission. Only because of Glenmede's actions and/or inactions were the ARSs not cash equivalents. As Laura LaRosa testified, "we had the whole portfolio in very short term paper."

20. The Court erred in that there is an inherent inconsistency in the findings. At page 9, the Court found that Richard Gale was not directed by Glenmede to liquidate the auction rate securities (see above). However, at page 24 of the Opinion, the Court, in finding a breach of fiduciary duty, stated that Glenmede "did a poor job in effectuating its investment decision made in February, 2007 to liquidate all of the ARSs..." There was an

investment decision made and Richard Gale was instructed to carry out that decision. The Court's finding was in error.

21. The Court erred in the method it used to calculate damages.

22. The Court erred in failing to award counsel fees. The reasoning stated at pages 26 and 27 of the Opinion is inapposite in Orphan's Court litigation such as this. The award of legal fees in a surcharge action is a well accepted deviation from the American Rule. *In re Rosenfeld Foundation Trust*, 2006 WL 3040020 (Phila., 2004), citing *Dardovitch v. Haltzman*, 190 F.3d 125, 145-147 (3d Cir); *Weiss Estate*, 4 Fid. Rep 2d 71, 77 (Phila., 1983).

23. The Court erred in finding at page 4 of its Opinion that "Auctions are held usually every 7, 28, or 35 days and interest on ARSs is paid at the end of each auction period." In fact, while the auctions are held every 7, 28, or 35 days, the interest was not paid following those auctions. Interest rates were reset by those auctions but the relevant thing that happens at the auctions is that the ARSs are bought and sold, the price of the ARS remaining stable, just like a money market investment as stated numerous times by Glenmede personnel.

24. The Court erred in implying at page 10 of its Opinion that because the maturation dates of the ARSs were noted on each statement, that somehow was notice of the long term of the investment even though Glenmede personnel testified repeatedly that all were cash equivalents. If the ARSs were properly managed by Glenmede, maturation dates were irrelevant because of the regular auctions at which the ARSs could readily be turned into cash.

Respectfully submitted,

By: ______________________

Steven A. Bergstein, Esquire
Engel, Wiener and Bergstein
825 North Twelfth Street
Allentown, PA 18102
Tel: 610-439-8430
Attorney I.D. #27658
Attorney for Petitioners

CERTIFICATE OF SERVICE

I HEREBY CERTIFY that, at my direction, a true and correct copy of the foregoing documents were served upon the following persons by depositing same in the United States Mail, regular, First Class Mail, postage prepaid, addressed as follows:

Karl Prior, Esquire
Mannion Prior, LLP
840 First Avenue, Suite 100
King of Prussia, PA 19406

Steven A. Bergstein

Dated: 12/21/2011

Lehigh County Court of Common Pleas
Orphans' Court Division
Lehigh County Courthouse
455 w. Hamilton Street
Allentown, Pennsylvania 18101-1614

Janet T. Woffindin, Esquire
Director of Orphans' Court Operations
(610) 782-3020
FAX (610) 820-2006

Wendy A.W. Parr
Clerk of Orphans' Court Division
(610) 782-3172
FAX (610) 782-3928
Assistant Clerks:
Minerva Diaz
Susan M. Brown
Kathleen Newett

FAX TRANSMITTAL SHEET

NUMBER OF SHEETS TRANSMITTED 28
(Including Cover Sheet)

_TO:_ **Steven A. Bergstein, Esquire 610-439-1235**

Karl Prior, Esquire 610-265-1204

FROM: **_Clerk of Orphans' Court Division_**

Wendy Parr

DATE TRANSMITTED: **December 8, 2011**

COMMENTS: **_NO HARD COPY WILL FOLLOW._**

IN THE COURT OF COMMON PLEAS OF LEHIGH COUNTY, PENNSYLVANIA
ORPHANS' COURT DIVISION

In re: JEROME MARKOWITZ TRUST B, under Agreement dated October 6, 1983, as amended February 19, 1985 : File No. . 1991-0304

FINAL ORDER RULING UPON EXCEPTIONS

AND NOW, this 16th day of April, 2012, upon consideration of the *Exceptions of Steven A. Markowitz, Trustee, to the Order and Opinion of the Honorable J. Brian Johnson Filed on December 8, 2011, filed* on December 21, 2012, the *Brief in Behalf of Steven A. Markowitz Trustee in Support of the Exceptions to the Order and Opinion of the Honorable J. Brian Johnson,* filed on April 3, 2012, the *Post-Trial Submission of the Glenmede Trust Company, N.A.,* filed on April 3, 2012, and after argument held on April 5, 2012;

IT IS ORDERED that the *Exceptions of Steven A. Markowitz, Trustee, to the Order and Opinion of the Honorable J. Brian Johnson Filed on December 8, 2011* are granted in part and denied in part as follows:

1. Exception #1 is granted. The record does contain evidence that the price at which the Jefferson ARS and the Mobile ARS could have been sold had auction rights been included in the transfer from Wachovia was their par value.

2. Exception #3 is granted. Joint Exhibit 1 reflects the parties' stipulation that Glenmede liquidated 3 ARSs during the period, February, 2007 through March, 2007.

3. Exception #5 is granted. Joint Exhibit 1 reflects that of the ARSs liquidated by Glenmede during the period May 6, 2009 and May 21, 2009, two of said ARSs were called and were not sold or tendered by Glenmede.

4. Exceptions #15 and #24 are granted. The inclusion of maturation dates on the monthly Glenmede account statements that were received by Steven Markowitz was neither an indication that certain investments were ARSs, nor that they were long-term investments.

5. Exceptions #2, #16 and #20 are denied. The plan formulated by Richard Gale and Laura LaRosa to eventually eliminate the ARS that had been transferred to Glenmede by Wachovia in February 2007, was not a **direction** from either their employer, Glenmede, (*See* NT. 11/9/2008 at pp. 129-131; 134; 156-157; 166; N.T. 5/12/2011 at pp. 104-105*)* or from Markowitz,(N.T. 5/12/2011 at pp. 99-100) to tender them by a date certain, which was intentionally disregarded. Thus, it is not evidence of gross negligence and a breach of the parties' contract. The particular breach of fiduciary duty found by the Court was not Glenmede's failure to obtain the auction rights for 14 months, but its choice not to tell Markowitz about the lack of auction rights in February, 2008 when it knew auctions had begun to fail, because it had not yet obtained all of the auction rights.

6. Exceptions #4 and #17 are denied. The record evidence did not establish whether or what "difficulties" in the ARS market were "openly discussed" at Glenmede during the 4th Quarter of 2007. The testimony that unspecified "difficulties" may have been mentioned at an in-house meeting of Glenmede personnel held some time in the last quarter of 2007 is not sufficient to establish that Glenmede knew or should have foreseen at that time that auctions would begin to fail. Rather, we found persuasive the testimony that the collapse of the auction rate securities market that began in February, 2008 was unprecedented; constituting an unforeseen consequence of the massive dislocation of the **mortgage** market which began in mid 2007 (*See,* N.T. 11/9/2010 at p. 131; 145; 170 152N.T.5/12/2011 at pp. 105-106; 109-110; 125). Markowitz presented no expert testimony to prove otherwise.

7. Exception #6 is denied. Markowitz used the par value of both the Mobile and the Jefferson ARS to calculate his commissions shortly after the account was removed from Glenmede in May, 2009.

8. Exception # 7 is denied. Because all of the breach of contract claims were dismissed, the court did not decide the amount of damages (set by the contract as losses to the account). Regarding the breach of fiduciary duty claim the Court determined that the proper remedy was the imposition of surcharge and rejected any "loss" as the proper measure of calculating it; finding instead that denial of compensation attributable to the two ARS remaining in the account when it was terminated by Markowitz was appropriate. Thus, the mention of Markowitz's sale of the Mobile ARS in late October 2009 and the subsequent call of the Mobile ARS in early December, 2009 that appears on page 12 of the Opinion to which this exception is directed is properly considered part of the chronology of this case.

9. Exceptions #8, #18 and #19 are denied. First regarding #8, as of the date that the account was removed from Glenmede, it held only 2 ARS the value of which represented 6% of its value and thus satisfied Markowitz's own definition of "liquidity": that the "lion's share" of the assets were cash or easily converted to cash. (*See,* N.T. 2/4/2011 at p. 224-228). Mention in #8 of the death of Mrs. Markowitz as evidence of the extent to which "liquidity" was a "requirement" of the trust, is misplaced. Martha Markowitz died in January, 2010 – after this litigation was

commenced and after the account had been removed from Glenmede. Second, #18 directed to the finding that "Markowitz produced no document in which the auction rate securities were identified as assts that Glenmede was to liquidate immediately upon taking possession or with a specified time thereafter" is disingenuous; the very next sentence of this exception concedes its accuracy: "While there was no document..." Finally, regarding exception #19 exceptant misstates the finding to which it is directed by quoting it as follows: "Because the majority of the ARS holdings were successfully liquidated by Glenmede well with the five (5) year investment horizon. There was no failure to meet the liquidity objective.". The Court's actual finding as it appears on page 22 of the Opinion reads as follows: "Because the majority of the ARS holdings were successfully liquidated by Glenmede well with the five (5) year investment horizon **articulated in the IPS, despite the delay in obtaining auctions rights, the lack of a primary market for the Mobile ARS and the Jefferson ARS, which represented slightly more than 6% of the Account,** there was no failure to meet the liquidity objective **contained in the IPS.**" This finding is well-supported in the record.

10. Exceptions #9 through #14 are denied. We reject the premise of all of these exceptions; that the finding of breach of fiduciary duty requires a finding of gross negligence and, therefore, breach of contract. As was discussed in our opinion, Markowitz failed to prove that Glenmede was not qualified to administer ARS, (*See, e.g.,* exception #15 which characterizes Laura LaRosa as Glenmede's "expert in the field"); that it violated any stated contractual duty or conducted itself in a grossly negligent manner. It was because we determined that Glenmede was a fiduciary subject to the duty, imposed as a matter of law by social policy and not by contract, to act with "scrupulous good faith and candor" and, that Glenmede breached that duty when it decided not to inform Markowitz of its lack of auction rights to the ARS as soon as it knew that not having them was anything more than an annoyance, (in February, 2008 when auctions had begun to fail), that the Court imposed a surcharge upon Glenmede.

11. Exception #21 is denied. Denial of compensation attributable to the par values of the ARS remaining when the account was removed from Glenmede is a reasonable and represents an ascertainable method of calculating a surcharge for the breach of fiduciary duty as found by the Court. (*See,* No. 10, *supra)*

12. Exception #22 is denied for the reasons stated in our Opinion.

13. Exception #23 is denied. When read in context with the sentence preceding it, the sentence to which this exception is directed is not inaccurate. That preceding sentence states: "An auction rate security ("ARS") typically refers to corporate or municipal bonds with a long-term nominal maturation date and **for which the interest rate is regularly resent through an auction."** (emphasis supplied).